Buckeye Schoolmaster

Buckeye Schoolmaster:
A Chronicle of Midwestern Rural Life, 1853-1865

edited by

J. Merton England

Copyright © 1996 by Bowling Green State University Popular Press

Cover design by Laura Darnell-Dumm

Library of Congress Cataloging-in-Publication Data

Roberts, John M., 1833-1914.
    Buckeye schoolmaster : a chronicle of midwestern rural life, 1853-1865 /
    edited by J. Merton England.
        p. cm.
    Includes index.
    ISBN 0-87972-695-4 (cloth). -- ISBN 0-87972-696-2 (pbk.)
    1. Roberts, John M., 1833-1914--Diaries. 2. Madison County (Ohio)--
Social life and customs. 3. Teachers--Ohio--Madison County--Diaries.
I. England, J. Merton (James Merton), 1915-   . II. Title.
F497.M17R63   1995
977.1'55041'092--dc20
    [B]   96-4279
                                                                   CIP

For my grandchildren—Teresa, Waheguru, Elizabeth, and Dharam—

with love and admiration

Contents

Preface

It was more than three decades ago that the manuscripts edited here came to my attention. Stephen M. Archer, Jr., one of my students in American University's School of International Service, where I was teaching for a year, knew that I was interested in the history of American education, and he let me read a journal and some diaries of a great-great-grandfather of his who had been a country teacher in Ohio in the nineteenth century. I found them interesting reading, and startlingly so when the name of my hometown in western Missouri suddenly appeared in a diary entry for 1878. Indeed, the diarist, John M. Roberts, moved to my hometown for a year or two and taught in rural schools in the county before returning to his old home in Ohio.

Except for making a note of a debate topic—of which more later—I made no scholarly use of Roberts's journals and diaries then. A few months later I left academic life for a government job, and while I still liked to think I was a historian, I found that making grants to college and university presidents for their use in strengthening their institutions' science programs was challenging and enjoyable work. When the Nixon administration wiped out my program in the early 1970s, however, the head of the agency kindly kept me on the payroll by returning me to my profession as the agency's historian. I managed to finish one volume of the organization's history before I retired in 1986 and left its completion in better hands.

Retired and wanting to do something of more worth than hunting for my ancestors, I thought of John Roberts's chronicles and wondered if I could track them down. Two letters sent to a California address for Steve Archer came back marked "Address unknown." Still, I suspected that most people who move to California stay there, and I asked a son of mine in Berkeley to search for Stephen Archer's name in California telephone directories. Fortunately, he found him in Sacramento and learned that his mother, Doris Archer, lived in Annapolis, Maryland, and probably had Roberts's journals and diaries. She did, and she generously let me use them.

The trove turned out to be much richer than I had thought. Instead of the one large, legal-size journal I had read years before, there was an even longer one recording Roberts's life, mainly in the form of birthday annals, from 1858 to 1913. And instead of the few diaries I had seen earlier, I learned that he had made a daily record of every day of his life from August 11, 1858, until a week before he died in July 1914, though diaries for three years (1860, 1861, and 1862) were not in the trunk with the others and may have been lost.

When transcribed, the two large journals and a short travel account resulted in a bulky 600-page double-spaced manuscript. To copy the diaries, which furnish the real details of Roberts's long life after his twenty-fifth year, would require far more time and energy than I have to devote to such a task. (My transcription of Roberts's Missouri diaries [July 8-September 16, 1878, and August 9, 1879-February 3, 1881] alone runs to 395 pages.) His diaries are a rich resource for historians of everyday life in rural America. I hope they will find a home where they will be available for scholarly research. Historians and other students of country life owe Roberts's descendants, especially the late Doris Archer, a large debt of gratitude for preserving the documents through so many years.

I have reduced the lengthy transcript of Roberts's journals by deleting most of his comments about the weather and many of his reflections which are repetitious of earlier ones, and I have occasionally deleted words and phrases that simply add clutter to his sentences. All deletions are indicated by ellipses (. . .).

Roberts's pages are full from top to bottom. There are no paragraphs, and it is necessary to guess where one sentence ends and another starts, since he often omits punctuation entirely and uses capital and lower-case initial letters indiscriminately. His punctuation is idiosyncratic and frequently unintelligible. He rarely uses an apostrophe, and when he does it often appears below the line as a comma. In his hurried writing, he sometimes omits or repeats words. His spelling is usually accurate but occasionally inconsistent.

Besides omissions, my editing amounts mainly to providing an intelligible document with conventional paragraphs and punctuation, though I have followed the original in omitting apostrophes. I have reproduced his spelling and have tried to avoid using the self-protective *sic*. When unsure of the spelling of a word or a name, I have followed it with a bracketed question mark. Roberts was inconsistent in linking many words (e.g., to day, fore noon, any how, school house), and I have silently joined them. I have occasionally inserted bracketed words where necessary to provide meaning or where I think Roberts unintentionally left them out. As an additional aid to the reader, I have arbitrarily divided Roberts's pre-Civil War journals and his and his wife's wartime diaries into chapters. (Since she kept a diary in 1862 and his is missing, I have included excerpts from her account.)

Another arbitrary decision: I decided to close Roberts's chronicle in the midst of his life, at the end of 1865. His annual birthday reflections, which are included along with diary entries for the war years in Chapter 10, continued until his eightieth birthday in 1913, but I believed they would not add enough of value to an already long book to include them.

One thing more: I mentioned above that I had made a note of a debate topic recorded in one of Roberts's diaries. While still pretending I was a scholar even as a bureaucrat, I gave a paper at a Southern Historical Association meeting in which I made a point of mid-nineteenth-century idolatry of George Washington by quoting Roberts's diary entry: "Polemic last night. . . . Question, Christ, Columbus & Washington. Washington gained the question." Luckily, before my paper was published I realized that what I had taken to be a comma after "Christ" was a period. The debate question surely was, "Resolved that Christopher Columbus deserves more praise for discovering America than George Washington for defending it"; and as usual Columbus lost. Not even Washington's deifiers went quite so far as to elevate him above Jesus. I apologize to any of my hearers who may remember the session, and I trust that none of them was so naive as to pass my foolish mistake on to his or her students.

Acknowledgments

I am sorry Doris Archer did not live to see this book published. She loved to read her great-grandfather's journals and diaries and believed they would interest other people too. She gladly let me use them without placing any restrictions on my editing or efforts to find a publisher. Her son, Stephen M. Archer, Jr., has kindly given me permission to photograph pages from the journals and diaries to use as illustrations in this book.

Ohio Magazine, in June 1989, published an article of mine entitled "A Buckeye Candide," a short version of the introduction and epilogue. The magazine's managing editor has given me full permission to reprint the material that appeared there.

Staff members of the Ohio Historical Society in Columbus made my visit to that excellent institution a productive one. Laura L. Chace of the Cincinnati Historical Society provided information on Farmers College. Residents of Summerford and London, Ohio, guided me to places mentioned by John Roberts and the site of the family gristmill on Roberts Mill Road and to the graveyard where he and many of the people he names are buried.

Two distinguished social historians, James Harvey Young and Thomas D. Clark, read the long manuscript and gave me helpful suggestions and encouragement. Another friend, Robert Harris Walker, gave good advice on the book's introduction and chapter openings. My daughter-in-law Ellen Blaik England transformed my confusing disks into the manuscript's final form.

I am grateful to them all.

J.M.E.
Washington, D.C.
July 17, 1995

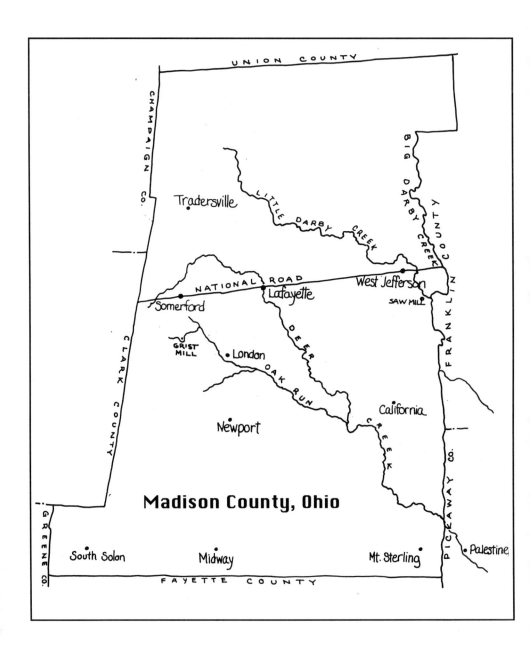

Madison County, Ohio

Introduction

"I love to note down the little facts of everyday life," John M. Roberts wrote in his journal on May 16, 1854. If not quite yet, his record keeping before long became a compulsive habit. Four years later he began keeping a diary, and he never failed to make a daily entry for the next fifty-six years, from his twenty-fifth year to a week before his death in his eighty-first.

Compared to that astonishing everyday chronicle, the edited journals and diaries reproduced here are only a fragment of Roberts's record of his journey through life. Even so, they reveal much about what he called "this little world of ours": his beliefs, fears, and hopes; his work as teacher, farmer, and miller; his and his neighbors' pursuit of happiness and a livelihood during years of rising sectional and community discord and, finally, war. For a time of alarming historical amnesia, Roberts's journal and diaries help restore our memory of country, village, and small-town life in representative midwestern communities.

Madison County, Ohio, where Roberts lived nearly all his life, was a rural area a little below the center of the state and just west of Franklin County, where the state capital, Columbus, is located. Enumerators of the eighth census in 1850 counted 10,015 inhabitants, only 78 of them African Americans. The population grew moderately in the ensuing years, reaching 13,015 in 1860 and 15,633 in 1870; the growth in the number of black residents, though small—there were still only 276 in 1860 and 705 ten years later—frightened Roberts and many of his white neighbors. Some of the older inhabitants were alarmed, too, by the influx of natives of Ireland, who came to work on the railroads that were linking the county seat, London, to the state's larger cities.

London was just a village when Roberts began keeping his journal. Yet its 513 inhabitants in 1850 contained, besides the usual county officials, an array of business and professional men—9 merchants, 7 attorneys, 6 physicians, 2 schoolteachers, 2 innkeepers, a grocery keeper, a druggist, a minister (Methodist)—and a wide range of artisans and others claiming special skills—11 saddlers, 8 shoemakers, 8 tailors, 8 carpenters, 7 clerks, 5 blacksmiths, 4 plasterers, 4 tanners, 3 tinners, 2 house joiners, 2 cabinetmakers, 2 printers, a brickmason, a butcher, a wagon maker, a potter, a cook, a hostler, a clothier, a stage driver, a

1

drover, a barber, a student, and a musician; in addition, the census recorded 18 laborers and 13 farmers among the town's residents.

London was over three miles away from the Roberts family home and gristmill on Oak Run. Closer was the village of Somerford (or Summerford), on the National Road from Cumberland, Maryland, to Vandalia, Illinois. Here, too, among the 139 inhabitants in 1850 their country neighbors could purchase some of the goods and services they could not supply by their own labors. On the eastern, opposite side of the county was the town of West Jefferson, near a Roberts family sawmill on Little Darby Creek which figures prominently in the young man's journal. Like Somerford, West Jefferson was on the national turnpike cutting through central Ohio. It was on Little Darby that young John Roberts lived with his father's family when the census taker came to their house in June 1850, though they moved not long after back to Oak Run.

John Roberts was born in Madison County on August 21, 1833, the son of Charles and Harriet Roberts, both Ohio natives. He was the oldest of eight children: John Macan (his mother's name was McCan, but he chose to alter it), William Henry, Catharine Margaret, Benjamin Franklin, Mary Elizabeth, Charles Cary, Harriet Maria, and Malvina Estelle. Their paternal grandfather, John J. Roberts, the son of a native of Wales, was born in Maryland in 1782. Many of the persons mentioned in his grandson's journals and diaries were natives of slave states of the upper South or their immediate descendants. Among them was the family of Handy Truitt, a Maryland native, who had married a Kentucky-born girl in her early teens. They had nine children, some of whose names often appear in John Roberts's record, especially that of Emarine, who became his bride in 1859.

Such large families as those of Charles and Harriet Roberts and of Handy and Mary Truitt seem large now but were not then in their rural neighborhood. Charles Roberts's sister—the diarist's Aunt Nancy—was the third wife of Valentine Wilson, the richest man in Madison County, and bore nine children by him to add to the ten borne by his first two wives; all but one of the nineteen grew to maturity. Handy Truitt's widowed mother had moved to Madison County from Maryland in 1818 with her fourteen daughters and two sons; she was said to have been 115 years old when she died in Illinois in 1858.

Her long life and the survival of eighteen of Valentine Wilson's children belie the abundant evidence of early mortality contained in John Roberts's record. Two of his and Emarine's children died in infancy. It was months after the birth of their first child before he wrote, "We think of calling her Flora." Early deaths of his recent schoolmates incited a number of the gloomy thoughts, and hopes for an afterlife, recorded in his journal. He had a low opinion of the healing powers of the local men who called themselves physicians. One of them, J. Randall, a family friend on Little Darby, was a hydropathic doctor, though "not a pure hydropath," Roberts said. Dr. Daniel Wilson, a botanic physician, also prescribed for the Roberts family occasionally. While Roberts blamed drugs and doctors for several untimely deaths, surely not Dr. Wilson, but the fecund Valentine was mainly responsible for the many tombstones bearing the family name in the graveyard just north of Summerford across Interstate 70.

Family names were often preserved in children's middle names, as in John's case and his brother Charles Cary's. Heroes of the Revolution and early republic provided names too, as that for their brother Benjamin Franklin (nicknamed Doc); whether or not their brother William Henry, usually called Henry, was named for the victor over Tecumseh ("Old Tippecanoe"), at least another William Henry who appears in Roberts's record was nicknamed Tip. The Bible and custom supplied still-familiar names with long antecedents. Strikingly unusual, however, were the mouth-filling names of some of John Roberts's acquaintances: Semproneous (Semp) and Gamaliel (Gam) Saunders, Selathiel (another Doc) Truitt, and Aquilla (Quill) Prugh.

Family traditions and skills learned from their fathers largely shaped young men's careers. Farming, milling, and teaching school were ways of earning a living often carried on simultaneously by male members of the Roberts family. Charles Roberts, the father, taught school in Madison and adjoining counties for eighteen years. In 1844 he bought and rebuilt a gristmill on Oak Run. As a deacon in the Christian Church and opposed to making and selling whiskey, he refused to buy a connected distillery. Five years later he bought land two miles south of West Jefferson and erected a sawmill on Little Darby Creek. His son's journal tells of the family's efforts to rebuild it, using the grandfather's knowledge of milling, while Charles lay dying.

John M. Roberts also farmed, milled, and taught. His main occupation in the years covered by the journals and diaries edited here was teaching in a one-room country school. His "journalism," as he referred to the act of writing down his private thoughts, began in such a schoolroom, where as a nineteen-year-old youth he studied arithmetic, grammar, and spelling and made feeble attempts to write rhyming verse.

He also engaged in public journalism. His obituary in the *Madison County Democrat* (July 17, 1914) says he contributed to the first issue of that London paper in 1857 and continued to cover the town's monthly livestock sales and report on local news as a country correspondent for more than half a century. In addition, he filled the columns of the *Democrat* and other papers with partisan attacks on Republicans, memories of old-time ways of living, reports on teachers' meetings, rejoinders to the jibes of anonymous critics, and essays on such diverse topics as education, socialism, imperialism, demonology, and religion. The newspaper became his latter-day classroom, another schoolmasterly means of enlightening the public and promoting democracy. To John Roberts, the teacher and the printer were the republic's guardians.

He dedicated himself to increasing the local citizenry's knowledge. Teaching in "the Brush" of Pleasant Township in the southeastern part of Madison County soon after his twenty-fifth birthday, he wrote: "My school is getting to be more interesting to me every day. . . . I love to see the minds of children expanding, growing, & refining . . . and although I am not as well qualified to give them the right kind of ideas as I should be, yet I feel like devoting my one talent to that noblest of professions, the training of the immortal mind." Again: "I love the schoolroom and its appurtenances. It is indeed a glorious occupation and one that is not patronized as it should be by the community. The profession needs more sympathy & hearty support from the American public, but I think that there is a better day dawning. God speed the happy day!"

That happy day never came, but Roberts's belief in the importance of schooling never faltered. For a quarter-century he taught in the district schools of Madison County, always hopeful of greater support from parents and taxpayers of teachers' efforts. After leaving the schoolmaster's desk, he continued his reform campaign—as district school director and clerk, participant in teachers' association meetings, truant officer, and newspaper advocate—to persuade Madison County citizens of their duty to bolster the very foundation of the American republic.

Free schools and a free press were essential to republican government; and the political party most committed to preserving those institutions, Roberts believed, was the party of Jefferson and Jackson. "He is a Democrat," Roberts wrote of himself in a family sketch he wrote for a county history published in 1883. Born during Jackson's presidency, Roberts remained faithful to the Democratic party—except for a misadventure with the Know-Nothings in the 1850s—through long, disheartening years of Republican dominance. Grover Cleveland's first term proved a welcome respite, but not his second; and Roberts's political idol, William Jennings Bryan, three times went down to defeat by goldbugs, monopolists, and imperialists. Woodrow Wilson's election in 1912 brightened Roberts's last years. It was good to have a schoolmaster in the White House.

Roberts was a lower-case democrat as well. He berated the local "aristocrats"—though who they were other than Uncle Valentine Wilson it is difficult to discern—and praised the virtuous poor—or at least those of the poor he thought virtuous and who had white skin. His tirades against blacks in the years covered by this book display the hateful racial bigotry of many midwestern whites. Madison County's difficulties in meeting its draft quotas during the war help explain why the North reluctantly came to accept the use of black soldiers in its armies. Roberts wrote that "Negroes wont make good soldiers nor good, substantial citizens." Most of his neighbors probably agreed. Still, if Roberts's views on blacks mark him as a man of his time and place, in other ways his vivid originality stands out when he describes and characterizes members of his community.

While Roberts intended his journal and diaries as aids to memory and often wrote with careless haste, he sometimes conceived of a future reader who might wonder what kind of person he was. About five feet ten inches tall and usually weighing between 140 and 150 pounds, he had dark hair, most of it gone before he reached middle age, and a full beard and mustache, somewhat sandy in color. One of his anonymous critics in the *London Times*, a Republican paper, called him "Old Baldy." Roberts showed his sensitivity about his baldness when he wrote in his diary (March 21, 1869): "I am using Ayres Hair Vigor to make my hair come in. I think it will do the work." Usually he disdained quack nostrums.

Through frequent practice, Roberts's writing gained in clarity, vigor, and sense. It reveals his personality. He enjoyed mimicking local speech, ridiculing ignorant notions, and using newly coined words and phrases. Less consciously, he resorted to vernacular expressions, familiar then but now strange, that had sprung from the country's recent frontier past. Diary entries had to be brief and factual, but the big blank pages of his journal gave his volubility and fun-loving whimsy room to ramble. He liked current slang words (e.g., "mizzled"), artificial ones ("absquatulate"), an archaic one ("comerogues" [fellow rogues]), and may have coined at least one ("raction" [evidently meaning nonsense]). Others words he used seemed quaint only a few years later to Edward Eggleston, who put them in quotation marks in his melodramatic tale of a Hoosier schoolmaster: "chunks" (of firewood); "sloped" (ran away or hid); "mitten" (a rejection); "saft sodder" [soft sawder] (ingratiating banter or blarney).

Roberts's journal entries often show abrupt shifts in subjects and moods, usually because he composed at different times, before school opened and during the noon dinner hour or morning and afternoon recesses. His crowded pages bear no warning signs to show the darting of his mind from tomfoolery to *timor mortis*. Thoughts about death and an afterlife fill a good deal of space in his big book. His comments about preachers and sinning members of their flocks reveal a critical attitude toward conventional piety, a distaste for hell-fire and brimstone sermons, and scorn for persons who swallowed obscure dogmas without question.

During one Somerford revival Roberts contemplated joining his friends at the mourner's bench; yet he seems never to have joined a church. He adopted the Universalist belief that a kind God gives everlasting life to all humankind. The local schoolhouse was the center of his religious community—and intellectual and recreational as well—and it was there rather than in chapels that he most often heard sermons by ministers of several denominations. In the postwar years his wife and children attended Dunkerd services in the nearby schoolhouse, and he liked to observe the sect's annual foot-washing service. (In one of his newspaper pieces he praised the Dunkerds as "good, quiet citizens" who "try to do as nearly as possible what Christ did in his social relations, as well as in his religious teachings.") His unquestioning faith in republican government and public common schools caused much of his distrust of London's Irish Catholics. He directed many of his barbs at Methodists, though what he called "the ne plus ultra of their great machine of passion stirrers," the camp meeting, provided the most riotous excitement of his bachelor days.

Weather and crops were Roberts's most constant concerns. As a miller as well as a farmer, he worried about the price of grain and the abundance of the harvest. Droughts and freezes could ruin crops, and torrential rains could wreak damage to milldams and head- and tailraces, the courses to and from the water wheel. Muddy or snow-covered roads made his long treks to and from the schoolhouse tiresome and cut school attendance, irregular at best, to a handful of "scholars." (Perhaps the girls should change their long petticoats for Amelia Bloomer's newfangled costume, he playfully suggested.) Dreary days cast a pall over the schoolroom and wiped out recesses. As a schoolboy himself, though, Roberts welcomed heavy snowfalls for the excitement of sleigh races; and when rain canceled farm work, it gave him a chance to write in his journal.

He snatched such chances when he could, and the schoolroom, whether he was pupil or teacher, offered them most often. Outside school, almost ceaseless labor was a primary, unquestioned fact of life for six days of the week.

Sunday was different. For Roberts, it was no day for a long face. Then came time for visiting, writing, and reading. He had no large stock of books, and rarely could afford to buy one, though his very first diary entry (August 11, 1858) records that he "Attended auction in Somerford. Purchased Rollins Ancient History, Dutch [German] & English hymn book." The tags of Burns and Shakespeare that dot his journal may well have come from school readers or elocution books rather than collections of their works, as did the sentimental pieces he enjoyed reciting at school exhibitions or literary society meetings. He thought *Uncle Tom's Cabin* a waste of time, no doubt because he disliked Mrs. Stowe's views of blacks, but he expressed no similar feelings about dime novels or one of Timothy Shay Arthur's moral tales. He borrowed books from neighbors occasionally, and by the end of 1863 there was a township library of sorts, as his diary notes that he had got Voltaire's life of Charles XII of Sweden there and thought it "a very fine composition."

The literary society, or lyceum or polemic, as he sometimes called it, provided another road to knowledge, and exciting contests as well. Debate topics ranged widely: Would there be life after death? Should Cuba be annexed? Was greater beauty to be found in nature or art? Who had suffered the greater ill treatment from whites, Indians or blacks? And for rural folk who valued animals highly, their arguments over the superior worth of the horse or the cow were spirited.

The candlelit schoolhouse provided the auditorium for debates, exciting spelling matches, and other kinds of entertainment and self-improvement as well. Nighttime singing and geography schools, organized by teachers wanting to supplement their income, attracted farm folk eager to learn or to visit with their neighbors. They also attracted disturbers of the peace, like some boys from a neighboring county who demanded admission to a singing school, or disgruntled local youths who pounded on the clapboards outside and whistled through a knothole. And to single young men and women the schools gave an opportunity to spark on the dark road home.

They flirted and courted at dances too, which were held in private homes rather than the schoolhouse. At these "frolicks," which were most frequent around Christmas and New Year's, Roberts found relief from his "ennui." Jealous rivalries among young males, fired by whiskey, provoked fights, even drawn pistols. After the fiddler left, couples sought out dark corners, where they talked and hugged, sometimes till "rooster crowed for day."

Unwanted pregnancies were frequent, and while some males accepted their approaching fatherhood by marriage, others skipped the country. Husbands, and wives too, sometimes forgot their vows of faithfulness and created neighborhood scandals. John Roberts, when single, worried that his intimacy with a girl on the creek across from the family sawmill might have blasted his dreams of success. (He wrote more frankly in his diary than in his journal: "I satisfied my passion & accomplished all that I went after.") But there was never a hint of infidelity in his marriage, on either side. One local wife's adultery—her plea of rape failed to convince—led Roberts to suggest that maybe Oak Run husbands should copy the Turks' practice of using eunuchs to guard their spouses, but he had no worries.

Although he did not advocate women's rights in a reformer's role, Roberts did plead for more attention to girls' schooling. He could not understand why parents had more interest in the education of their sons—and all too little there—than in that of their daughters. Women, after all, as mothers largely shaped the coming generation. "As the twig is bent the tree's inclined" is one of his many oft-quoted adages.

There was a strong-minded woman at home before his marriage, and Roberts complained that she treated him meanly. His mother expected him, her oldest son, to do the work of his ailing, and soon deceased, father; but she made decisions without consulting him. He wanted to go away to school, perhaps to Antioch College in Yellow Springs, Ohio, or to Farmers College near Cincinnati, where he could live with his Uncle Cary. His uncle, Freeman Grant Cary, had founded the college in 1846, hoping to meet the educational needs of farmers and young men entering business. When Roberts visited the school in April 1853, its 87-acre experimental farm, botanical garden, and instruction in agricultural chemistry attracted a substanial number of students. (If he had visited the school a year or two earlier he might have encountered a future president of the United States, Benjamin Harrison, and his secretary of the interior, John W. Noble.) A sharp drop in enrollments during the Civil War contributed to the school's decline. A successor institution, Belmont College, operated for a few years in the 1880s, but then the still remaining ten acres and buildings—one of them Cary Hall—were transferred to the new Ohio Military Institute.

For Roberts a college education was a fading dream. When he reached the age of twenty-one in August 1853 and told himself he was now legally free to leave home, his mother's reminder of his family duties kept him there. He resented being tied down and fretted under her discipline. After his marriage, his mother agreed to let the young couple have a good milk cow, but then, as he saw the matter, reneged on her promise. As long as she lived, John found himself caught in the middle of her quarrels with mill workers and tenants.

The other member of his immediate family most often mentioned in John's journal was his brother William Henry. Two years younger than John, Henry was something of a wild colt. He thought some of becoming a teacher and did fill in for John a little when they bached at the Utopian schoolhouse in the Brush, but instead took up carpentering (another Roberts family occupation) and daguerreotyping. Henry later moved to Clinton, Missouri, where he continued to do carpentering and photography (along with Anson Corey, his partner in Ohio) and tended an orchard after marrying a widow with property. He encouraged John to move to Missouri and was his landlord there for a while. Their disputes over family property and national politics continued until Henry's death.

John's relations with his father's youngest brother, James H. Roberts, only two years John's senior, were friendlier. Uncle Jim also moved to southwestern Missouri, and unlike Henry, whose itchy feet carried him to Oregon, then back to Clinton, and finally to Durango, Colorado, remained there until his death. The lure of the West and the hope of better fortune there tempted members of the Roberts family and many of their neighbors; as John Roberts's journal and diaries show, they often returned to Madison County after experiencing hard times, severe weather, and racking ague on the western prairies.

There was plenty of illness, including the chills and fevers of ague, back in Ohio, too. Although the deadly frontier malady of milk sickness was rare by mid-century, Roberts records a few instances of it. Consumption, dropsy, cholera morbus, smallpox, measles, mumps, liver and heart diseases caused by heavy drinking, all appear in his references to sickness among his neighbors and family members. The outbreak of smallpox caused the abrupt closing of one of his schools in Missouri. For his own physical disorders, Roberts relied on fasting and hydropathy. Again and again he castigated medical doctors and druggists, nearly all of whom he considered quacks. For an aching tooth, until he could get it "plugged," he resorted to chewing tobacco.

But the use of tobacco Roberts called his most grievous and unhealthful vice. Time and again he vowed, and failed, to break his habit of smoking and chewing. (A page cut out of his journal was perhaps a shameful reminder of his failure.) He was fortunate in having a weak stomach for alcohol and had no real worry about becoming a drunkard, as so many of his neighbors did. Although the Maine Liquor Law failed in Ohio to bring the reform Roberts hoped for, he continued to believe the temperance movement would triumph. Like his optimism about Democratic victories at the polls, his faith in social progress rebounded after every defeat.

Indeed, John Roberts was a Buckeye Candide in many ways. He needed no Dr. Pangloss to assure him that "this little world of ours," the pure country of Madison County, was the best of all possible worlds. He always wished in his end-of-the-year diary reflections that the coming year would treat him as well as the past one had done, no matter how badly that had been. A new year brought the hopeful prospect of change and opportunity.

His "little world" now seems like a foreign country. Could a young American man or woman today imagine getting excited about walking a muddy road to a debate or a singing class in a candlelit schoolroom? And how, an elementary teacher must wonder, could she possibly cope with as many as fifty restless "scholars" ranging in age from five to twenty in classes reciting lessons from the primer to algebra?

Yet many of John Roberts's whimsical musings and considered reflections, particularly those about the importance of education and on a teacher's troubles and rewards, have remarkable present relevance. Other issues that concerned him have their counterparts today, among them addiction to tobacco and alcohol, religious and patriotic zealotry, fear of immigrants, inequality of rich people and poor, and burdensome debt resulting from easy access to credit. His prejudices also connect the past to the present. Anyone probing for the roots of America's enduring racism can find them abundantly revealed in his record. Roberts's furious, abusive words are no longer tolerable in civil discourse, but the fear and loathing they express still divide American society.

It is time, though, to let John Roberts speak in his own words. So, back to January 1853 and a country schoolroom . . .

1

Schoolboy Musings
January 17–March 3, 1853

John M. Roberts, a nineteen-year-old schoolboy studying grammar, Ray's Arithmetic, *and spelling, sits on a bench on the boys' side of the room and writes in his book while other "scholars," some as young as five, recite. Their noise and stumbling reading often bother him and muddle his thoughts.*

He writes in a big, legal-size book purchased for the Ciceronian Literary Society; when the members thought it too large for their needs, John, the secretary, decided to keep it for his "journaling." The first page shows the book's original purpose; it records a Ciceronian Society's debate topic, "Resolved that there is no punishment after death," with John Roberts, Semp Saunders, Henry Roberts, and William Tingley on the affirmative side against Gamaliel Saunders, Addison Cornwell, William Orpet, Andrew Turner, and David Garrard on the negative. On the next few pages appear several versions of Roberts's signature, autographs and brief descriptions of several friends, exercises in penmanship, Jaques's "All the world's a stage" speech, and a few "Poetic Effusions of Jno. M. Roberts," among them the following rhymes, composed in his upstairs room at home, which may serve as a prologue to his musings in the schoolroom over the next month and a half:

> *This book is of many truths and errors full;*
> *It makes with reason & sense a tight pull.*
> *The writer can tell a bag of cheese from a bag of wool.*
> *This is a journal of the times and it takes*
> *A man to read it who is up to all kinds of shakes.*
> *Now, dear reader, you may turn over and read of snakes.*
> *But here ends this rhyming clatter,*
> *For some may think the writer wants to chatter*
> *About himself & then cry, O, what is the matter?*
> *Now I will lay my book in my trunk*
> *And go downstairs and kick up a chunk.*

That is, I will show my great spunk.
One to look at this poetry would think I was drunk,
But here I will leave it all in a great lump.
 Here you see that I duly
 Subscribe myself yours truly,

                                          John M. Roberts

Obviously not a candidate for Parnassas, as he thought his friend John Allen was, Roberts is an earnest student who regrets his friends' poor attendance in school and their indifference to learning. Some days, especially when mud or snow "most to[o] deep for pettycoats" makes walking the country roads difficult, only a handful of pupils come to the "temple"; on fair days as many as fifty fill the room, if parents don't keep them home to perform farm or household chores.

Roberts studies mainly on his own, and while showing no esteem for schoolmaster Lowry, blames himself for slow progress in his studies. In the village of Somerford, a little to the north of Roberts's school, rebellious pupils oust their teacher, but Lowry's let him off with a warning posted on the schoolhouse door.

Juvenile playfulness gains joyful release during morning and afternoon recesses and noon dinner hours. Girls run across the yard playing a game called black man, trying to dodge being tagged by those in the middle; boys throw snowballs or skate on a nearby creek. One noon hour, half a dozen girls and two or three boys snatch Roberts's shabby hat and gleefully demolish it.

The schoolhouse is the center of Roberts's life and the community's. It provides a meeting place for the weekly candlelight debates of the Ciceronian Literary Society and for the singing, spelling, and geography schools he regularly attends. Some nights, boisterous or drunken pranksters disrupt singing classes or, on the dark road to the schoolhouse, frighten a boy walking alone. On another night, Roberts and his friends have an exciting sleigh race and run their competitors off a bridge.

Work fills daytime hours out of school. Roberts cuts wood, chops ice at the family's frozen gristmill, and hauls flour barrels to the mill, but he chooses not to help Henry Peck and Semp Saunders drive Jacob Garns's hogs to Pickaway County.

Sunday sermons offering the opposing views of Messrs. Cotterel and Miller stimulate Roberts's emerging skepticism about religious dogmas. He and Henry Peck argue with two Catholics about "their priests infallibility." And among Protestants, Roberts notes a falling away of the zeal fired by recent revivals and camp meetings.

Although he claims to dislike gossip, Roberts records tales and rumors of his neighbors' peccadilloes and fancies. California gold fields still lure some of his companions; other former residents of the community return to Madison County after disappointment on Illinois or Iowa prairies. In the final entry of this chapter, Roberts relates his own family's earlier moves. Here, and often later, he shows his bitter feelings toward Mrs. Fleming for burning his father's sawmill on Little Darby Creek.

[Monday] January 17th, Anno Domini 1853

Going to school to Thadeus M. Lowry, studying arithmetic, grammar, & orthography. Making poor progress. All my own fault; nobody to blame but my own procrastination, which is indeed the thief of time. . . .

Good preaching & practising are two [different] things. I have & always will have, I am in hopes, enough of effrontery to carry me through this world. What is the use of wasting breath in argument when talking to dolts & blockheads? No use, no, not a bit. All that is required of you is to keep up appearances; best foot foremost and you will succeed. That is the motto of all from the schoolgirl up to the city belle. Yes, a man must blow & bulley if he wants to get along. Nothing like it. Brag is a good dog & one which if managed right will carry you through to Eureka. What a grand thing for doctors, lawyers, & printers commencing & pertaining to one & all of them. Whew, just listen to the doctor: "Ah, I have done wonders in my time. Why, sir, I can cure a man who has lost his liver & stomach, no mistake, sir." "Ah," says his patient, "how did you do it?" Dr.: "Do what, sir? I have done it. Thats enough." . . . Poor patient swallows the pill along with the rest of the Drs narcotics, which makes him no better. M.D. gives him up & he recovers. M.D. goes to him and says, "Ah, my dear fellow, how well you look. I knew that that last dose would do the business. That was a preparation of my own."

[Tuesday] January 18th

Today read Uncle Tom's Cabin through. Labor lost & time thrown away on that raction, but I dont know but what others have done the same. Whew, what a load of imaginary evil one can think of. . . .

No grammar lesson today. Dry work, for my classmates do not take hold of it. Why not say, "I do not see that it will ever be of any use to me." Well, I have no objection, but dont look back with reproach upon your teacher when you see your error. Just remember that when you want to grumble about your ignorance. . . .

[Wednesday] January 19th

. . . Parsed some today. Not good in grammar; neither am I good in anything. All gone off into the regions of abstraction; nothing real, nothing solid, all fading & ethereal.

Geography school tonight. Wm. Romigh, teacher, bred & born here. . . . Nothing of importance has ever been done by him yet, but there may be. . . . Jonah W. Trowbridge, Jac. Forbess, Saml. Trowbridge, & Henry Peck all sit on the same bench with myself, all fine fellows made of good stuff, but not very good schollars. No fault of theirs, however, for they cant see the use of it. . . .

[Thursday] Janr. 20th, [18]53

Last night geography school. Disturbance got up by some small boys on account of not being allowed to come. George Wilson, Harris Markley, Thomas Cornwell, & Valentine H. Prugh chief ones in the disturbance, which was making a noise outside whistling & whooping in through a knothole in the weather boarding. John M. Allen & myself caught one of the chaps; fetched him into the house by force. Give us two or three curses & then behaved the rest of the evening. Thomas Cornwell snatched H. Pecks hat; got well kicked for so doing. . . .

[Friday] January the 21st, A.D. 1853

Last night debate. Had refreshing time. Spoke till midnight. Lost some sleep & breath but had the satisfaction to be on the right side although that side did not convince the judges. Everything passed off quietly.

Letter writing all the rage here now. Schoolboys are getting sentimental. Several letters have fallen into the hands of the teacher, who has made the authors of the said letters read the same to all the schollars. Some of them quite pithy, full of fun. Well, I have no objections. . . . Dont listen to those old saws who were just as bad as you were when they were young. Now they croak up their noses because they have passed the Rubicon of their pleasures. Ah, say they, how I would like to be a boy again. Well now, just let us boys be boys. Dont make old men of us when you yourselves own that childhood is the time when one can have the most pleasure for the least money & the least trouble. Oh, you old envious porcupines, how glad it would make you if you could only make us as austere & sour as yourselves.

Today I am going to quit chewing tobacco for one year, but I must still smoke some. Cant give the critter up entirely. I love the beast and cant help it, but here is the resolution. . . .

[Monday] January 24th, 1853

Today as sleepy as I want to be. Went to Somerford last night in a sleigh with Gam Saunders. Went to Patrick Powers. Had some oysters & ale. Enjoyed myself very well but staid up most too late to enjoy myself very well today, but the pleasure has overbalanced the pain & I am content.

I cant cipher today. Eyes feel like as thoug[h] half the sand of Sahara was in them. Got as far as the adjective in my grammar.

Noah Marsh has gone crazy & has not eat any for ten days nor drank anything for three days. Noah moved west . . . year before last. . . . Bought a good place in Iowa but was not satisfied. The reasons he gives are that the wind blows to[o] hard there for him to light. He says wind would blow me off. He come back again & bought his old place again. Paid out all his money for his land & thought that he was broke up & ruined forever, which threw his mind off its balanced, though some say it was lopsided before. . . .

Not many girls here today. Some to[o] proud to come & others too lazy. That accounts for the absence of most of them. Stay at home if you want to, but if you cant weigh a pound of butter or tell the day of the month by the almanac, dont say that you had no chance to learn anything when you were young. . . .

[Tuesday] January 25th

Up last night as usual. Got home at twelve o'clock exactly. Myself & Gam Saunders were at a debate up at the Turner schoolhouse. Had a good time of it, take it all in all. . . .

Semp Saunders is here today, which makes the first time for him. Teacher has got him among the little boys.

It is s[n]owing yet & we are going to have fine times yet, I am in hopes. Must get Paddy [the family's horse?] on the track tonight. Must keep up the excitement. Cant live without I have something to stir the blood, which if it was not excited sometimes would eventually get so cold & insipid that man would degenerate, become senseless clods. The fact is that it is better for man to "wear out than it is for him to rust out."

There are more girls here today than there were yesterday. Some hopes yet for them. . . .

Got as far as the adverb in my grammar today. I hope that I will be able to conjugate all the verbs before I get many months older. . . .

My studies are too much disconnected for them to be very beneficial. Grammar & arithmetic all jumbled together, but maybe light will spring up from out of chaos. Who knows the luck of a lousy calf? It may live all winter & then die in the spring. . . .

Just nineteen years, 5 months, & four days old today. Where will I be when another 19 years shall have passed? I perhaps under the sod, myself & [this] book both forgotten, or perhaps between the plow handles working out my salvation in this world if not in the world to come. But come what may, I am ready. If death, why then my troubles will be over. If not, why then I can only die some other time. . . .

[Wednesday] January 26th

The last night went to spelling school. Had a refreshing time. Went sleigh riding. Got home as usual late enough. Feel the effects of the same today; but no matter, the pleasure overbalances all other considerations. . . . Must keep up the excitement. "Whoopee"! Nothing like it.

Geography school here tonight. Have to come, I guess. . . .

Danl. Wallace & his brother have got back from Illinois. They are not going to . . . live out there. . . . Madison Co. against Ohio & Ohio against the world for pleasant recreation & profitable instruction. Whew! Nothing like this place for big babies & corn dodgers [small baked or fried corncakes].

Have not done much in my arithmetic. Felt a little kind of wooly headed. Must try & do better tomorrow. . . .

Mr. Cotterel moved here today. He has rented a house of Jno. Forbess. Come from Jamestown in Green County & is a Baptist preacher, an old regular Baptist. Dont know anything more about him now, but more anon. . . .

Miss Mary Jane Harper & Miss Elizabeth Hewitt, both natives of the far famed vale of Little Darby, they both go to school here now. . . .

[Thursday] January 27th

. . . Last night had a geography school. Had a tall time of it. Jno. Wilson came over drunk & wanted to fight J.M. Allen for tumbling his George into the schoolhouse the other night he was here. J. Wilson fetched a butcher knife with him, but we got rid of him without fighting. Myself & Jno. Allen asked his pardon & got it along with a blessing. Such is the inconsistency of human nature. . . .

No girls here last night. It got to[o] cold for them. Well, I have no objections to be sure. What are they to me? Nothing now, hereafter much. Got throug[h] analysis in Rays Arithmetic today. Guess I shall get through this winter if I try, & if I dont, why of course I wont.

Mill froze up last night. Had to help chop it loose this morning. Did not get to school untill after it had taken up.

Not many schollars here today. They would rather live in ignorance than come to school. Well, where little is given, little is required. But every one ought to feel as if he was the pillar of the state & do all he can to promulgate true principles & promote the happiness of others. . . .

Confound the everlasting ill & carping aristocrat of this country or any other. I naturally hate to see them poor bloats. They can puff & blow about respectability & religion when if they were tried to the full of measure, they would fall as far behind the common run of farmers as they now think themselves ahead. . . .

[Friday] January 28th

. . . Had a debate last night. Had a juicy & refreshing time. The reason was because we were victorious. Who does not feel complacent after having come off conqueror? It makes one feel about a head & shoulders taller than the rest of mankind, but when defeat comes and his cherished sc[h]emes are bottled down, then the thing is reversed. . . .

Getting along pretty well in my arithmetic today. Working in the exchange business today. What I shall do Monday I know not; perhaps go into a select company & do a driving business, that is if the company is a drove of hogs.

. . . Grammar lesson in the personal pronoun. Got along pretty well with it, though I do not practice it as much as I should.

Henry Peck here today. He wants to go away again at recess to fix for a sleigh ride. Have spelling school here every Friday afternoon. The schollars are not very good spellers, so that there is no time lost there. . . .

[Monday] January the 31, 1853

. . . Since I last made an entry in this book several things have transpired which may make a decided difference in my future transactions on this mundane sphere. . . .

On Saturday I chopped some wood. Staid at home that night & got a good sleep. Sunday I got up, read awhile, & then went to here [*sic*] Mr. Miller preach. He made out tolerably well. He took his text . . . from the eighth Psalm. He made out that man has all the power within himself to make his bed in misery or immortal glory. In the afternoon went to hear the Rev. Mr. Cotterel. He preached exactly the reverse of that of Mr. Miller. Both of them appear to have been in earnest about what they preached. Now who is going to decide when "Doctors disagree"? If you know, just shove him over this way so that we that are all in the dark over here may get some light on this & other subjects of equal importance.

Last Saturday [Friday?] evening started to go a sleighing. Went to Mrs. Saunders. Got there in company with Henry Peck, & Semp Saunders got our crowd together at Mrs. Saunders, which were as follows: Henry Peck, Semp Saunders, Jonah Trowbridge, Henry Roberts, Frank Roberts, & myself. We started in two sleighs, one one horse sleigh and one two horse sleigh. Went to Somerford. Some of the boys had a bowl of oysters. We got there without any accident, but when we come back we come the long pull over a stump with the one horse sleigh & broke it all to smithereens. Come on a little farther, we met two fellows coming full drive. They past us & turned around & wanted to pass us but did not come it over as easy as they thought they could. We run them about two miles & a half. Succeeded in getting them to run off of a bridge and break one of their sleighs, one in which was a woman that said she had the toothache & could not go with us. Well, the punishment followed her close, for she got well doused in the snow. . . .

[Tuesday] February the 1, 1853

Last night had a spelling school. About 60 schollars, some from other schools. I suppose they thought they could beat us, but they could not do it, and thank the Lord for it. . . . All of the Deer Creek scolars were over. . . . If they had of beaten us, they would have crowed for a week anyhow. Well, I guess it is not following the Scriptures to get up these rivalries, for it says, "Little children, love one another."

Have got along first rate in my arithmetic today. I am working in the extraction of the square root, which takes a little more intellectual labor than the extraction of hickory roots. . . .

Today I heard of something out of the common in the shape of a staid member of the M.E. Church who happened not to have that respect for the property of others. She absquatulated . . . with a bolt of calico, pair of shoes, & also some cotton shirting. Widow she is, but that was no excuse for the crime. . . .

Some of the boys have staid at home today to work, so we are not quite as much crowded today as usual. Well, I have no objection. Ignorance may be bliss, but I have yet to find out in what manner. Miss Rhoda Roderick is here today which, by the by, is something out of the common. I am afraid that it is portentous of some great thing, perhaps an earthquake. The reason I think so is that all of the young ladies around here have got too proud to go to school.

I am getting along pretty well in my grammar. I am still in the pronouns. Get through them this week if I do not get to[o] dilatory. . . .

[Wednesday] February 2d

Last night went after a load of flour barrels. Wm. Anderson went along with me. He has just come from Darby. All right down there according to what he says. The folks down there about two years ago all belonged to meeting. Now there are none there who make the least pretensions to religion. They have all took to dancing & drinking since then. Well, who would a thunk it? Not I. An overheat is very apt to have an overcool to ballance it. Humph! How little did I think that those folks down there who done so much ground & hasty tumbling [at camp meeting?] would again be found among the shoals of sin. But as the old proverb goes, Whatever man has done, man may do.

Wm. Anderson is here [in school] today. He has not been here before for six months. He is just as ignorant as he was six years ago. Well, there must be hewers of wood & drawers of water, & I suppose that he is one of them. . . .

The weather today is wet and gloomy. Well, the bright side of creation ought to be out of sight sometimes, for if it was not the case, we would be bored to death by the monotonous aspect of things. "Yes, whatever is, is right." I believe that sentence, for why did not the Creator who created the world & all that is therein say something to the contrary when He first made them? I leave that for theologians to solve if they can. . . .

Have got as far as the cube root in my arithmetic. I guess that I shall get through this winter now certain. Grammar progresses along with the rest. Got as far as the adjective pronouns or pronominal adjectives. . . .

[Thursday] February 3d, 1853

. . . Last night we had a geography school here which passed off in as humdrum a way as it usually does. No girls here, which is one of the reasons why it was not interesting. . . . If a man has not the approving smile of woman to cheer him in his labors, he is an undone & miserable creature. Indeed, I would hardly want to go to Heaven if I thought that there would not be any women there.

Henry Peck is here today. He talks of going down to Pickaway County with a drove of hogs & wants me to go with him. I do not know if I will go or not, for the roads are so confounded muddy & my boots are none of the best. But who knows what money can make people do?

Jonah Trowbridge was here this forenoon, but he has gone. The why & the wherefore is that he loves money better than knowledge. . . . There are not many girls here today. I guess the roads are most to[o] muddy for them to turn out.

We are going to have a debate here tonight. The question up for the lear[n]ed savan[t]s of this neck of woods to spout upon is, Resolved that slavery has been a greater curse than the intemperate use of ardent spirits. For my part, I take the negative of this question. . . .

I have got along pretty well in my arithmetic today. Managed to get the cube root all done & commenced a fearful warfare against arithmetical progression. . . .

One of my old schoolmates died yesterday evening. He has always been feeble & weak, so he is better off as he is. His name is Jeremiah Wilson. . . . Peace to thy ashes, say I, for you never did me any harm. . . .

[Friday] February 4th

. . . Last night had a debate here which [went] off as rich as cream. But there were some drawbacks which were interspersed through the whole which were not as palatable as I would have had if I should be called upon to choose for myself. One of the greatest was the rain, which came down upon my devoted head most unmercifully, but I had companions who were in the same fix with myself, so I was not entirely afoot and alone amid the jeers of an inconstant world. I got home and got [to] bed at just precisely ten o'clock. Blowed out the light & shut my eyes, then snored away untill the sun did rise.

The roads are still as muddy as old Sam. . . . I have concluded not to go with Garns hogs. Most too muddy to make an attempt on those everlasting beech woods & elm flats.

Mrs. Ships is the womans name who stole the goods that I mentioned. She was not in want, I believe, at the time. Well now, [let] the one who is without sin cast the first stone, say I, & if you cant find none that are in that happy state, why then say unto her, Woman, go thy way but sin no more. But no, that will not be the way with you. No, it will only be who can throw the most stones that will receive the benedictions of the fathers of the church. Curse the man, say I, who will willfully malign the fame of woman, whether she be found in the drawing room or in the kitchen. Yes, the man who would thus attack the fame of the gentler sex would be fit for nothing but "treason, stratagems, & spoils."

Henry Peck, Semp Saunders, & Wm. Anderson are going with those hogs. They are going to Bloomsfield on the Scioto River. . . .

All our girls are not here today. Some of them staying away on account of bad weather, I suppose. No grammar lesson yet today nor none yesterday. I shall get behind the times, I am afraid, if I do not stir my stumps.

[Monday] February 7th

Today has passed off pleasantly enough. The sun shines out gloriously over the snow which fell last Saturday & Saturday night.

Henry Peck & Semp have had a hard time of it [driving hogs] this time, I think. . . .

Last Friday night I went after a physician for the Allens wife who has the winter fever. It was as dark [as] a stack of black cats. I got to the doctor, roused him out of his warm bed, helped him catch old grey, got upon my mare, & took it liesurely enough.

No grammar lesson today. Guess I shall not get one, for the first spelling class is taking their place to spell. Not many of the fair sex here today. The snow was most to[o] deep for pettycoats. Guess the bloomer will have to be adopted yet by the ladies.

I have made good progress today considering the time that I have been here. . . . There is not going to be any school tomorrow, for the teacher is sick.

[Tuesday] February 8th

No school today. Hauled wood all day.

There is a protracted meeting being held over at Somerford. . . .

[Wednesday] Feb. 9th

Come to school. Found some schollars here who were enjoying themselves fine. They say that there is not going to be any school untill Monday. . . . There is going to be a geography school here tonight. . . .

Good by book, good by school, untill Monday anyhow. . . .

[Monday] February 14th

Today I have made some progress in my various studies. . . .

Noah Marsh is dead. He died last week from the effects of insanity.

Mary Ann Wilson married last week to a Mr. Cheny. So mote it be. But where, oh where will those other two aspirants for her hand [go]? . . . I expect that they will not go entirely crazy & hang themselves. Poor D.T.G. & T.R., you have been lured on by the siren, but you will know better next time.

Last Saturday hauled wood. The next day I staid at home like a good boy & kept house. The next day I came to school but there was none. Rode up to James Porters in Jas. Fullertons wagon. Loitered around there for awhile, then went home. I did not do anything that day. Either laziness or something else was the cause. . . .

I have not got my grammar lesson today. I guess that I will not do anything more in grammar this quarter, but I think that I will study it thoroughly next summer if I can get to go to school, which I think perhaps I shall. This school will be out in two weeks and three days. I will then have to go to work, which, by the by, will not be very pleasant at first. . . .

Jonah Trowbridge is here today. He has not been here for some time before. Semp Saunders is not coming anymore. Neither is Miss Roderick. I shall mark those two persons after this & see what they will do for a livelihood.

I was up to Plattsburg Friday evening last. They had an exhibition there. The house was crammed full. The affair went off very well. They had some pretty good compositions and some pretty smart little boys. The larger ones, however, were only ordinary chaps to my notion, although I am no great hand to judge. . . .

[Tuesday] February 15th

. . . All the boys here today, I guess, but these boys are just like the rest of mankind, so they are not much to write about. Some of them appear to take no interest in anything whatever. They will set for hours in a state of perfect nonchalance gazing upon the ceiling. . . .

Jas. Porter is threshing wheat today. He will have a fine day for the work, I am sure. Wm. Todd talks of going to California this spring. . . .

I did not get any grammar lesson yesterday. Neither have I done my duty today in that line. Well, I believe that I will let the grammar slide this term and give it particular Jessie sometime soon after this.

My old schoolmate Sam Morris is keeping school at the same place that he and I studied together. He is married now. . . .

School will soon be let out for dinner, & I for one will not be dissatisfied. I have done tolerably well today considering the circumstances under which I began this morning. I am now working in the plasterers & printers rule [in arithmetic], which is hard enough for me now. . . . Perhaps it may . . . be very plain to me after a while. . . .

[Wednesday] February 16th

Today is dark & rainy. The fire of enthusiasm which snowballing has imparted to the boys give them a bright and happy expression.

Last night we had a spelling school here. . . . We got along very well, that is when we take into consideration the fact of their [there] being nobody here but the schollars. I learnt something myself last night which I intend to store up for future use. I can still live and learn. Thank goodness for the privelige. I find that there are a great many persons who are overnice & also a great many more who are not. There are a great many Pharisees yet in this world of ours. They lay burdens of very grievous nature, but they never lay hold of them themselves.

Henry Peck has been bother[ing] me ever since I commenced [writing].

I was there last night. We had a big argument with a couple of Catholics. They stoutly maintained their priests infallibility. At least they thought that they did, while we argued directly to the contrary. But what did we gain by the controversy? Nothing but the mortifying fact that not one of us knew anything about religion, neither the theoretical or practical part of it.

> It was but throwing words away,
> And thoughts were cast aloof and sent astray.
> But poetry like this will outshine the bright orb of day
> If it is left to its own all powerful and intricate way.

. . . Gamaliel Saunders says that he is going to California this spring. . . . If he does, he will find that the diggings are not the place to go to make ones living by his wits. It must be nothing short of hard work there and no mistake. Henry Peck says that he will go if Gam does, but I do not believe that either of them will ever go, although I may be mistaken. Gams mother does not want him to go off if she can help it anyway at all. So I think it will finally pass of[f] in talk, which is the general fate of all such air built schemes. . . .

[Thursday] February 17th
. . . Last night we had a geography school here, which went off as well as I could wish, although there were no girls here. Well, I am of the opinion that we learnt more than if there had of been girls here. We learn devilment enough as it is anyhow. I got home about eleven o'clock last night but did not get to sleep any untill twelve o'clock, which makes me feel a little sort of owly today. But I had enough sport last night to make up for the bad feelings of today.

I have made considerable progress in my arithmetic today. . . .

Jane Ann Harper is here today. She appears rather glum, however. She is at the outs with me about the spelling school, I believe. Well, what care I for that? Nothing now. Perhaps I may care hereafter, but why run on errands to the future for misery? My good gracious, I for one am glad that I am no prophet, for the miseries of the present are enough to bear. But why moralize at or on these things? It only makes one feel their littleness & weakness.

The drawling noise of the boys almost puts an end to my joys.
The thing is a nuisance which a great deal of usance
Has made a real swaybacked looseness & turned all my sharp
Points into blank obtuseness. But for fear that my keenness
May show you my greenness, I will just quit this rhyming,
For it['s] nothing less than timeing.
If you do not believe it, why just go and ask our Siming[?].

Henry Peck is here today. He is deeply engrossed in Rays Arithmetic. Well, it is not often the case with [him], so it will be best for him if he is let alone this time. My righthand man, Jonah, is also busily engaged in Talbot. . . . I think Jonah will make a first rate fellow yet. He is as steady as an ox & as saving as the next fellow. Well, I would be glad to see him prospering anyhow, whether in mental or spiritual [ways], but here we are again at the end of the rope [the bottom of the page].

[Friday] February 18th, 1853

We had a debate here last night which came very [near] being a fizzle, but by dint of perseverence we managed to wag through it, though. I got home at ten minutes past 12 o'clock, which makes me feel a little kind of owly today. . . . The drawling mode of reading which some of the schollars here have fallen into is almost insupportable. It will take some time for them [to] unlearn their errors if they keep on getting no better as fast as they have done for the last three months. . . .

I have got this book used up pretty badly . . . by having it thumbed over by every brat that comes along. I do not care if people handle it that know how, but then to have a bodys private property trampled and torn up by every blockhead. Last night I had this page greased over by some boys so that I can hardly make the first mark upon it. . . .

[Monday] February 21st

Today is about as dull as any other that has passed for some time. But yet this is one link in the chain of life & [one] more step towards the grave, which is the common leveler of all things from the least unto the greatest. . . . No bail there, no, none. It is touch and go. No dutiful officers are sent after the culprit, but old death comes along & here we have to give in, and we might as well do so with cheerful face as any other way, for it must come, anyhow. . . .

Last Sunday I passed at home in peace and quietude. I did not, however, have any more of either than I could bear. No, I never have any more pleasure than I want to. No, I find that I have but few friends, & it seems the more I do for anybody the easier they get at the outs with me. The fact is, the more you do for a selfish person, the more they will require of you. If you drive the hogs out of a mans cornfield & and lay up by the fence, he will just like as any other way curse you for not fixing his fence before the hogs got in. That is just the way I have been served, and I suppose others have been served the same way. I guess that nothing but iron rule will do, for the Golden one is either lost or never has been put to any use yet. The one which has been substituted for it is, never do a good deed if you lose money by it. Keep all you have got and get all you can.

Tonight there is going to be a geographical school here. This makes the seventh night and there will be six more. It is a first rate plan, and if the scholars do not learn, it will be their own faults.

There are no new scholars here today but the school is pretty full. There are somewhere near fifty here today, some tolerably little chaps too.

. . . Tis education forms the common mind. Just as the twig is bent the trees inclined.

[Tuesday] February 22d

. . . One boy has left today for fear he should have to take a thrashing—Harrison Ayres. He went out without asking. The teacher told him to stay in in the afternoon. He did not obey the injunction, however, but went out and then went home. Well, he is a wild chap anyhow, so it will make no difference if he never comes back.

I am getting along tolerably well in my arithmetic. I have five more leaves to turn and then I will be through. I do not know whether anyone else will get through or not, but I suspect that there will not be many, if any.

We had a geography school here last night. It was carried on pretty well, but I think that some of the scholars learnt more how to whoop & yell than they did anything else. Well, if man has the strength and inclination to make night hideous by hallooing [with] all his might, I have no objections. The fact is, I like to let my loungs expand. There is nothing like it.

There were about sixteen persons here last night, amongst the rest Wm. Orpet, who raised a little excitement by trying to disturb the school. He fired off a pistol, threw a club against the house, & yelled in at a knothole in the weather boarding. He then ran off as fast as his legs could carry him.

. . . One boy has just been thrashed for disobeying orders. I know how that goes, for I have been served the same way myself, but it never done me much good. I always played pranks whenever I felt like doing so. I never counted the cost untill I was called upon to pay. . . . I think that the rod will be banished from every schoolhouse in the land. Well, may God speed the day, for I consider that it has been used long enough, and strong enough to[o]. I, to be sure, will not perhaps be benefited by the change, but then someone else will. . . .

[Wednesday] February 23, 1853

The weather today is somewhat on the snowy & blustery order. The roads here are horrible. The mud is deep, deeper, deepest.

There was a man here today soliciting subscribers for Prescotts Home Book. It is a very good book, I expect, but I have not got the dino[?] to buy it, so I did not subscribe for it. . . . Henry Peck subscribed to the book, which is as good a use as he could put it to.

I am here today without a hat. Well, the thing that I did have was of not much account. I had some fun at the des[t]ruction of it anyhow. Poor thing, it had seen a great many hard fights in its time. I think if it could write it might draw some very soul stirring incidents of the wars that its inhabitants have been engaged in and of their wise plans to avoid their common enemy, a fine tooth comb. I expect that I will have to get another hat. If I can get a sheet iron one, I think perhaps I can keep it whole. My last hat was fast approaching its dissolution when I traded it off for one in the same fix.

However, the change made it somewhat better than it otherwise would have been, but now it is gone, gone, gone. To where? Why to shreds and strings. It departed itself from this world at 12 o'clock today. The cause of its dissolution was five or six girls and two or three boys. They tried the water cure upon it after everything else had failed, but neither sitz nor douch baths would stop its rapidly approaching dissolution. But, hat, thou art gone, and that too forever, but peace to thy ashes, for thou hast indeed been a good and faithful servant. But now thou art gone, and I feel for my lengthened years. But rest, thy warfares are sleep, the sleep that knows no breaking, morn of strife, and night of shaking. Old cap, rest, thy race is done.

We have about thirty three scholars here today. Well, I am glad of that, for it shows that they have a little of the spirit of improvement, which ought to animate every one of them to the highest degree. . . .

There is going to be another geography school here tonight. I guess that I shall attend if I can, and if I cant I wont, thats all. There are no females to be here anyhow, so it will not make much difference. . . .

[Thursday] February 24th, 1853

. . . Last night we had a geography school here. . . . I enjoyed myself first rate. I learned . . . some geographical knowledge besides. James Roderick was here last night. He was shown the elephant before he got my comerogues [fellow rogues]. H. & S. made up a plot to scare him. One of them got behind a tree at the side of the road and acted a robber to perfection. Jimmy was by himself. He looked at the fellow for some time, and he took to his heels, which were very nimble. Just then he ran over to where the boys were who I came with and told them that he saw a large man over by the road who wanted to shoot him. They laughed at him and told him to go on, that it was no one that wished to hurt him. Well, over he comes and seen someone again who he told to come out, whoever he was. But his courage all oozed out at his fingers ends when he saw that [he] was coming sure enough. So away he goes again at the rate of about ten knots an hour, when the friend in the brush hallooed after him, but it was of no avail. He only ran the faster. Now one would like to think he would own up to the corn, but not he. He says that he was not scared the least bit in the world.

. . . They have been kicking up their heels in Somerford lately, that is, the juvenile portion. They turned their schoolmaster out and took possession of the temple themselves. . . . I am of the opinion that when they get older . . . they will be able to thrash the whole world and the rest of mankind.

We are going to have a debate here tonight, which I expect will be the last. I do not know, though. If this goes off right, it may hold out some longer, but if it does not, then we will have to say, Hic jacet lyceum. The question tonight is, Resolved that all mankind will be finally holy and happy after death, which is a fact, I expect.

[Friday] February 25th, 1853

. . . Last night we had a debate here which I enjoyed first rate and no mistake. The question which we discussed was, Resolved that all mankind will finally be holy and happy, which was handled pretty well. . . .

There is quite an excitement got up among the relatives of Jackson Wilson in regard to his orphan children. They are now under the guardian care of one of their aunts, who the other party thinks is not capable of bringing them up as well as they could. Now, my candid opinion is that their love for the friendless orphans is not so great as their great love for the orphans money. Shame upon them and all others who would take advantage of helpless children.

. . . We have a pretty full school today, which makes things look businesslike if nothing more. This day is Friday and we always have a spelling school in the afternoon. Now, if we only had the fonetic way, we could do without these same spelling matches, which are very good as things now are, but then if the labor of learning to spell was only devoted to some other purpose, we would be that much the gainer. Anyhow, I should like to see fonetics tryd in scul. I *thinc* [JMR uses a symbol for th] it wud sun tak the pan from the old orthadox wa. Wel, I *think that the* tim iz ner at hand hwen it wil be luct in tu and tryd. I sa God sped *the* da, for cum hwen it ma, it wil alwaz pa. But no more, for I must stil[l] keep in the beggarly elements of the old plan, which I must follow until imperious custom shall cry, Hold, enough!

We are going to have four days and a half more school, which will then adjourn without day, and then John will have to go to work. . . .

[Monday] February 28th, 1853

Today is dull, stale, and profitless. . . . Egad! I have got a fit of ennui which will last me all day, I am thinking.

Spelling forenoon. Now, I dont spell anymore. Why it is I do not know. Perhaps I am good enough in that now.

Yesterday I was over on Deer Creek. Saw the folks, had some fun, and saw some streaks of human nature in the natural state, which is refreshing to one who has always look[ed] for the work of nature, which, by the by, I hardly ever get to see myself. Everything is affectation, nothing real, nothing natural, all assumed, all overstrained. Yes, man has frittered away to mere automatons, all for form and nothing for utility. Your coat is not made to make you warm, but it is made to be looked at. Apes and ape makers are all that now remain of what was once the noblest work of God.

Someone wrote a sentence upon the door the other night which awakened the sleeping lion in the breast of the pedagogue governer that presides here as master of ceremonies. Well, I know little about the matter and care less. I am blamed for the writing, but I suppose it would not consign me to the penitentiary if they were proven guilty. The hand on the wall may prove instructive to the governer, perhaps. If he has a Daniels perception, he may read a great lesson in those words. There is one thing certain about the thing, and that is, it shows that the kingdom is divided and must fall, here anyhow, if not in some other place; for whenever a man loses the respect of his subjects, open rebellion is most sure to follow, and one against many is hard work.

I have been talked about by certain individuals. Now, whether it is best for me to lay low and keep dark or not, I do not know, but I suppose that . . . prudent, cautious self control is wisdoms root. So I wont make bad worse by giving the authors a regular overhauling. Will let them go this time, but if the dose is repeated, I may fling back the thing in their teeth with interest, and that will be all. . . .

[Tuesday] March 1st, 1853

Today! Yes, today! There is more meaning in those words than most people think. What was it that raised Napoleon from being a poor Corsican corporal to be the First Consul of France? Nothing more nor less than making a good use of today. What is it that raises every man that ever has done any immortal or glorious action? The prom[p]t action and economy of the todays that have passed. Then, today is the time for us to enjoy ourselves. Let us not wait untill tomorrow or untill next week. My motto is:

> Let come what will, let come what may,
> I will laugh at fools who borrow from tomorrow
> And thus mar the pleasures of today.

For it is as Burns says:

> Catch the moments as they fly
> And use them as you ought, man,
> For happiness is shy
> And comes not a' when sought, man.

There is three more days of school and then it will be out, which is looked forward to by some with delight and by others with dread. . . .

Last night we had a geography school here . . . which went off quietly and peaceably, which is a little more than [it] has done every time. . . .

I have not made much progress today, but I may do something yet. It is now ten minutes of 12 o'clock, and the classes are spelling for noon. Well, here is another half day gone and nothing done, but [I] am not the only one that has been slack.

So here we are after noon and nothing done of any great consequence. I have just got myself into a sweat, which makes me feel ten per cent better than I did before I went out. And I think that it is not much of a curse after all to have to earn ones bread by the sweat of his brow. It makes one feel as though he was a new man to sweat real good sweat. . . .

[Wednesday] March 2d, 1853

Today shows no new thing except that things are on the rise or on the decline. The fact is, this is a world of change. The farmer breaks up his ground and there is a change. He plants his ground, which in the process of time makes another change. Then comes harvest; he cuts down his grain, which makes another change. He then exchanges the proceeds of all these changes for change, which makes him feel about him to see what part of himself needs changeing. But enough of this changeable subject, for I am not on change.

Wm. Orpet was here today. He was a little on the elevated order, caused by imbibing the essence of corn. Bill is now at work for Gam Saunders making rails at fifty cents per hundred. He is well calculated for the business, for his animal faculties overballance his intellect. He had his bottle stolen while he was here. It was a pint bottle which he got of someone and was about half full. Well, if he can enjoy himself by getting drunk, I have no objections, I am sure.

I got through my arithmetic today. It was a pretty hard squeeze, though, for I have had some blind times this winter. In one way and another I have at last staggered through, which is just two days before [Franklin] Pierce goes into the presidential chair, which will be an important epoch in the history of this republic.

The weather today is squally, and though it is snowing at this time pretty rapidly, the girls are taking their recess. At this very moment they are playing black man or something like it. Well, exercise is a great thing, and I like to see them run. . . .

There is going to be a geography school here tonight. . . . I have learned a great deal at those same geography schools. Let me see: There are five grand divisions, five oceans, five zones, and five more lectures if I recollect rightly.

There are a good many schollars here today. They hang on first rate, which I like to see, for it shows that they have some aspirations for an education. I will not give the place up yet, for I think that there is some of the great good leaven here yet. . . .

[Thursday] March 3d, 1853

This is the next to the last day of this school, and I expect that it will be the last of my journaling for some time to come. I will, however, look back upon what has past and see what I have done in my short life.

I do not recollect of having many hard times in my early years. I passed some seven years upon the banks of Deer Creek, where I was born, and then I was brought here and lived here about six years. I have no reason to complain of the neighborhood. The people are generally honest and industrious. They are true republicans and ardent lovers of their country. I have met with some slight checks from some of them, but I forgive them all, for I have been a little unruly at times, and perverseness ought always to be frowned at by everyone.

We moved to Little Darby in 1849 and staid there three years. I came near being drowned there while we lived there. I, however, escaped with a good ducking. I there witnessed the effects of jealousy, which made the whole neighborhood feel uncomfortable. Father suffered more from it than anyone else. The excitement got to so high a pitch that one party tried to burn the other out and did so effectually. The she Hecate [Mrs. Fleming] burned up a mill which my father and one Randall had built, which is a loss to Father of about five hundred dollars.

I went to school about five months while we lived there. Since we have lived here I have went to school about six months, which is all I have went for the last two years.

This is the sum of all my life, and it is a very small one at that. . . . Perhaps I am destined for something great yet. Great oaks from little acorns grow. . . .

Last night there was a geography sc[h]ool here. We come very near breaking down in the middle of it, for the boys all laid on the benches except myself and John Allen. But we tugged on untill we got through. Towards the latter part of the evening the scholars wakened up and we had a pretty good time. There will be [two] or three more lectures and then we will be through. . . .

2

Work, Sermons, and the Joys
of Country Life
March 13–October 16, 1853

School is out, and Roberts's journal entries have a more serious tone as he writes in his upstairs room at home or in the family gristmill in work-free periods. His father's illness, friends' deaths, and preachers' dogmas, all stir his curiosity about mortality and about human behavior here on earth. They do not, however, stifle his optimism or his ambition. A trip to Uncle Cary's at College Hill outside Cincinnati and a visit to Farmers College make him eager to continue his schooling there or at Antioch College in Yellow Springs. But the bustle and noise of the Queen City bother him; he much prefers the peace and quiet of Oak Run. He rhapsodizes at the coming of spring in the country.

Yet if Roberts delights in rural quiet and simplicity, and if serious thoughts displace most of his schoolboy nonsense as he writes in his journal, he continues to crave amusement and excitement. He relates local gossip and scandals, mimics rustic speech, and pokes fun, and occasionally ridicule, at some of his neighbors. He joins with them in cooperative roadwork and a barn-raising. He worries about the growing number of Irish Catholics who settle in the county while building Ohio's new railroads, one of which provides a job for him and offers the prospect of added value for his family's property.

As town and rural population increase, so do social class differences. Roberts complains about the snobbery and pretense of local "aristocrats." He finds a decided contrast to them among the slovenly, backwoodsy, and hospitable Clifton family, who will later be the source of relaxing pleasure and satisfaction.

[Sunday] March 13, 1853

Today is Sunday, the day of rest and enjoyment. That is, it ought to be, but it sometimes happens to be directly the reverse. As far as I am concerned, it is a day of rest.

I have heard one sermon today and expect to hear another. The one I heard today was a regular orthodocs Baptist sermon laid down with emphatic and iron firmness. The text was, if "The Son make you free, then you will be free indeed," which was handled pretty well. The preacher brought up some new ideas. One was about sending Bibles to the heathen. ["]Now," said he, ["]suppose you throw a ten cent piece into the box for printing the Scriptures in the Burmese language. Now, some old heathen gets the Bible after it is sent and is saved from everlasting woe. Which saved the man, the ten cent piece or the grace of God?" Of course, it is the latter that saves and not the money.

. . . An old fellow named Clifton is going to live on the [Roberts family] place [on Darby]. He is a regular hard case, I guess, but so much the better, for the people need another hard one to make out a set. I like to see the goats all together. It does me good to see them pawing one another.

I was at the old place last week. . . . I saw Miss A. Roe while I was on Darby. She is going to set up dressmaking in Jefferson. . . .

Mr. Wm. Cullumber and Miss Louisa Fleming were married last week. Well, all I have to say is that if good looks were necessary to have to get to Heaven, their chance would be very poor. Mr. Wm. Anderson [JMR's error: William Godfrey] was also married the same week to Miss [Mahala] Truitt, both good people, and I hope that they may live a long and happy life. I myself think that I might get married and have a great deal of comfort, but time and chance will have to settle that.

Our school ended peaceably and satisfactorily to all. We had some fun and no trouble, which is more than a great many people can say of themselves. I myself will always look back upon that day as one of my sunny spots.

But I must quit & go to meeting.

[Sunday] April 3d, 1853

Today I again take up my pen and lay open my journal. It has been some time since I took up the book, but there has things happened since I last wrote which I shall never forget.

I have been at all kinds of work since I left school. I have dug and delved in the earth, chopped down trees, hauled rails, plowed, & all the various other things that appertain to farming. I have seen death stalk into this neighborhood & take one of its members. . . .

I have been traveling some since I last made an entry in my journal. I have been to the great Queen City of the West and saw the mighty hum of business and the incessant turmoil of city life. But I would rather breathe the pure air and drink the clear water of the country than live in the city. To[o] much noise and smoke there for me. Indeed, I felt a kind of loneliness while I was there. It seemed to me that I would cirtenly be forgotten if I should happen to get killed in there. The very houses have a gloomy look about them. It made me feel as though I was such a small atom in such a mass that I was glad when I heard the bell ring for the engine to start. Well, then it was such a relief to see the country. The houses looked bright. The people all seemed to look as though they were never in a hurry. No noise to disturb one. All was quiet, peace, and contentment. The country is the place for me at last.

I started from home on Tuesday morning with Henry, Paddy, and the buggy. We got into Springfield at half past eleven o'clock. I went down to the depot of the Hamilton, Dayton, & Cincinnati Railroad, bought me a through ticket for Cincinnati, paid two dollars for it. Started on the cars, which left Springfield at four o'clock, got to Cumminsville at quarter past seven, & then walked two miles and a half to College Hill. Got there against eight o'clock, found Uncle Cary in a grocery, went home with him. Aunt Malvina was sick. I did not get to see her for two days after I went there. I had a very fine time, take it all in all, while I was there. I staid there from Tuesday untill Saturday evening.

I went into Farmers College. Was in the recitation room where there were some students reciting in Latin, which was all Latin to me sure enough. There are some two hundred and thirty students in Farmers College. There is at the same place a female college called the Ohio Female College. It is about a quarter of a mile from the male college and is a large square brick building. There are about two hundred students in it, I believe, but as to that I am unable to say, for I did not get to learn the exact number. There may be more for aught I know.

I will just set this visit down as one of my shiny streaks which I can look back upon in after years with pleasure. . . .

Yesterday I helped C. Hornbeck roll logs all day, and some of them were logs for certain, for they were about as heavy and as large as any that I ever had anything to do with. But we got them piled up at last, and now they will not have to be piled again. . . .

Last Sunday was Easter, and I just got home and expected to have a fine time, but death had just entered one of our nearest neighbors mansion and had left one less there than there was before. Martin Hornbeck died on Easter Sunday. He had been sick for some time with a tumor in his throat. It broke and then run on the inside. He then took an inflammation in the bowels which terminated his short life. Well, the Good Book says, "Blessed are the early dead," and why should we repine when we know a truth so sweet that the departed one is better off now than when he was here below? But man, weak man, cant always see what is the best. If he could, this world would be a paradise, but since

Adams fall this thing is out of the question, and if God did not design that it should be so, it never would have been so. Martin was about six years old when he died.

Henry has went into the grocery business on a small scale. . . .

Mr. Wm. Tingley is not expected to live. He has been sick nearly 3 months. He has killed himself at hard work, poor man. I think he ought to have a monument reared for him. Why ought not the honest toiler be honored as well as the soldier who gains so much fame for plundering and butchering his fellows? I do not see why they should not laud the one who builds up more than he tears down.

> "But the brave sodger never despise,
> Nor count him as a stranger.
> Remember he is his countrys stay
> In day and hour of danger."

So says Burns, and I agree with him there, but there ought to be some praise for one who toils through thick and thin for the benefit of his race. . . .

[Monday] April 4th, 1853

Today the weather is dark and gloomy. The wind is from the northeast and the rain patters incessantly upon the roof.

Last night had a prayer meeting here. Had quite an excitement, take it all together. Some half dozen shouted. . . .

Today I will not get to plow any. It will be too wet. We are only going to put in eight acres anyhow, so it wont make much difference whether we get it in this week or not. . . .

I have not eaten my breakfast yet, but I think it will be pretty shortly, for the kettle begins to sing for tea.

There is a thundering lot of work to do on this place this spring. . . . Let me see: There is the sheep pasture fence to lay up right off, & then the dam ought to be fixed, by all means as soon as possible. Eight acres of oats must be sowed or the horses will have to be put upon short allowance. The tail and headraces must be cleaned out, & that ought to be done immediately; but we will have to put that off untill warm weather commences, for working in the water when the ice is still upon the margin is a little too cool for this chicken. I must do some grafting this very day, for I got some very fine grafts of Uncle Cary. I must put them in, for they are of a superior quality.

I hear them getting the chairs at the table, so I must hurry. . . .

[Saturday] April 9th, 1853

. . . I feel as though there has not been a sadder day than this for some time. I am sick and weak today. I took a chill yesterday about noon & I have eaten nothing since. Nor do I intend to eat anything untill tomorrow, which will, I think, cook out my sickness. . . .

There was a man killed in South Charleston last week by the railroad cars. He had both of his legs cut off & one of his arms. He lived about two hours after the accident occurred. He was a brakesman upon the wood train. He was going to be married the next day, so says madam rumor. . . .

[Tuesday] April 19th, 1853

Today is another rainy day & I have stole off upstairs to write.

I have got over the ague and feel very weak. There has not been much of importance done since I last took up my pen to write in my journal. There has been some change, though. Miss Mary Jane Harper has left for Darby. She is a funny girl, full of frolick. But then her intellect is only about common. She is an orphan and poor, which goes a great ways in this world. It is, in fact, one of the greatest crimes a man can be guilty of. Poverty is the greatest of all crimes, for if you are so unfortunate as to plead guilty, you cannot get any further hearing. You are condemned at once to neglect and contempt.

I am poor, but if riches are to be had, I must have them. But why should one trouble oneself about the fleeting shadows and pompous hollowness of wealth? . . . I believe a competency is enough. . . . But it is well enough to have some grasping minds. If we had not, everything would stagnate and business of every kind would soon stop, or so near it that there would be but little doing. The fact is, the great men move the little ones, and the little men move the world. The importer would soon be nothing. The sailors and shipmasters would refuse to act. They would soon sink into insignificant pedlars & hawkers. But they all hang together and pull the same way, so they move one another. But the dignity of one is a little below that of the other.

. . . The reason why one occupation is more honorable than another is a problem of hard and intricate composition. Why the man that makes shoes is not equal to the one that deals in moire shawls, shoes, hats, caps, pins, needles, & other fancy articles I do not know. . . . In the shoemaker the secret of the whole thing [is that] he does not smell quite as strong of money as the shopkeeper. He is a little harder in the palms of his hands. He carries his own marketing home rather than pay a great lazy fellow for doing it for him. He, in fact, is a different creature from the other entirely. He is termed a senseless snob by the storekeeper, while the fact is, it is directly the reverse. The storekeeper is the snob and the other is the gentleman. . . .

[Saturday] April 22d, 1853

Today is dark & rainy. Many days do I expect to pass upon this earth, but rainy days are not of a necessity dark and gloomy. Indeed, they are and ought to be days of rejoicing. . . .

I have seen many changes in my brief lifetime, but none was ever as great as that I have seen in Mary Ann Wilsons situation and fortunes. A few months ago she was surrounded by admirers. Now she has none. There she is, the neglected & abused wife. She, the proud, the rich, and by many called lovely, is now cast down but not destroyed. . . . Yes, it is a hard blow to her after having cast all her hopes upon the worthless scamp that is now her husband. Little did she think six months ago that she would be served as she is. She has been most shamefully treated and abused, so madam rumor has it.

. . . They are calling me downstairs and I must go. They are very much troubled anyhow about what I do. If [I] appropriate one minute to myself, there is a little war raised about it. . . . This is the first time in several days that I have had a minute to myself.

I was in a logrolling yesterday and worked like a Turk. I am a little the worse of it today, but not much. Thanks to a good constitution I am not very easily made sick. . . .

[Sunday] April 24th, 1853

. . . Miss Nancy Allen & Mr. Parrot were married this last week. There is something queer about marriage that I do not understand, & that is that little women pick for the biggest men that they can find. . . . And the disposition of the two generally differ. The high strung woman generally gets a very prosy kind of a slip and go easy fellow, one who does not care a fig whether he stands upon his head or upon his heels and feels perfectly at home when he has all the buttons off his coat, makes no noise about anything, but just pursues the even tenor of his way, neither turning to the right nor to the left. The women are, when they have such men, always fidgeting and fussing, driving everything before them, cant bear to see anything out of order, must have everything "comme il faut," or they are in the suds and cant do anything.

But to Miss Nancy. . . . She is a nice, fine girl, and I wish her all the happiness that she is capable of containing, & I think that that will be considerable, & may she live long in the bliss of wedded life, and may she have the charge over a whole nest of Parrots. . . .

Spring is here. She has cast her magic wand upon the earth, and all things are changed, & that too for the better. . . . The grass looks green. The flowers are nodding gracefully in the gentle zephyr. The invalid looks out and smiles. The farmer drives his horses along with a merry whistle. The birds carol among the branches of the trees, some of which are now loaded with blossoms. The cattle have a contented look. In fact, everything looks cheerful and gay. . . .

I do not know, but everything is just as God designed it to be from the first. I think that God makes man do these things to show him how weak and puerile he is and of how little account he is when compared with the powers that are in Heaven. . . .

[Thursday] May 5th, 1853

. . . This is the glorious month of May. The birds & bees keep holiday now. But what is that to me? I have no holiday. The fiat has gone forth that I must earn my living by the sweat of my brow. I have to work, but I am not the only one that has to, so there is some consolation after all.

Father is very sick at this time. He has got the liver complaint, & it is doubtful whether he will ever get well again. . . . Aunt Rachel Roberts is here helping to tend to Father. . . .

We are fixing the mill at this time. We have one David Jones working for us. He is a Welchman. He is putting in some cogs in the master wheel. He will get done today. He will then leave for some other place. He is a man of sound parts but not very many. He has just come from Wales for the second time. He is a travelled man and a pretty good millwright. . . .

I have been plowing some today. I am going to help Wm. Allen plant corn tomorrow. . . .

[Sunday] May 22d, 1853

. . . I have been toiling on in the same old way all this summer. I have been plowing, hoeing, & various other things that a farmer has to do. For the last few days, however, I have been cleaning the mud out of the races. Bill Orpet has been helping me. He works along, takes medicine, and drinks redeye as usual. He will kill himself yet if he does not desist. . . .

I got a letter from [Uncle] James the other day. He is not doing as well as he might have done had he of staid here in Ohio. . . . I for my part think that Ohio is large enough for me yet, but it may be that I will leave the bonnie Buckeye state yet before I get to be ninety years of age. Perhaps I may be soaring away in the spirit land before I get to be that old. . . .

Our summer school will take up tomorrow. Miss Ankhellen will preside as chief pedagoguess. Well, the little ones must pack and be gone tomorrow. I would like to go myself, but the world has got to be so selfish and narrow contracted that it would be the next thing to an impossibility for poor John to go. He must grind & ditch & work all the time. But there is a good time coming perhaps, & I must have my bowl right side up if I can.

[Saturday] June 25th, 1853

. . . I have been doing various things since I last wrote in this book. I had Allen Anderson hired for a half month. He & I worked at the culvert below the mill. We dug up the old puncheons & put in new ones. We had some pretty hard work there. The clay stuck to the shovels pretty bad, but [we] managed to get it through with.

Hornbecks stock has been pothering us for some time past. Yet that is no more than what ours have done to him, & therefore we ought not to complain.

I was at a barn raising this week. They had about 30 hands but did not get it up. Col. Brush offered to pay the hands, but no one took any money except Roderick & son, which is what everyone would expect of them. I consider that if I can do a little job that way for a neighbor . . . his thanks & provision is enough. The fact is, if a man would ask pay for every little act of kindness, we would be at a sorry pass. I am afraid that if Roderick had to pay back for the many little jobs that have been done for him gratis, he would have to work pretty busy for some time to come. . . .

I have been laying track upon the London railroad for the last three days. I have fine times over there. We lay about a half mile a day. The track is laid up as far as Harmony.

Grandfathers folks are coming in this summer. They have got into a sickly part of the West, I guess, if all accounts are true.

Bill Anderson has left Pecks and went home. He is a poor devil, of no account to anyone. He is so lazy and worthless that no one will have anything to do with him. . . .

[Sunday] July 3d, 1853

Today I again take up my pen to jot down a few items & take a review of the past, dream of the future, & make use of the present, which will make three in one & one in three, & if I follow up my preface, I will fill up this sheet sure.

The past is all a man has to look at. He cant have no idea of what the future will be, only by the past. Experience is a dear school, & it is the only one in which a man can learn anything. Whether he is to be wise or foolish, it is all the same. He must be experienced if he wants to have the truth to go by. The past is gone. Let it go. The future? What shall we do for that? Why, dream of it, & that is about all that we can do. Building of air castles is not a very bad notion after all, for if one can have a few hours pleasure, it makes no difference whether it is real or ideal.

Hope is an angel of very good quality. Hope—of what use would a man be if he had no hopes of the future being better than the present? No man would have the heart to labor in this world if he did not expect to have a better hereafter. . . . If a man who does not believe in a Heaven or in a God was to have no hopes in this world, he would commit suicide. Man always thinks that tomorrow will be better than today, & it is a good thing for him too.

The present is not taken into consideration. People do not see the time going. They either dream of the future or brood over the misfortunes of the past. If one could only perceive the advantage of taking hold of [the] present, we would be much better off than what we are now. But the thing of it is, I never know when to strike. I stand & study how to strike. While I am doing this, someone else strikes in my place.

Father is very sick at this time. He has got the consumption. I am afraid he will never be able to do anything anymore. He has taken more than a wagonload of drugs, yet he is no better; rather, worse from the effects of the medicine, I think. . . .

[Sunday] July 10th, 1853
Today I was at meeting & heard two sermons, one by the Reverend Mr. Miller, Methodist, the other by the Rev. Mr. Cotterel. Rev. Mr. Morris also said a few words. The last two are Calvinist Baptists.

It is something singular that men will differ so much upon religions when they can come very near agreeing in every other particular. All men agree about the mathematical calculations that are made in regard to the planets; yet these very men when they come to read the Scriptures interpret it as far from one another as the poles.

The Rev. Mr. Miller today preached all his sermon upon the hypothesis of mans ability to save himself from a future state of misery while here below. He went on to show that man was a very powerful engine. Yet he was as weak as he could be, not able to do anything. Yet he must & can do everything. He preached in glowing terms of the happiness, of the righteousness and goodness of God, & said that He would be far more merciful & far easier to appease than man. Yet an age of misery uncounted would not satisfy him. He talked a good deal about circus shows, horse races, & card tables being Satans great invention to entice poor humanity down into endless punishment. Well, he went on to preach a regular orthodox sermon, & as a matter of course his Heaven must have a smokehouse attached to it to make the enjoyment of its inhabitants sweeter by witnessing the suf[f]erings of creatures once equal & perhaps superior to themselves.

The Rev. Mr. Cotterel, then. The stand he said: a man could do nothing either by way of saving or damning himself. He said man was dead to everything spiritual and that no power could save or sink him. Anything that was done of benefit was done by God, & He foreordained who should be saved & who should be damned, & man could not alter one iota of Gods laws in regard to his future state. Sin has no effect upon the man, but if God said a man should be damned before the foundation of the world, all his prayers were as chaff and would avail him nothing.

Fathers health is very poor at this time. He appears to be gradually growing weaker every day. I do not believe he will live long. It is a very sad spectacle to see a strong man moulder and shrink away. A friend will pass from ones sight almost imperceptably. Gradually one sees ones friends taking their leave, yet seldom thinks about himself.

[Friday] July 15th, 1853

Today I have done but little, although I have rode about ten miles and dug as many pounds of medical roots and plants. Father is no better yet, & I am afraid he never will be. He is going now to try syrup compounded of several things: cumfrey, alecampaigne, spikenard, wandering milkweed, and honey. Perhaps it may help him & perhaps not. No one knows how these medicines will operate, perhaps to the advantage or perhaps to disadvantage of the patient. I do not believe much in these quack nostrums. . . .

I must quit this, as the call for stove wood begins to strike on the tympanum of my not always the sharpest ears. . . .

[Sunday] July 17th, 1853

. . . This week has passed smoothly enough. I have mowed some and rode some. The last part of the work was easier than the first. . . .

The neighbors are all at peace. No war of words, I believe, except it is a little tattle among the old women, & then there is a small, one horse battle going on between Lud Roderick & Gam Saunders. There has been no blood shed yet. Neither do I think there will be.

Roderick is playing a picayune part in the game, & I think that he will come out at the little end of the horn. He wanted to bore us out of eight bushels of bran but did not succeed. . . . The way he tried to do it this time was by trumping up an old contract between himself & Gam Saunders. He said he had paid Gam fifty cents for eight bushels of bran & that Gam was to let him have this bran this fall. Well, he never called for or mentioned anything about the bran untill this summer. He came to me and said that Gam said that he should have the bran. I gave him two bushels. Saw Gam in a day or two afterward and asked him about it. He said he did not know anything about the trade & that if he made the bargain, he did not mean to get out of it. But he denied the whole thing in toto and said that if we let Roderick have the bran, we must look to him for the pay, for he was not going to pay for it. We told Roderick of it. He ranted around considerable but finally cooled down and drawed in his horns.

The great thorn that troubles Roderick is a gun trade that he made with Semp Saunders (Gams brother). He traded guns & got wofully bitten. The whole transaction was a cooler. Semp, he happened to pass by Rodericks one evening with a smoothbored rifle, one that some Irish had had, but he had just bought it. Well, Roderick saw the gun and thought that it was a rifle and asked Semp if he would trade. Yes, Semp said, he would trade if he would give him three dollars to boot. Done, says Roderick, so the trade was soon made, Roderick all the time thinking that he was cheating Semp, when, lo, it turned out that he was the man that had lost by the transaction. Instead of a rifle he got bored with a shotgun, not worth as much as the one he traded for it, and he also gave fifty cents on the three dollars to boot. Now, that was rich, but the nub of the thing was, he thought he could make us pay the fifty cents back to him. But he could not come that load of poles over us. Well, he was bored all around, so I will just drop the subject.

Henry has got into a stew with some folks up above here. He went sleighing with Semp Saunders and took along a couple of girls. They had a rich, racy, grand, & peculiar time, I guess, from what they say themselves. Well, Henry fell out with some of the small fry. They went and told a great yarn to one of the girls about what he should have said concerning himself and herself. Well, frog town was raised. Everyone of the family bristled up, looked rope and ratsbane at Henry. He did not know what was the matter. His love, a charming girl of 15 with a turnup nose, reddish hair, and sage look, looked daggers at him. . . . Well, the storm is about over now. Miss Elizabeth has softened down. There is one wrinkle less in the old womans forehead as she passes. The old man has got on speaking terms again. That is, he can say, "How dy du, ows yer dad?" The small fry have got farther along. They ap[p]ear to have forgotten past errors and will even take a hand at marbles with poor Harry. As to him, he still has a pretty good appetite and thinks he may be happy yet. He looks forward to a speedy reunion of hearts. I look forward with considerable interest to the denoument. A wedding perhaps, who knows?

The Methodist meetinghouse caved in the other day. The gable fell in and damaged the house right smart.

We grind about 15 bushels per day here now. The wheat this year is not as good as the people thought. The fly and the rust hurt it considerable; yet there is a plenty. Yet I think that wheat will be about 75 cents a bushel this fall. Perhaps it may be more.

Link has got his boiler placed and will have his mill running in about three weeks. He may do well, but I think he will not make it pay as well as he expects. It will cost him a good deal and maybe will bring him in a good return, but it is only maybe.

[Saturday] July 23d, 1853

. . . I have been doing a great many different things within the last few days, but the most that I have done is in the haying line. We got our grass cut & put up in good order this season. We did not have much to put up, yet it took us some time to do it. I believe we were at it about seven days. Four days and a half Jesse Waldron helped us. The rest I done myself. Henry hired Jesse & gave him thirty seven cents per day. He is not a very stout chap and is of not much account nohow. Yet he will count one on the census list & one on the election day perhaps if he does not get put in the penitentiary or get killed before he gets to be of age. I do not think he will ever be of any great force in this world, & I am not prepared to say what will be done with him in the next. Perhaps he may be a bright luminary there, but if he does not shine any better there than what he does here, I do not think his light will eclipse the sun or put the stars to shame, not by any means.

I see Wesley Allen and his family going past just now. They were going to see Nancy Parrot, I suppose. . . . Mrs. Parrot is a married lady now. . . . Jimmeny! I intend to marry some of these days myself, just for the fun of the thing perhaps. Now, I might get bit in the transaction, so I guess I had better let it alone yet awhile . . . for fear I run on the breakers and have to go on broken timbers the rest of my voyage through life. I suppose that the marriage rite is a good thing when it unites good people together, but when it does otherwise, it is a bad operation. . . .

I must give Darby a review: Old Clifton was here day before yesterday. He says old John Fleming still goes to Randall's. He has moved his washing away from home. He neither eats nor sleeps at home anymore. . . . I hear Miss Alice Roe has not the best character down there that is in the world. . . .

The railroad has at length been located from London to Columbus. It goes right strait through our place near the creek. We will make something by that operation, I think. We ought to begin to make something, for we have had a run of bad luck down there that ought to turn sometime or other. This thing of having good luck is something not to be grinned at by them which has no teeth.

I guess we will have to go down and saw wood for the railroad. There will be a fine chance to make money. If Jim Roberts was here we could make money fast. Jim writes that he will come in in September. . . . I do not know whether Jim will go in with us on Darby or not. I expect he will. If he does not, I must go down and work like all fury for two or three months. . . .

I heard a good story told about the prudery of two women in this neck of woods. They were at home alone when a pedler happened to call. Just as he came in at one door, they run out at the other. Well, the pedlar thought that they had just went out to do some little job of work and would be back again. But instead of coming back, they left the house. Well, on they went untill they came across one of our neighbors riding along the road. They stopped him and told him that there was a man in the house. Well, he went on to the house to rout the pedlar, asked him what he wanted, what he was doing there. The pedlar told him his business and requested him to ask the ladies to come in so that they might see that he took nothing away with him. No, no, they said, he must go away; they were afraid of him. Well, he finally left and left the neighbor in the house. Well, they got afraid of him; come to the door and told him to lift a kettle [of] tallow off of the fire and then sloped out again. He went out and told them to come back and help him, but they would not. He then had to evacuate the premises. He had the ingratitude, however, to leave the tallow on the fire. Poor man, after vanquishing the pedler he had to leave the field. The guns were left to the enemy. He left the diggins pretty well convinced that a chap about his size and weight had been put up and sold. . . .

Time wags and the cry is still a little more. A little more fun, a little more money, a little more land, a little more time, a little more power, a little more wind or a little more calm, a little more war, a little more peace, a little more of everything. A mans soul is never satisfied in this world. He always wants something more than he has got. I want a little better pen, a little more water, a little more grinding, & a little more time to write in this book, for I hear a little more noise made on account of not having a little more stove wood. The bread has raised enough and a little more so. If there is not wood cut, we will have to do with a little less to eat, which is none of the pleasantest things in the world. . . .

Death! I have thought of thee many times, and oft. What is death? The infidel says that it is the end of man. After he is dead he is forever done. He moulders away & is forgotten. No future realm for him to perfect himself in. No happiness, no misery, no nothing. Dead, gone, destroyed, annihilated. The Christian says it is but the beginning of life, that man is put, as it were, low down in a pit, but at the top all is sunshine, joy, life, light, gladness, glory, and immortality. Peace and fullness there await him. Hope is there at an end because man has nothing to hope for. Despair is forever banished. The great source of all living things looks on the picture and smiles, smiles on the happiness and goodness of His works. All earthly thoughts are driven away after death. It is this that makes Him seek out many plans and ways to get what is designed for all.

Now, which is right, the one who believes that death is the end or the one that it is the beginning of life? I think the last has the best of the bargain. Anyhow, if a man could only see beyond the grave, he would be better satisfied to see the latter true.

[Saturday] July 29th, 1853

Today I am in the mill again. I have not been doing much of late. I do not expect to stay in these parts longer than next year. Then I am going to go to some far off country where I will not be so well known, then & there to build up my fortune and fame. . . .

This settlement has overrun with lies lately. I have been lied on by a set of harpies who are ever ready to pounce upon a poor, weak individual who is unable to help himself. . . . I have done some mean acts, I expect, yet I do not think that I am entirely mean. . . .

Addison Cornwell went along here this morning pretty well drunk. He was in Somerford yesterday & got drunk on some of their whiskey. They then fell upon him & tore his clothes, blacked his face, & hauled him around over the turnpike. He is going to London today to sue all Somerford for letting him get drunk in there & also for letting the citizens use him up after he got drunk. Poor Ad! He will go to town again and get drunk, fall among another set of Philistines, and be used up again. I do not pity him much, for he might learn in the sc[h]ool that fools generally have to go to if they ever learn anything.

There is going to be a camp meeting on Darby in about three weeks. . . . I will try & see if I cant get off. I do not know as it will do me much good, but then there will be a good chance to study human nature. A man can always learn something of human nature by going to someplace where the passions are let out and where they have completely overcome the other & nobler part of man. The wild excitement of a camp meeting will just suit me for a while. I have been to a great many Methodist revivals, yet I have never seen the ne plus ultra of their great machine of passion stirrers. I have never been to a camp meeting yet, but if I live and keep my health, I think that I will go to this one, anyhow. . . .

Henry is working upon the millstones today & is now wanting me to grind the mill picks. . . .

[Christian Church] Conference is about to commence in Somerford. Then & there we will be enlightened on the subject of a future life and how the same is to be obtained. . . .

How long will it take me to write this book through? Perhaps the sands of life may have run out with me ere I write twenty pages more in it. I do not know whether these pages will ever benefit me or not, yet it will be a satisfaction to me in after years to look on these pages and see how many of my plans have failed & how many have been carried out. Perhaps years since some boy may pick this book up and look at the pages, wonder what kind of an individual wrote the lines he sees here. Well, he is a boy & has boyish thoughts. He has had some dreams of future glory, but they were only dreams. He had passions and weak places in his nature which led him hither & thither at their will. But, boy, I never yet have gone so far from the paths of rectitude but what I could see my way back.

I am five feet ten inches high & have a pretty good proportion of flesh along with it. I have not got a rotten tooth in my head; have some beard and am not very good looking; black hair and eyebrows, beard on the sandy order. But a description of myself will, I am afraid, never be published in a very large number of books. So I guess I will leave off & get at something else.

Father is sick. He will never get well, I think. He looks like a shadow, pale, thin, and weak. His life has got to be a burthen to him, yet I believe he would like to live on even in the situation he now is.

There is something so gloomy about death that no one, however well he may be prepared for it, can face it without feeling afraid. Is it possible we all have to die? It makes me feel cold all over to think about it. Yet it is so & there is no help for it. These fingers that hold this pen will someday be useless, cold, and lifeless. It seems as though life was nothing but a dream to mock one with. I do not know what man was designed for, but I think it is for some noble purpose. Perhaps the troubles and vexations of this world will be cleared up in the next. Well, that is some consolation, anyhow. I think God will not forget us in the last great day.

I have the fragment of a letter before me, one I started to write to Miss Jane Harper. She was here last winter. Her mother is dead and her father is crazy at times, so she is not the best off for natural protectors as she might be. I do not know as I loved her, yet she was one of those funny creatures that always interest me. I like someone to be lively if I am in a crowd. She was so & [I] am a little inclined that way myself, so everything seemed to gee the right way. Some of the old women, however, have given her character a pretty thorough overhauling & have fished up some dirty trash out of their never to be exhausted brains. Some people love slander. The reason why it is, is because their minds neve[r] soar any higher than the gross dark paths of sensual pleasure, or misery, just as you may wish to term it. This girl may be far better than her traducers. I expect she is, too, if the truth was known. I think they had better sweep their own doorways before they go crying out the awful condition of their neighbors.

I am not quite ready to commence a fire against these slanderers yet. I must look into my private patch first to see if the weeds of vice are not getting to[o] strong a hold there. I guess I had better not throw stones when I have such a large glass house myself. So I will have to let them slip this time, at least those who pass me by. I do to others as they do to me. I think that that is the way the Golden Rule reads nowadays, so I must keep up with the fashion. So Stubbs says, and he ought to know. Fashion is a tyrant and is submitted to by a great many who would not be under any tyrant. If they could be forced to serve a man as faithful as they do the tyrant fashion, there would be no end to the revolutions and bloodshed that would follow. . . .

Well, I have just heard some more concerning Conference. I hear that one woman has sold her cow to buy a silk mantle and dress. She has quit work so that she may have white hands. Well now, that kind o[f] gets me. I think perhaps she might take a lesson from [Lorenzo] Dow on that subject. It appears that Peggy D. was a little sort o[f] fond of finery and teased the old reverend for a new bonnet. Well, at last the old codger had to knock under. Well, she gets all the cash in the house, but that would not suffice, so she turns in and sells the bureau. Well, Sunday comes and the bonnet must be worn to church. Well, it happened that Peggy did not get to church as soon as usual, a fault which some of our modern Peggies have sometimes when they get a new dress. Well, in she comes full sail, when the old Rev. stopped, hemmed once or twice, and bawled out, "Please make room for Sister Dow with the bureau on her head." . . .

[Sunday] July 31st, 1853

. . . Yesterday I went to Somerford & to Uncle Wilsons & dug some roots & raked some moss out of the headrace. Our oats must be cut this next week. Wm. Orpet will do the cradling and we will do the rest ourselves. Oats are very short but tolerably heavy. We have about seven acres and a half to cut. Some of them are not more than a foot high, which will make them very hard to cut, yet cut they must be, for oats are now worth 31 cts. per bushel, so I hear. I do not know whether we will have any to sell or not. I guess not, though, for we have got no corn in this season. Corn is not very good anyhow, so we will have to feed our oats to our horses.

I have not heard from Jim for some time. I guess he has found out that the West is something less than a perfect paradise. I have an idea that the West is great, but people put to[o] high an estimate on it before they get there, so they get disappointed & likewise get discontented.

I think Ohio is as good a place as I want to live in. Perhaps it is not the garden of the world, yet I think it comes the next thing to it. The great and inexhaustible resources of Ohio are yet to be brought to light; yet there are some of them now being used. Our timber is hardly thought of by us yet. If it was used up economically, it would always last and always be a source of profit. Our railroads are getting to be finished, so we will soon have the best of markets for all we have to sell, and we will also have good markets to buy. Ohio will be the first state in the Union yet. She has the advantage of almost every other one in a natural way, and then she is fast outgrowing them in the artificial. . . .

I heard a rumor about the railroad between London & Columbus. They say that it will not go through. . . . I think that they have went to[o] far with it to stop now. . . .

I see Jesse Waldron last night. He is working for Watson over on the pike. . . . He is a real sot & would not stoop much to steal. He is an ignorant and debauched serf, a tool for sharpers & knaves, one whose mind never extended farther than to the nearest grocery, & whose genius never attempted anything higher than how to diddle the grocery keeper out of a dram. Poor Jesse. He has had a bad example set him by his mother who is a _____ and his father who is a thief & a drunkard. Like father, like son. He is not so much to blame for these tricks as others who have been taught better things.

Addison Cornwell went past here yesterday night. He stopped at Wm. Allens. He had got his profile or daguerreotype taken in London. It was a very well done concern & showed out Add to the life. I think when he gets sober he will look at his miniature with anything but pleasure. He talks of running for an office. I believe it is to be representative. He will make a grand one. He will be drunk half his time if he should be elected, but I think there is no danger [of] anything like that happening. . . .

There are some half dozen small boys here [at the mill] today. They are going to be our men some of these days, and how important it is that they should be the right kind of men. Our country needs good men & a great many of them, for with the great influx of foreigners we also have to put up with a great deal of the refuse portion of Uropes population. There are some, however, of our foreign people who are of the true metal and ring in with us very well with regard to the rights of men. Yet we will have to rid them of the leaven of monarchy, which still clings to them in spite of the charms of republicanism.

[Monday] August 1st, 1853

. . . Patrick Dailey & David Garrard came to see me [yesterday]. They staid here for some time, the whole afternoon in fact. Patrick is a real Irishman & no mistake. There is nothing good out of the Green Isle to his notion, yet he appears to be a pretty fine kind of a fellow, fond of fun and money. He does not drink any whiskey or chew any tobacco. He works for Cyrus Hornbeck at 150 dollars a year. He will have his year out next September.

David Garrard is an old schoolmate of mine. He is a plain, plodding kind of a fellow who loves money and women pretty well. He loves money a little the best. If he could only get both together he would be satisfied, I think.

America has a great many plodders, & likewise a great many go ahead fellows who do not care for anybody or anything providing there is no money to be made by it. Well, we need them, so let them rip, for the country needs all that can be done to make things brisk and lively.

. . . John D. Henderson is here today with his family. John D. is not a very great man, although he thinks that he is some punkins, anyhow & anyway or anywhere. He shoemakes some and farms some. I am inclined to think he is a little kind of lazy. Tact and perseverance are two great things which are found wanting in John D's head.

Mrs. Wallace & Aunt Rachel are here today also. Old Mrs. Wallace has sold out & is going to move away from Somerford. The old man is getting pretty frail, and I think he had better stay where he is. Perhaps he knows best what is good for him to do. He is an Irishman and has done a great deal of hard work in his day and time, but I think he will never do much more. . . .

I have not heard from any of my friends for some time. I do not know why they do not write. . . . Uncle Cary has not written & may have forgotten my letter. It has been some time since I have written to him, & no answer.

John D. came in awhile ago & I just had time enough to shut up my book before he looked in it. He is now getting some flour for Quill Prugh.

Mrs. Romigh was here yesterday. I would never have known her if I had not have been told. She looked some older and some fleshier in the face. She lived in the same house with us some 12 years ago. Her husband done the digging of the mill races. For 2 years he worked for us at the rates of about ten dollars per month. We found him a house to live in. . . .

[Tuesday] Aug. 2d, 1853

I am in the mill today again. I have not done much today, but I will have to pitch into the millstones this afternoon, for we are going to take up the corn stones & give them a dressing.

Henry has sold right smart out of the grocery today. Mr. Williams bought 31-1/2 pounds of pork at six and a fourth cents per pound.

Gam Saunders has gone to the West to buy Amelia Porters farm. I guess he will get it this time, for he was bound to buy it if he could when he left.

. . . Mrs. Henderson has a wonderful smart baby, so she says. It is a perfect keener. She says it began to notice things when it was three days old; could distinguish the rest of the family across the pike. To[o] smart to live, I think, just like its dad & the very image of its mam, & they are not to be grinned at by them what aint got no teeth. Well, we need a few more smart chaps, so the aforesaid article will be just in the very niche of time to suit the country. I must write to President Pierce and let him know about it. I think he can give it an office or its mother a pension. Either would do. . . .

[Tuesday] August 9th, 1853

. . . Grandfather [Roberts] is here. He came last Wednesday. He looks some older than he did when he went away. He does not like the West none of the best, I think. He and Uncle Jim toc ov [talk of] going in with us to build the [saw]mill on Darby.

Lance Peck is going to take a drove of cattle over the mountains for Wm. Watson. Allen Anderson talks of going along.

There is going to be a meeting here this afternoon. Rev. D. Somers will give us a preach. Well, all right with me anyhow. I do not object to having ministers and have to hear them preach. The fact is that they that preach and they that listen are two; so one is not bound to believe, nor is the other bound to come and go at every beck & call. Man is naturally inclined to hope, & it is a very good thing, for without it man would be a miserable creature indeed. . . .

I was at Darby this week. I seen the folks and scratched out some of those old mill irons. I inwardly cursed old Mrs. Fleming, the old she devil. I would like to see her in the penitentiary. Mr. Teller, he still takes her part. He is blinded with her flatteries and cant see her faults. I told him if he lived ten years longer by her side he would find her out. I do not know how she has stuffed him, but she has done it effectually.

Alice Roe is there yet. She does not have the very best times in the world, I guess. Well, one must expect to be a little slandered if they go among a certain set down there . . . some of them hard enough for any place.

I had an invite to a dance down there, but the girls mother would not let her go, so I did not go. They do not have any very great balls down there, but they can raise a pretty tall kind of a spree. They always have whiskey at all of their parties. They sometimes fight and tear up jack.

I went while I was down there to Cliftons. He has six girls, three big ones and three of the small fry. I never saw such a string of dirty faces in my life. The oldest one had a new dress on and took some airs while I was there. She was a great, tall, rawboned damsel and looked like a Samson. They say that she can run a wild turkey down & I do not doubt it, for she looks as though her wind was good. The next oldest girl looked like a pile of rags and grease piled up together. She generally sloped into some corner and there she would set with her chin in her hands. She eyed us pretty close. The rest were about ditto with the second one, though some of them had faces a little dirtier. The old man himself looked like some Arab. He was a little kind of crestfallen. He did not say much. He had an old handkerchief tied to his suspenders & kept continually wiping his eyes. I think he is nothing more than a poor old serf. He is a friend of Mrs. Flemings & takes her part on all occasions. His two sons look as though they would do to represent the fever & ague. They are poor specimens of humanity and ought to be taken to some show.

[Friday] Aug. 12, 1853

Today it rains and I have some time to write in this book.

Grandfather Roberts is here. He does not look as bad as he did when he first came. He wants to go down to Darby to see that mill. . . .

I was at Springfield on the 10th. I went & got my money of Wright. He kept me waiting till dark before he would pay me. I think Mr. Wright will find out that he will not make much by keeping people out of their money. A railroad contractor is not a king, and he will find it out some of these days.

Brownell is working in Iowa. He will carry on there untill he breaks, & then he will retire to some other corner and commence again. How he manages to diddle the Irish so much I am at a loss to know, but the thing is done, and done to perfection, by that same Brownell. I think the Irish are not very bright, or they would not be fooled so much by those "down Aysters," as they call them.

I saw in Springfield the other day about one of the best looking females that my eyes have been on for a long time. Perhaps she may have as hard a heart as the rest of earths children, yet a lovelier face I never saw. She was some great belle, I suppose, for she was dressed up in the very height of fashion. Pish, now! What good will she ever do me? None. I suppose she may never have a thought about me.

I saw a great many Irish girls in Springfield, but they are not pretty nor intelligent, so I did not pay any attention to them. The Irish all look alike to me. They all have a kind of heavy, sodden look.

I hear Pat Finneran has joined the Methodist Church. If he has, the Catholics have lost one of their once most superstitious members. . . .

I got Henry 8 pounds of tobacco and 18 pounds of candy. He sells right smart for to have so little a capital. I bought a wooden bucket in Springfield just to get a bill changed. I believe those fellows there have more change than they let on to have. I had to make change for Wright when he paid me.

They have not got their passenger cars on the London road yet. I do not know why they are not doing more business on that road. Randall says that he is going to work on it and that it is going through to Columbus strait on from London. I guess that they will have the cars running by the first of September.

I have been threshing oats for the last three or four days. Oats this year are very short. We have got ours cut down and part of them threshed. They turn out very well. We have threshed only six floorings and have got about half of seven acres done.

The assesor was here this morning. He is an old fellow by the name of Rob Amos. Land here he reckons at about fifteen dollars an acre and other things in proportion. He layed ours and C. Hornbecks at fifteen. Land here is high enough. The railroad has made everything come right up.

There was an Irishman who went along with me a piece this side of Springfield. He was a little drunk and went around the tollgates. He did not ride back when I did, but I heard the gatekeeper say he was going to fine him when he came back. His name was John McDonough. Perhaps he may find out that going around a gate is not such fun as he might get otherwheres, and for less money. He lives in London and boards Irish.

Well, there is no pity for him I know. Hugh Sweeny still keeps the gate there. He is always very accommodating to me. . . .

[Sunday] August 14th, 1853

Today is Sunday, a day for long faces and devout actions. There is no day in the whole week so much abused as Sunday. . . .

Old Chas. Clifton was here yesterday. He wants to take a lease on our place on Darby. He says he will clear up fifteen acres; put a good stout fence eight rails high on it; let us have the saw logs and wood on it; build a house on it twenty by twenty two; have it all in corn the second year. He will do all this for the use of it five years. . . . He is a pretty good hand at a lease, I guess, for he has always been at it & ought to be good. Practice makes perfect. I do not see why the old chap is not worth more than he is. He has always lived in this country and had a good chance to make money. But then some men wont be rich. You cant make them so. I suppose he has had Fortune to rap at his door several times and he has been asleep.

He has a large family of girls, but they are great to work out of doors. They maul rails, chop cordwood, grub, & do sundry other outdoor jobs which fall to the lot of men generally. I expect perhaps he will burn our fingers yet. But we must look out for breakers and watch the old chap.

Father & Grandfather will make a trade out of that Darby property yet, I think. The land case is not yet decided, & we do not know what to do.

I would like to go to school and learn a little more, for I am as ignorant as a horse. I want to be so that I can hold my own with [the] rest of the boys in this neck of woods. The great thing that I lack is money & time. If I only could go to school about nine months, I would then be able to go on my own hook. I am on a stand whether to go to Darby to work or go to school. I might learn a great deal there if I would set my head rightly at it, but one cant study and work both at once. I have a notion to get me some books and go to work and study to[o]. Father, he is sick, and I cant do anything at studying untill he gets better.

Bill Anderson & his mother are up here. Bill has got to be a perfect dog. He wont work or tell the truth anymore. He will come to some bad end yet, I am thinking. He lays around old man Sidners all the time. He is in his natural element when he is there. Birds of a feather will flock together.

Miranda, I hear, shows signs of a connexion before she was married. Well, it is about as I expected she would do. She was very keen to get John Sidner, and at last did get him, but he got her first. Nancy is on the carpet now. She will be married next, I suppose. . . .

I hear we are going to have another war with Mexico. The news came to London yesterday that the president had ordered twenty thousand men to go down on the Mexican frontier. Well, if they want to be whipped, let them come ahead. Uncle Sam is ready and willing to give them another joe darter. I would like to go down there myself if it was not so hot. I do not like these hot places. Mexico will be no more if she tries us another hitch. We will take all of her this time and make a Yankee state out of her.

The Whigs will make a great hurrah about the Democrats raising this war. Well, it is to be so, I suppose. Thom. Corwin will have another chance to make another war speech. I guess he had better go down and help his brother Santa Anna, the wooden legged dictator of Mexico. If Pierce makes as good a haul as Polk did, he will make the United States one of the richest nations on the globe.

There is meeting in Somerford today. Mr. Tingleys funeral is to be preached. He was a fine man, & the honour done to his remains and to his memory speak well of the people here. He was a firm believer in the doctrines of the Dunkard Church. He was a good neighbor & a warm friend to all that knew him. He was a man of great physical power. He was about six feet 4 inches in h[e]ight. I never knew aught said against him. He lived and died a simple farmer and left nothing but an honest name behind him.

. . . I have not finished threshing my oats. They will not turn out very well, not so well as I thought they would. We will have about sixty bushels, I think.

I have not seen Henry Peck for some time. I guess he has been putting up hay at home.

Roderick is going to the camp meeting on Darby. I wish I could get to go but am afraid that I will not get to go anywhere soon. Roderick needs some more of the good spirit, so I think no one ought to try to stop him from going. He is a selfish man, I think, & selfishness ought not to belong to a religious man. He is a little bigoted to[o], I think. So I think if he goes and gets cleansed from these two things, he will have great cause to be rejoiced. I do not know of anyone else that is going to go.

I hear that Mr. John Cheeny is cutting a wide swath. He and some others just like him broke up a camp meeting at Mechanicsburg. He is a poor excuse anyway you can take him. He is a smart fellow & by his cuteness generally manages to elude the law, but I think the chap will get into limbo yet for some of his tricks. He can talk with all the gravity of a preacher and act with the impudence of a Satan. I never was deceived in anyone so much as I was in him. He talked so fair & everything about him seemed to be so gentleman like that you would almost want to make a confident of him at first sight. Yet he was a double dealer in every sense. He and Mrs. Fleming are just about alike. They both talk fair and do their tricks in the dark as much as possible. They are both getting their dues now.

Long John Hunters wife is dead. She has been lingering all summer with the consumption. She I think was a fine woman. John, I do not know but what he is a little kind of on the Pharisaical order. He is a man that loves the dollar very well. They say he made some advances to Miss Margaret Doane before his wife died. How true it is I am unable to say. She was a fine girl, I hear.

[Saturday] Aug. 20th, 1853

. . . I am writing before breakfast this morning. Mrs. Randall is here with her family. She looks about as well as usual and still can rail out on Mrs. Fleming, who by the way needs it if anyone ever did. The infernal old Hecate has burned us five hundred dollars worse off than we were before we saw her ugly mug. Mr. Fleming & Mr. Randall have gone up to Hardin County to see about that piece of land that Mr. Fleming owns up there.

Louisa Cullumber, the wife of William Cullumber, has, it seems, took a jealous fit. She has to set by Bill all the time to see that he does not run away from her. . . . She has got to be a little jealous of Nancy Anderson. Ha! That is a good joke. . . .

Henry Peck, Gam Saunders, Semp Saunders, and John B. Garrard have all gone to camp meeting on Darby.

[Sunday] August 21st, 1853

I am twenty years old today & am alive and well. I look back upon my past life & find a great many shadows and dark places; yet I have my share of happiness with the rest of the world. Twenty years hence and where will I be? Perhaps settled down on a farm with a wife and—well, I wont say anything about the other peculiar pucuniary platter cleaners that generally follow the union of male and female together.

Long ago I was a little madcap chap delighting in nothing but mischief and mischief makers. I recollect the time I used to go to school with Rachel Marsh. What long walks and long stories she would have on a Saturday. I have seen many a happy time, but none could come up with them. Poor Rachel. She has gone the way of all flesh. Perhaps she may now be recounting over in her spirit home the joys of her youth. She married Isaac Potee and lived with him some year or two, then died. Peace to her ashes.

I have seen the happiness of some of my playmates dimmed and some of them cut off by death. There was Joe Young. He went [to school] to Webb in Somerford. He used to be a wild kind of a youth. Joe, he has gone to some place remote from this. I do not hear anything more about him of late. Joe lost his arm after he left school here. Lige and Ebenezer Hutchinson have left too. They had a good many small tricks in them when they were young. They were very proud boys and wanted to boss the school. Ebenezer is one of the head men in the Whig party in this state now, but I think him & his party too will go by the board. Lige does not make much of a stir.

Jim Ryan used to go to school there too. He went to Mexico and is since dead. Weldons boys went there too, Lawrence and Christopher. I see them well paddled one day for sticking straws in horseflies and then letting them go in the schoolhouse. They have come out since. One of them keeps a wholesale store in London, while the other is studying law in the same place. The old man still lives in Somerford. He keeps the [toll]gate there. One of the girls married last winter. She used to work for us some years since. She was a good natured and industrious girl. She married a Morris. He boarded here in 1847. He is a pretty fair kind of a fellow, I guess. He lives up about Plattsburg and has some property.

I hear that old Jimmy Mathews does not do so well in the West. He used to live on Deer Creek. I went one night along with a lot of other fellows to paddy [toast?] one of his daughters. We thought she was going to be married. We were sold that time sure. Pet Heffley married one of his girls. I guess it was the same one we went to paddy. He was in the crowd, anyhow.

Running back to the former things in ones life will give me pleasure, I think, so I will just keep on writing in this book, and perhaps I may derive some benefit from it yet. I bought it for the Ciceronian Society to use, but they did not want so large a one, so thought I would just keep it myself. We had a deal of fine sport in our debates. I must have some more fun [this] winter if I can raise another [literary society].

Grandfather left here today. He went over to Uncle Wilsons. He has not made any bargain yet with Father about that mill.

[Saturday] September 3d, 1853
. . . The Conference has come & gone. . . . I [at]tended every day while it lasted. There were some very smart men there. I heard right good sermons while the Conference lasted. They had some of their lead horses there sure.

John Phillips, the great Antioch agent, was there. He is all mettal & all original. He is a great man for anecdotes. He got about seventy five dollars for Antioch. He appears to be wrapped up body & soul in the enterprize. I guess it will be a mammoth concern when it gets to be finished. They talk of extending the building across the twenty acre lot. If they do I must certainly go & see it. I will anyhow if I live & can get there. I would like to go there myself about three years & just get myself finished enough to do business on my own hook, but I have almost give that up as an impossibility. . . .

The yellow fever is raging in New Orleans pretty bad. One of old David Hulls boys are there. I think it will be a pretty hard time on him. I expect he will never get back. I would not go there for half of the city. Some people are fond of such places, but I know I am not.

Old Joe Melvin has got to be our P[ost] M[aster] in Somerford. I do not know as we will be benefited by the change, but we cant help that, so it is of no use to grumble.

[Sunday] Sept. 18th, 1853

Today I again set down to write in this my only friend who neither flatters nor reproves. I have been through a variety of adventures since I last wrote. I have been humbugged pretty cutely & have humbugged others.

I was at the Hippodrome on the 14th. I saw some tolerably good performances. They [had] all kinds of races, monkeys on ponies and women in chariots. I saw some of the greatest charriot [*sic*] races ever. They just went with the wind. Mad. Poline & several other French women cut up some antics. One of the men got killed while performing, or injured so that he died soon after.

Mr. [Miller?] holds forth today up at the schoolhouse. I do not know whether to go or not. I am kind of an eyesore to him, I guess, so I had better not.

On the 13th of this month I got decently humbugged by one Henry Peck & Watsons boys. I will, however, make no mention of the particulars here, for I did not cut a very high figure in the spree. I must give them a high strike some of these days. I do not much like the idea of letting them pass without a stiff return of the compliment.

Jim is going to come in in October. He writes to me that they have all been sick. The ague out there [in Illinois] is plenty enough, I guess, if all the accounts be true.

Everything here is on a stand. No excitement. No life. Everything seems to have taken a Rip Van Winkle snoose. No deaths nor no weddings. All the people appear to know is to plow & to mow, to reap and to sow.

Cass Tingley & Steve Sweet were married in Springfield this week. They have the infair [infare, the reception of a bride in her new home] today at the widow Tingleys. I hope Steve has had it in fair before this. . . .

[Monday] September 19th, 1853

. . . I was at Welsh'es Parisian Hippodrome on the 14th of this month. . . . Races & chases were the order of the day. They whizzed around in charriots, four horses abreast. It looked kind of scary to me to see four or five women ride as though Old Nick was after them. They had some of the most commonplace looking women there that I ever clapped my eyes on. One of the men got killed there that night. He was swinging on the slack rope by one foot when it broke. He fell about twenty feet right on his back. He died next day in Urbana. His name was Franklin.

They had quite a row with the Irish. It appears that the Irish were raising a row, as is usual with them. It ended in a serious manner. Sixteen Paddies & four showmen were sent to figure on another stage, then shuffled off their mortal coil & took up their march to that unknown country.

The Irish are getting to be pretty thick in this country lately, & I am afraid we will have hot times with them before many years will have passed over our heads. I see that the Irish are beginning to get discontented with the Americans & want to have all the government in their hands. The priests are stirring them up in many places, and they are getting to think that the Americans want to undermine & distress them. Pat Dailey, an Irishman who works for Cyrus Hornbeck, he is a strong Catholic & prays fervently to the Virgin Mary. He thinks, however, that the priest is a little too avaricious & too proud happy. Will the day be when all Catholics will begin to see the same way?

The bright days appear to have flown from my page in lifes great book. We have sickness on every hand. Father is still on the decline & will soon be passing through the shadow of death. Emeline Richmond is very sick. She is not expected to live. She was confined with a female child some time ago, & it is the same old tale of quacks & nostrums of many grades and many colors. Poor humanity must suffer these days with the man traps & health destroying practices of a set of drivelers called doctors.

I hear that David T. Garrard is again paying his addresses to Mary Ann Wilson. If it is indeed the case I do not know where his wisdom has gone to. He must certainly be out of his mind, for she once refused him, & that before the whole world & that too in a very pointed manner. If she shows him any encouragement, I am at a loss to know how she can do it without acting the hypocrite, for it has not been long since she has left Cheny, & how could she vary as quick as that? Perhaps I am too hasty in my opinions. Yet if not, I think D.T. Garrard is a knave or a fool. He cant help but be one or the other.

His brother John has not acted the part of a man of honor & prudence. He left his wife in the first year of his marriage. What the cause was no one knows, except it is the family. He is going to go to Illinois tomorrow. He has sold off all his stock & is going to make his residence permanent in the West, so I hear. . . .

Wesley Allen has a large watermelon patch this year. He has sold about eight dollars worth already. I hear a good joke on Henry Peck & Wm. Forbess. They went over there, it appears, to get some watermelons & Wesley was in the patch. He told them to hold on but they concluded to run on. He had a dog which tore one of their pantaloon legs etc. . . .

[Sunday] September 25th, 1853

. . . Andrew & Lewellen Fleming are on Darby once more. Well, I have no very particular good love for them, so it makes no difference to me where they are. I would like them all the better if they would only take their mother out of the state. She has caused us a great deal of trouble and vexation. The Bible says, "Do unto others as you would have them do to you." It is hard to do this if one is [not of?] a mind to. I can never forgive Mrs. Fleming for the injury she has done us. She has struck us a blow from which we will always feel the effects.

Mr. Randall was here this morning. He is going to Springfield today. He has the superintending of some work on the railroad near Columbus. He borrowed Henrys mare to ride. He got here this morning before breakfast. He is going to superintend for Degraffe on the Xenia and Columbus Railroad. I hear that the Springfield railroad is not going to be finished through to Columbus for three years, so it will be of no use to count on its doing us any good. . . .

Mr. Randall has got back from Springfield. He is superintendent for A. Degraffe at forty dollars per month & board. He will make some money now, I suppose, for he has got into a paying business. I hope he will, for he has had a hard run of luck ever since he came to Darby, & it is no more than right that he should have some good luck. . . .

Henry Peck talks of going to Saint Louis this fall, but I think it will be like his going to California. It will be a windy concern and blow over in the same way that that did. He says he has been lied on by the people of this neighborhood. Well, he is not the only one, so he need not be grieved overmuch about it.

Pat Daileys time with Cyrus Hornbeck is out today. He has put in a crop of wheat with Cy.

[Friday] Sept. 30th, 1853

. . . Sickness still hangs over our family its dark and gloomy mantle. I wish it were not so, yet it must be & there is no help for it. Father is very low at this time, & I do not think he will ever recover. . . .

I hear a report going the rounds that Will Heffley & Mary Wilson are going to get married. This is the talk now among the kitchen girls & busy old women. I do not fancy this thing of marrying first cousins. Their children, if they ever be so unfortunate as to have any, are always sure to be deformed or idiotic, and we always have enough of that kind of people anyhow. So I think it would be best not to marry at all if you cant do without having your couzin [sic].

The state & county fairs have come and gone, and I have not been to either. Wesley Allen took the premium on potatoes. Well, I am glad of it. The honest farmer ought to have his dues, & he is one of the sort. But it is not always the case at these fairs that the deserving ones get the premium.

Sunday, October 3d, 1853

. . . There is not any sickness in the neighborhood at this time except some old cases of long standing. Eli Wilson ran a pitchfork into his foot about a month ago. He has not got over it yet, & some think that his foot will have to come off. I hear that his wife says she would rather have him die than see him have his leg taken off. A great deal of affection for Eli! Truly this is an age of sensibility and benevolence. Eli will think more of his wife after her charitable declaration. . . .

One of Col. Garrards boys have run away. He started about a week ago for parts unknown, & there has been nothing heard of him since. He told his folks that he was going to work for one Mr. Blann, who lives close to where the Col. lives. He got up several times during the night before he started & pretended that he was sick, but all the time he was getting his clothes for to run away in the morning. He started, as they supposed, to work for Blann. He went into the corn field, stripped off his work clothes and put on his Sunday suit, went to London, bought a suit of clothes on his fathers credit, got on the cars, & sloped. . . .

I had thought once of going to college this winter, but I guess that that will have to be given up for the present, & perhaps forever. I would like to go very well, but there are so many difficulties & trials in the way that I have almost got out of heart. I think I can eat, drink, & sleep as soft as students do. The rugged paths of life might be softened a little by knowing more of its ways. . . .

The wave that Mr. Miller & Mr. Cotterel caused in the sluggish pool of events in this neighborhood has subsided into a gentle ripple. All is now as calm as a duck pond. Mr. Miller, of course, thinks that he has forever settled the hash with Mr. Cotterel, & Cotterel thinks he has done the same with Miller.

[Sunday] October 9th, 1853

. . . Father still keeps poorly; no better all the time. He has just heard of a famous remedy and has commenced using it. I believe they call it Dr. Halls Lung Syrup. I do not believe that it will ever do him any good. . . .

Grandfather is here yet. We have made no arrangements about that mill business yet. I do not know what the result will be, but I think that we will be apt to let things stand as they are, for awhile yet anyhow.

Aunt Malvina Cary is here now. She came last Friday on the cars. All well down there, I believe. . . . College Hill is a place I should like to live at. The country is just suited to my fancy exactly. I now intend to go to school there after I get to be of age. I must go somewhere anyhow, so I will make my arrangements to do so. I want to get an education so that I can be independent and not have to ask others to do me favors in the way of doing business.

I worked on the road Saturday afternoon. We had a pretty good time over on the road. Henry Peck, Jonah Trowbridge, Pat Dailey, Cy Hornbeck, Dav. T. Garrard, Jam. Porter, and myself constituted the squad & Grubber Jones acted as supervisor. Jones does very well in that capacity. . . . We loaded gravel and hauled it on to the Springfield road. I am going to work a half day tomorrow, and then I will be free from the roads, this year anyhow.

Old man Clifton still vegetates down there on our place on Darby. Guess the old fellow will do about right with us down there, because he wants us to let him have that house on the side of the creek that Flemings live on. Old Aunt Sally still stays there, and I guess she always will, because she seems to want to stay there for fear Mr. Randall would happen to move in. I do think the old creature will turn perfectly green before she dies. She is so full of the green eyed monster jealousy that she can hardly live. She is so smooth and insinuating that one would think she was one of the finest women in the whole world. . . .

[Sunday] Oct. 16th, 1853

. . . I have been doing some hard work since I last wrote. I have been digging in the tailrace and working at a ditch that runs into the milldam.

This world does not change me much. I know a little more than I did when I wrote in this book before. I am particularly green about women and womens ways. I had a most luscious time with one the other night. I came very nigh— Well, its no use to talk, thats all. I must do more and talk less. I find that it pays a great deal better.

Susan Tingley is working here now. She is a pretty fair kind of a girl, I guess, from what I have seen of her. I must try and get a little better acquainted with her and see if we cant agree well enough to— Well, shoh, here I am running on at a great rate about nothing at all. She says she is going to be married before the year is out. Well, we shall see what is what after awhile.

Day before yesterday I helped Gam Saunders with his sheep. He bought four hogs of us and paid us thirty dollars for them. Gam is a fine fellow & I like him, but I am afraid he will put off his education untill it will be too late. He is doing a very good business now, I think, and will have a pile to go upon if he keeps on.

Miller preaches today at the schoolhouse. I was not able to go in the forenoon, but Henry said that the house was full and overflowing. I do not think he will get up much of an excitement here this time on account of him and Cotterel having that little battle. There is a great deal of froth about Miller, more of that than anything else. The Methodists are losing ground here now, and it will take something of a blow to raise them up as high as they were some time since.

The flour market is very good at this time. I think we will make money if it keeps up, although barrels are very high now and wages are very high. We have to pay 35 cents per barrel and one dollar for wheat.

Grandfather had quite a turn of the cholera morbus last night. He is getting too old to stand much now. He says that he is seventy two years of age. That is as old as I expect to live, and it may be that I may not live to be half that old.

The weather today is very fine. Indian summer is here, I think, for everything looks smokey. Uncle Jim and the rest are having a fine time to move in. If it only holds on this way for a week or ten days, I think that they will be here. I have not heard from them for some time, so they must be on the road somewhere between here and Chillicothe. I hope so, anyhow.

Father is no better. He is very weak & feeble.

3

Studying Human Nature
November 12, 1853–August 15, 1854

John Roberts returns to his journal soon after his father's death. The death, the onset of winter weather, and disappointment at not being able to go to college might have caused prolonged melancholy, but it gradually fades. Writing in his journal seems to have served him as an anachronistic psychiatrist's couch. Although mortality often weighs on John's mind, his thoughts about the changing seasons contribute to his belief in universal salvation. "I am now a believer in Universalism, hydropathy, democracy, & progression in everything," he writes in July 1854.

While continuing to operate a gristmill on Oak Run, the Roberts family moves for a time to Darby, where John farms and works at rebuilding the sawmill his father had erected there in 1849. (When he writes "to Darby" or "on Darby" he means the family homestead on Little Darby Creek and its general neighborhood.) He remains enthusiastic about the peace and simplicity of life in the country. Dance parties, though, are hardly peaceful affairs; young men's antagonisms, fired by liquor, sometimes erupt in fights and drawn pistols.

On Darby, John experiences "life among the lowly" at the Cliftons' fireside and hears a tale of true grit from the mother of the illiterate brood. His efforts to teach them to read and write show his desire to become a schoolteacher.

John studies for a short period under an eccentric grammarian with a rapid-fire delivery of the rules of parsing. The literary society falters, but John's desire for personal and social improvement grows stronger. He is still determined to go to college when he comes of age and feels free to leave home. His two-year-younger brother Henry continues to annoy him.

In his patriotic outbursts about the "old despots of Urope" and the glories of his own country, John reflects the growing fear of many native Americans that a flood of immigrants—especially Irish Catholics—endangers the democratic republic and its free institutions. London's doggeries (cheap saloons) are another threat. Too many of his neighbors

*are drunken fools, he believes, doomed to an early death. He thinks
Ohio's adoption of the Maine Liquor Law will bring a needed reform,
but in early court trials the saloonkeepers' money and influence dash his
hopes.*

[Saturday] November 12, 1853

Today I again set down to write in thee, old book. I and you have
been strangers of late.

The face of things are changed since I last wrote. The leaves have
fell to the ground and all nature seems bare & desolate. All is wrapt in
the mantle of decay and death. It seems as though we ought to keep on
living in this world, but it is not so, and I must abide by the law.

Father is dead. He died Oct. 20th, 1853, at ten minutes of eight
o'clock p.m. He passed off peacefully and calmly & with a firm
conviction that Heaven would be his home after this life was done. He
had the consumption and was drugged till life got to be a burthen to him.

I feel a kind of loneliness steal over me when I look around and
find his bed of suffering unoccupied by him. Peace to his ashes, & may
my end be as satisfactory as his was to myself and friends.

Grandmother & Uncle Jim are not here yet. They are expected
every day. I would be glad to see them, & yet I feel sad on that account.
They will find things so much changed that it will be to them like
moving into a strange land when they get back.

Aunt Malvina Cary was here some time ago. She was going to
Chillicothe to see some of her relatives. I had some notion of going
down there [to Uncle Cary's] this winter to live. I do not like, however,
to be dependent upon anyone for my bread. I want to be independent if I
can of everybody and everything as far as possible.

Alice Roe is married, so I hear. I guess she is suited at last. Mr.
Bartlett is the man she made happy or miserable, I do not know which.
Neither do I care. I hear that she had a very long and hot chase before
she got him. He is a blacksmith, I believe, humpbacked and a widower
to boot.

. . . Old Mrs. Fleming has gone west. The old harridan could not
live among white folks any longer. Mr. Fleming gave her three hundred
dollars and let her shoot for the West. May she live a life devoid of peace
and comfort and at last sink into an ignominious grave cursed both [in]
body and memory. But may God take her at last up to Heaven and teach
her the way and the truth is all I have to say about the old thing, and I
presume that that will be or is enough.

[Friday] Nov. 25th, 1853

This day we finished a chimney in the west end of the house. Uncle Jim & Henry laid the bricks and I carried the mortar. It is a tolerably good chimney & will draw very well, I guess.

Uncle Jim is sick with the headache and has been in bed ever since dark. I think bad diet is the chief cause. I do not feel very well myself. I have a pain in my stomach. . . .

I have been run to death by Henry. He has blotted my book and various other inconveniences too tedious to mention here or any other place. He has so much wind & self importance about him that I can hardly stand it. I have to bear with him because he is my brother, but on no other consideration. There is nothing bad about him, but he is a little too important to suit me altogether.

Mother is going over to Uncle Tine Wilsons tomorrow & Grandmother is going to come over then. She has been over there for two weeks.

Emeline Richmond has been sick for four months. Old Dr. Dan will keep her in tow untill she has wound her brief life to a close. I do not see why people do not see the fatality of medicine and quacks. I do not believe in them.

[Sunday] Nov. 27th, 1853

. . . I have had a long talk with John Cheny. He appears still to harbor a hope that he & Mary Ann will & can live together. The fact is, all he knows is Mary Ann, Mary Ann, & that is the theme and all the theme that he can talk on. If you talk of the weather, he will tell you that the weather was good when he was married. If you talk on politics & womens rights, he will wind up on the propriety of a womans obeying her husband & tell over his sorrows. He thinks that old Jobs afflictions were nothing compared to his. He neither eats nor drinks, sleeps nor works, but what Mary Ann is ever ready at his tongues end to be doled out with a pathos that is truly surprizing. He will take no insults nor hints from relatives. He is always the same incomprehensible self, the same John Cheny, nothing changed, nothing daunted. He still stands immutably fixed on obtaining the grand and object of his heart, Mary Ann Wilson, his woman, as he calls her. Well, he has a whole catalogue of sorrows to stand up under & no heart to feel or eye to pity him. He is in a wretched way. That green eyed monster cankers his every enjoymen[t]. I envy him not.

Dec. 4th, 1853, Sunday

Old Boreas has commenced his blasts at last. We have winter here & a pretty raw time of it too. . . .

I have been doing various kinds of work since I last wrote in this book. I was down on Darby some two days ago along with Uncle James. We hauled two loads of corn from there and we had a pretty rough time of it. We staid all night at old Charlie Cliftons. He is a regular old cock of the woods & no mistake. He can beat me all hollow in telling smutty stories. He is, I think, nothing but an old serf who never had a thought about the morrow. Jim talks of getting one of the girls to live with him. I think that one will be a dose. The old fellow has a regiment of girls, and they are all ready for anything from a bear fight to a footrace. I saw something of life among the lowly while I was down there. Old Mrs. Clifton is a very good match for old Charlie, & he is a match for any man I ever saw. . . .

Mr. Randall is about to move into Mr. Flemings house. I do not like such proceedings myself. I would if I were Randall do otherwise, that is if I still had the same mind that I now have; but perhaps he knows best what is good for him & his. Mr. Fleming looked kind of sheepish when I saw him. I suppose he saw the awkwardness of his situation. Old Mrs. Fleming will turn entirely green & explode with rage when she gets to hear of it. . . . I have no bowels of compassion for her, I know, & I do [not] think that there are many who have. She has made herself miserable by her folly, & she may as well lay on the bed now as she has made it as anyone else. They are all out in the West but Mr. Fleming, & may they never return is my prair. They are a set of ignoramuses & knave[s], I verily believe, & the more they injure themselves by their deviltries the better.

Corn is now worth thirty cents per bushel in the field and is still coming up. We have ten acres to sell, so let it rip.

Sunday, December 18th, 1853

The old year is fast passing away & with it our pleasant weather.

. . . Man is indeed a vapor, fleeting and etherial in his nature and in practice. But man has inculculated the idea that he will be like the grass. He will spring up with renewed beauty after the winter is over; that [while] this earthly tabernacle is dissolved, we have a home eternal in the heavens and which passeth not away. What a blessed and cheering thought, that of immortality! . . .

Talk not to me about the hardness of the doctrine of universal benevolence & universal happiness. If anything would make me love God, it would most assuredly be on account of His love and mercy. Oh, when will the good time come when all men shall have a knowledge of God as He is? . . . He has made us in His infinite wisdom & mercy, and will He punish us forever? The Scripture says no. Reason & nature speak in tones of thunder the stern denial of such a doctrine. . . . He has always done the best, the very best, for us in times past & gone by, & we may rely upon Him in future years.

. . . Yes, blessed is the doctrine of universal benevolence, universal love, universal salvation. It cheers the brokenhearted widow to think that her husband is in the land of the blessed. It consoles the disconsolate orphan to think that its earthly protector is covered with Gods love. Who would rob them of the blessed thought? . . .

Franklin Cary was here this week. He is going to try the egg business. I suspect that he will not make much by the operation.

James & Henry have gone to Darby after corn.

[Tuesday] December 27th, 1853

John Forbess is going to move west. He will start today. He intends to move into Vermillion Co., Illinois. Well, he is and always has been a good citizen and a kind neighbor, and we will all feel his loss. . . . I do not know what we will do for a shoemaker after Mr. Forbess leaves. . . . He sold his place to Uncle Tine Wilson for 20 dollars an acre, which is a good price and I think not much of a bargain to the buyer. Perhaps I am mistaken. Land here has been coming up for the last three years very fast. Land that could have been bought 3 years ago for five dollars cant be bought for less than fifteen at this very time.

Aunt Rachel Roberts came near being burnt to death on Christmas. Her clothes were burnt entirely off of her, and she was burned considerable in the arms and on the body. Mother rode over yesterday to see her and was glad to learn that the first report was far greater than the reality.

Valentine Wilson, Jun., was here this morning enquiring about his spouse. He looked as stout as a major and appeared to have a great desire to see his dearly beloved but much abused wife. He is a real brute and no mistake, for he has thumped his wife most unmercifully in times past, & it is my opinion that he will do so again. Yet she still clings to him with a constancy that is truly wonderful. I do not see what she can see in him so enticing. He is not beautiful nor is he virtuous. He wont work and will get drunk. The fact is, he is good for nothing under the shining sun without it is a warning to others not to let whiskey reign over their reason and make beasts of them [in] every sense of the word. May I never come to such a pass as he is in at the present time. If I do, I ask some kind friend to put an end to my worthless existence. I would not want to stand on the face of the earth if I was a slave to my passions & especially to the love of strong drink. There is no good in it now, nor there never was any good in it. . . .

December 27th [Thursday, December 29th?], 1853
 . . . Hamilton Wilson lost a horse on Christmas Eve. He was in Springfield at the time. He takes it like a philosopher & never makes the first wry face about it. Well, it is the best plan to take things as they come, in a good humor & with cheerfulness if possible. Hamilton must be a happy fellow surely.

Valentine got into a scrape with some of the Irish denizens of Somerford on Christmas Eve. Old Dr. Wilson had a frolick and they all got drunk, and of course they could not keep from having a muss. A fellow by the name of Mansfield got pretty badly used up. He is a kind of a bully and people do not pity him much. These sprees do not turn out very profitable to everyone every time and on all occasions.

We have not had a very great Christmas here this year. To be sure, we have had enough fights to make variety; yet solid pleasure we have had none and will have none till we reform some in our way of carrying things on. We must have more refinement if we want to have pleasure.

James and I have been to Darby amongst old Cliftons stock. We had a good time, taking everything into consideration. I think there are not many who enjoyed themselves better than we did, but as for intellectual enjoyments we are not disposed to boast. I saw more of human nature while I was down there than I ever did before. I saw & heard things that I never saw nor heard of before. Old Charlies girls, however, do not always speak the truth. We had a specimen of that by their promising to come up with us and then backing out. . . . Jim has engaged Miss Elizabeth Robinson to work for him. She is to come next week, which will be the beginning of the new year. Elizabeth has got to be quite a large girl since I first knew her. . . . She has a notion to go to school here this winter if she is suited & everything works right. . . .

Saturday, December 31st, Anno Domini 1853
 Today is the last day of the year. . . . What a crowd of misery this year has brought forth. How many hearts have been broken and how many souls have sickened and grew weary of this world. I myself have saw many of my hopeful anticipations come to nought. I have seen friends leave this world for a better and have been chided for the bitter tears of regret. I have seen & endured all this within the short space of 12 months, & yet I feel that there is much pleasure here below.

There is much to be done here in this little world of ours. I would to God that I was better qualified to enjoy the pleasure and endure the pain of this world, but the good God who made all things knew the proper qualities & propensities that were necessary for His own good, & why should I repine and grieve over what I cannot help & do not know how to help? . . .

Uncle James has gone to Darby. He is going to try once more to see if he can get a girl to live with his folks. I guess that girls are getting tolerably scarce or very proud, one of the two, I dont know which.

I was at a party last night at Wm. Todds. We had a good time. There were about 14 girls there, and everything went as mer[r]y as a marriage bell.

[Monday] January 16th, A.D. 1854

The night is dark and rainy & I have exhausted all my newspapers, so the only thing I have left is this book. . . .

I was on Darby last Saturday and Sunday. I saw & heard a great many things while I was there.

Fielding Lynn is dead. He died a miserable wretch, unwept and uncared for by his former associates. He was a wild, reckless sort of a man; made every thing but the right thing, and that was a good man and a useful citizen. His own brother would not take him into his house untill he was shamed into it by others. Poor fellow, he has had a hard row to hoe in this life, & I will, I am sure, not begrudge him all the happiness he can get or have in the next. He died with the consumption. He was not 30 years of age when he died, and I think some of his associates will follow him sooner than they expect to if they do not reform. Truly the way of the transgressor is hard.

Charles Clifton has rented our place on Darby for another year. He is a regular old fellow & has a great deal of originality about him. He is extremely ignorant and of course extremely poor. Neither of them are very desireable companions in the rugged path of life, yet he seems to enjoy himself & can crack as [many] jokes as a circus clown. Well, I do not know but what he is about half right. They say that "care killed a cat," and I guess it has killed men too before now. . . .

Elizabeth Robinson is still working for Grandfathers folks. She seems to be a fine girl for business and warm hearted, but she is poor and the world will never hear of her good qualities even if they were ever so conspicuous. . . . There is now more real virtue among the poor than among any one class of people upon the earth. The fact is, honesty & benevolence will make a man very poor if he follows them up closely, not poor in real worth and satisfaction, but poor in gold. There is more real enjoyment in a rustic party than in a splendid ballroom with their thousand dollar slippers & splendid bands of music. But true pleasure is hardly to be come at in this world by us. It needs something of a purer nature, something nearer Heaven to make us happy.

There is a debate at the brick [schoolhouse] tonight, but the weather is so bad that I do not suppose that I would have been profited much more than I am now if I had went. Gam Saunders is at the head of affairs down there at our schoolhouse. He was not on hands the other night. How well he will attend in future, let time determine, for I know nothing about it.

Sunday, [no date] 1854

. . . Our schoolmaster has been turned off and we are without a schoolteacher in this district. Poor Pease, I suspect that pride & self esteem have been his greatest enemies. He spoke very well of the school & schollars. He regretted the leaving of the school very much. I do not know why they turned him off. He introduced a new order of things into the school. He is a man who wants to have everything done up in book style. He wants everything his own way. . . .

Friday night I spent in revelry and mirth among as jolly a set of boys as one will have the pleasure of meeting in these diggings. Wm. T. Jones, commonly called Grubber, had a wood chopping & of course all the elite were out. I started at noon and got there just as they quit. I felt kind of cheap when I found myself there with my ax on my shoulder and the wood all chopped. But then I knew that "Grubber" was one of natures noblemen and it would be all right.

Well, there were some 7 or 8 girls there, and we had a pretty tall time till 8 or nine o'clock, when there was a damper put upon the proceedings by the announcement of the fiddler, a saffron colored specimen of humanity, who looked as though he had not slept any for the last week. He come and the most of the girls went home. Four stayed and danced untill midnight & then sparked till daylight.

Our debating society has went on pretty well of late, but it seems as though there is not enough interest taken in it to make it prosper. I would like to see it go on if it were possible . . . for I will die of ennui if I do not have some place to go to of an evening. Gam Saunders is president, James H. Roberts vice president, & I am the secretary. Some of the boys take delight in breaking down everything that comes along. I am not one of that kind. I go in for all the new improvements that are beneficial to the public. I do believe that a debate properly carried on would be a great benefit to mankind. The public mind would soon be enlightened so that deception would never have the least respect paid to it.

Some of the boys proposed to have compositions read before the lyceum. . . . John Allen wrote a couple of splendid compositions, one on the beauty of nature & the other a piece of poetry on the flowers. John has the stuff for a good writer, but I fear his diffidence will spoil him yet. He is so bashful and retiring that I suspect he will never aspire to the higher and nobler sphere of a writer. He is somewhat cast down by a criticism or two offered by some of the boys on his composition. He told me the other night that he would never try to write another composition as long as he lived.

. . . My legs are extremely sore caused by excessive exercise over at Grubbers. Dancing will lay me up if I do much more of it. I made a great many new acquaintances while I was over there. The ladies were charming. They almost got me into a notion of marrying. Some of them were very pretty and all very sensible. I must extend my acquaintance a little farther in that direction.

Henry Peck & William Forbess had a few words but did not come to blows. Henry challenged Bill to fight a duel with pistols, but that did not seem to be as good a way to settle the matter as Forbess wanted. He wanted to take his fists and pummel one another. In that way they, however, did not come to any terms, & each one went his way, not rejoicing but peaceably.

By the way, Henry Peck talks of going to California. I do not hardly think he will go, for he talked of that once before but never went. Henry is a pretty good sort of a fellow, but he is most to[o] visionary, to[o] shiftless to get along first rate, that is in the money line. He dresses fine and spends his money free & is altogether a fine fellow to be with.

I cant help but think of those girls over at Jones'es. They made an impression upon some of the swains there, one in particular named Norris, who was pretty well elevated with the whiskey he had drank. He appeared to be on needles all the time. Well, a mans heart is like a mud turtles egg, susceptible of being considerably dented without getting broken. One girl comes along and makes a dint in one side which stays there untill some prettier girl comes along and makes a deeper impression on the other side, which cures the old dint entirely.

[Sunday] Feb. 12th, 1854

. . . I am now attending a course of grammar lectures in Somerford. We have a very good teacher, Dr. Simmerman. He understands the science of English grammar perfectly. I think he is the best grammarian in the state. He has memorized several grammars. Kirkham he has memorized to a "T" & no mistake. He is the most industrious man I ever saw. He is never idle when in the lecture room. He will come in & pull off his coat & immediately proceed with the exercises of the school. He does not waste a minute of his time in useless talk but says everything quick & short & always to the point.

We go through the ten parts of speech every day. In fact, we go through the book every day. I do not see but how we can help but learn. We are now parsing in the back part of the book. Some of the schollars have been through the book twice before this time, which makes the thing more interesting than it otherwise would be. There are about twenty one schollars. . . . We have a first rate set of fellows, take them "bye & large." I enjoy life first rate. I walk home every night, which is a very good exercise. . . .

London has become almost defunct in the abstract. A fire broke out in London about a week or ten days ago. It first started in Chamberlains clothing store and took a northerly direction; took all the houses on that block and on the one north of it. London looks as desolate as Edom, I suppose, but it will be of some benefit to the town. After the loss is made up a new energy will be imparted to things there. Men will not be quite as independent as the[y] were heretofore.

One thing certain about it is that a great many sinks of iniquity have been broken up by the fire. There were a lot of low doggeries that ought to have been suspended long ago by the authorities. They were receptacles of filth and vice. I always felt bad whenever I went past them. Bloated Irish, sodden headed Dutch, and villainous looking Americans in troops were always to be seen in their vicinity. I would be glad to hear of every doggery in the state being closed by the state authorities. . . .

Our polemic [society] has nearly fizzled out. Gam Saunders does not take enough interest in the thing to make it interesting to the boys. I want to get up a club if I can to encourage debating & foster a spirit of improvement in the minds of the youth of this vicinity. I think if I can get the thing started that we can have a first rate school. I want to get up a meeting once in two weeks anyhow. If two weeks is to[o] often, then try 3 weeks.

Mr. Peters will preach to the "little flock" today at 11 o'clock and I must attend if I can.

[Wednesday] February 15th, A.D. 1854

Dr. Simmermans mode of parsing *i.e.*: *i.e.* is a contraction of *id est*, a Latin pronoun & verb; *i.*, a contraction of *id*, is a pronoun, a word used instead of a noun relative. It relates to the foregoing phrase for its antecedent; neuter gender, third person, singular number, because the foregoing phrase is with which it agrees. According to rule 14th, relative pronouns must agree with their nouns antecedents &c., & note 2d under rule 16th, & in the nominative case it represents the subject of a verb, *e.*, a contraction of *est*, & governs it according to rule 3d and rule 15th and note 1st under rule 6th; *e.*, a contraction of *est*, is a verb which signifies to be; neuter, it expresses neither action or passion, but being or state of being; singular, it will not form its imperfect tense of the indicative mood in *ed* [?]; indicative mood, it simply indicates or declares a thing; present tense represents an action or event as taking place at the time in which it is mentioned; 3d person, singular number because the nominative *i.*, a contraction of *id*, signifying that, is with which it agrees according to rule 4th & note 1st under rule 4th. . . . [JMR continues at some length showing Simmerman's parsing of *Amen, Hallelujah, &c., as,* and *methinks.*]

The American Grammar published by Morgan & Co. in Cincinnati has all these examples fully illustrated and explained. Our teacher, Dr. H. Simmerman, is the author. He is going to have some brought on in a few days. He has some in Lafayette, price 62-1/2 cents. I must have one if I can possibly raise money enough to buy it.

The school at Somerford get[s] along first rate & [we] are progressing finely. The Dr. gives the praise to John Allen as being the best schollar in the school. John is a first rate fellow & studies like a hero. We have parsed all the exercises in Kirkham [Samuel Kirkham's *English Grammar*, a book Abraham Lincoln studied] & are now parsing the rules of syntax. I have committed [to memory] all the coarse print as far as the conjunction. There is more in the book than I had any idea there was. Kirkham is very explicit in everything, more so than what I thought when I first commenced. He gives the most copious rules of syntax of any author now out. Simmerman has every one of them in his head. He has the whole book committed to memory. . . .

[Sunday] February 26th, A.D. 1854

. . . The old states of Urope are at this time convulsed in war. The chains of the serf are about to be unloosed or bound tighter by the despots of the old world. I think freedom will at last find a home in the old states of Urope. She has long been hovering over but has never lit upon the toil worn & famished sons of the old world. But it seems as though there was a faint glimmering of hope & that it is again making its appearance. Well, all I have to say is, may God speed the right.

Grandfather is going back to Lasalle in a few days to attend to his ferry. He talks of staying there all summer. I do not know whether he will or not. Jim thinks he had better sell the ferry on account of there being a bridge being built near it.

Grandmother still has the ague. She is going to try Dr. Randall, who says he can cure her up right off & no mistake. I think that it is an obstinate case and will take something more than ordinary to remove it. Jim has to go to Somerford today to get the medicine which Mr. Randall promised to send by mail from Jefferson.

I see a great deal of life every day in the grammar school. We have as lively a set of chaps as could be scared up anywhere. There is a good deal of sickening sparking going on sometimes, which is very hard to look at, but not particularly obnoxious to a person when he goes into it himself. I do not like to swell much in that line for fear I would flatter the girls so much that they would get too proud to speak to common people here. . . .

[Friday] March 10th, 1854
. . . This world is a queer kind of a machine filled up with many queer things. Man is the queerest of all the rest & will admit of more investigation than any other creature upon the face of the globe. There is a greater variety in the conditions of different men than one would at first suppose. The prince & the president, the Pope & the bishop, the favored sons of luxury & the ragged sons of want are all alike. They all come to the same end. . . .

I was on Darby not long since & there saw more of humanity than I expected to. There was one little occurrence happened which I must note down, for it is one that I never heard of before. James & I stoppped at old Charlies & staid all night with that worthy. In the night one of the children was taken sick with the cholic, & thereby hangs a tale. After they had tried various remedies in vain, they at last hit upon a happy expedient. They, I suppose like all physiologists, thought that there was not enough vital warmth in the parts affected, so they thought that the best way to do would be to get some there by an outside application. Well, a stool was resorted to, which availeth nothing, so that estimable old lady, Mrs. Clifton, opened her mouth, & her melodious [voice] uttered the following enchanting sentence: "G-d d-mn you, Barb, git the jonny-cake board and put [it] to the fire & put it on that younguns belly.["]

. . . Wm. Orpet is here today. He has been working for Mrs. Tingley. He talks of helping us when we go to Darby to rebuild the mill there. He is a pretty good sort of a fellow & is not overburdened by a super-abundance of good sound sense. That, however, is not his fault & I am not going to fall out with Dame Nature about it.

Henry & James are parsing. They appear to get along very well with it, but nevertheless Simmermans influence is bound to be a great help. The old man is one of the best grammarians that I ever saw. He has a peculiar way of teaching, which is perfectly amazing in its way and one that I think cannot be surpassed by any other system now in vogue. We are going to have a grammar school & lecture in Somerford on next Saturday & Sunday. Thos. Guthrie [and?] William Romigh will deliver a short address, & perhaps I will try to deliver one myself.

I really do think that the peasantry of the United States are the great mainspring of the republic, & we ought to educate and improve the present golden opportunity & educate ourselves up [to] the highest degree. All the world now look up to America as the great dispenser of knowledge, light, & liberty. If this be the case, then let us be up & doing.

I consider myself one of that favored few & intend to improve my birthright. Let the old despots of Urope tremble in their seats, for the sons of enlightened America will scatter the mists of ignorance from the face of the habitable globe. [Czar] Nicholas may look out if America takes him into hand & uses not cannons but the schoolmaster, & his pen will come down upon their old antiquated notions & dispel them like the sun does the morning fogs in July. [The time] may come, & that too speedily, when the sons of education will have representatives in every country in the world. Let every man, woman, & child have a good education, & if crime is to be found anywhere, it will not be so disgusting in its form or so frequent in its visitations.

The rain has ceased for this time, I guess, but the snow has taken its place. May God help the wretched inhabitants in our large [cities] who are poor, for flour is high & fuel is also high.

I was at Lafayette last Sunday to a grammar lecture. They had it in the Newlight church there & had quite an interesting time of it, take [it] all together. Jim & Henry were a little disappointed in their expectations. They had made their calculations pretty strong & were expecting to take a lot of girls down in a wagon, but the "best laid schemes of mice & men gang aft agley."

Sunday, March 19th, 1854

. . . The latest piece of gossip is about Miss Elizabeth Orpet. . . . Miss Betty is in a bad situation. Not bad either, for she has been going in *accordance* with the *Scripture*, which says, "Be fruitful, multiply, & replenish." Well, I suppose she is enceinte & no mistake. Now, the question is, where is the other individual that will have to stand up & say, it is mine? Some say that Hamilton Wilson is the man. I am inclined to doubt it. I think that he would not have anything to do with her, but there is no accounting for the taste, and this may be an instance of this kind.

Mother & myself staid all night with Mr. William Hollar at his residence on Deer Creek last evening. Mother has some idea of hiring him to frame our mill on Darby. He offers to put it up for $100.00. . . . I think that the terms are about as reasonable as we could expect the way things are at this time. We intend to hire Allen Anderson to help him.

I was on Darby all of last week. I boarded at Mr. Randalls. He is over in Columbus & is going to set up a Dr. shop. They have a queer kind of arrangement over there. Mr. Randall is off at Columbus & Mr. Fleming stays with Mrs. Randall & no one else with them. Well a day!

. . . Nancy Porter is sick with the consumption. I do not think that she will ever get well again. Dr. Wilson tends on her.

[Sunday] April 2d, 1854

. . . We have at last moved to Darby, & I have been cleaning up ground for the last week. The weather, however, has been so bad that I could not do much at it. . . .

Mr. Randall & family were here this evening. They appear to be in good spirits & in good health, which is one of the greatest blessings that man can have. Mr. Randall is now doctoring in Columbus. I do not know how he gets along, but I guess that he is doing a pretty good business. Mr. Fleming still stays with them, which creates as much talk as ever. I do not know anything about their private affairs, but I think that they give people room to talk, & if that is done we all know that they will take it upon themselves to talk.

. . . Catherine Margaret, Charlie, Harriet Maria, & Doc have all gone back to Oak Run, but Doc & Charlie intend to come back again. We have hired Allen Anderson to work three months for us. He is to commence tomorrow morning. We are to give him sixteen dollars for a dry month. Allen is a good hand and cheap at that price. . . .

James Roberts had liked to have got me into a combat with old Mrs. Clifton. He had wrote some nonsense upon a book there, & they happened to lend it to Mr. Garns, who read it and then told them what it was. I, however, got clear & now he will have to catch jesse for it.

[Friday] April 14th, A.D. 1854

. . . There is not much stirring in these parts. We have a singing school over at the Archer schoolhouse, Mr. Elmer Morris teacher. The boys appear a little inclined to be progressive.

I have come across one or two choice spirits down here. One of them is Clark Garns, who lives with his father on the Dunn Plain. He appears to be of the right kind of metal & he is a Universalist. These are the right kind of folks. I wish the world was full of that kind. . . .

I was at singing school last Tuesday & had a refreshing time, a decidedly invigorating, truly enchanting, felicitously endearing [time]. I had the good luck to fall in with Miss Lydia Robinson, who by the by is a buxom lass of 24 & weighs 180 lbs. avoirdupoise. Well, I went over to old Auntie Barbara's & found Mr. Charlie Burke, a young man excessively verdant, waiting to escort Damoiselle to the singing school. She was not at home at the time of our arrival, & Allen Anderson, Mr. Burke, [and I] all started to the singing school, when who should we meet but Madamoiselle going home. Of course we stopped & went back with her; when Mr. Burke clinched her & we all started, she & he leading the crowd. Well, we got there after considerable walking without any accident. Well, by & [by] the singing school broke up & Mr. Burke stood around & kept Madamoiselle waiting. She got tired & started & said, ["]Come along, John.["] Of course I was not going to back out, so I just goes up & clinches, expecting her to give me the mitten & take her partner, but he got miffed and off he went full drive. So home I goes with Damoiselle, & talk to me about tall sparking, will ye?, & I will give you my experience, which is some if not [more?] than a few. Shoh! It is of no use talking, thats all, & language fails me. Shakespeare & Milton would be lost if the[y] even tried to give a hint. Time of quitting: rooster crowed for day.

[Sunday] April 16th, 1854

Today is Easter & it is cold enough to be Easter. The Deutch will have a fine time of it today eating aggs & ham. They will have a general spree.

I was in Jefferson yesterday & had my boots mended, & it cost me like smoke too, for I had to pay 70 cts. to get them half soled & a patch put on the toe of one. I think that shoemakers cannot grumble at the low price of work. The tradesmen of all sorts have raised their prices. The prices of the products of the farmer have been very good for some time past, & I think that they will keep up at the present good rates for some time to come.

Uncle James is going to school in London at this time. He intends to keep the Oak Run school this summer. He is to get 16 dollars p[e]r month & is going to teach four months. He will make a pretty good pile this summer if he manages right, & I think he will.

I heard from Dr. H. Simmerman yesterday. He started a few days ago for the renowned Antioch at Yellow Springs. He is going to teach a grammar school there & also one in Cincinnati. He says that he will charge them four dollars p[e]r schollar. He gives general satisfaction wherever he teaches. I saw several of his pupils from the Upper Glade yesterday & they all spoke in his favor. I think that he cannot be beaten on grammar by any man in the United States. He seems to understand it perfectly & no mistake.

We have a new neighbor. His name is Bently Burdett. He is going to work for Mr. Hollar at the rate of 75 cents per diem. Mr. Burdett appears to be a kind of braggadocio of a fellow, fond of telling about his exploits & hairbreadth escapes. He is not a very wise man, & I think less wise by his talk. He cant read a word nor make a letter with a pen. He has no books of any kind, not even a Bible. His family consists of his wife Barbara & three very small children, the eldest named Nicholas Greenbury, the second one James Mahomet. . . .

[Sunday] April 23d, 1854

. . . We have been working at the sawmill frame for the last two weeks. The weather has been very wet for some time past, but I think that we will have some dry weather now. . . .

I must quit and go to dinner, for they say that [it] is ready and I do not like to keep the cooks waiting, so I guess that I will finish this chapter after dinner.

Today has passed away pleasantly & proffitably. I have been over to Cliftons all day & have had a lot of fun, . . . & that is what I like. Miss Nancy & Barbara Clifton are here tonight. They are good meaning girls & are just as good as though they were worth their tens of thousands. Aristocracy is on the raise in this country. Shallow brained, monied aristocracy, wilt thou ever pervade in this country, or wilt thou go down with the far famed doctrine of endless misery and various other dogmas of ancient date?

I saw Mrs. Street for the first time. She was talking to me about teaching her boys how to spell & read this summer. I have agreed to teach them of nights & Sunday. Nancy & Barbara may take a notion to study some too. I am in hopes that they will, for I would like to dispense some of my little knowledge amongst some of my fellows. . . . Mr. Clifton has hired the widow Hauns horse. His mare has got the distemper. . . .

[Monday] May 1st, A.D. 1854

Today finished hauling the timber for the mill. Mr. Fleming helped me. We had four horses in the team. We have got all the timbers hauled, little and big, and I am glad of it, for we have had quite a time of it getting out those timbers. But at last the thing is finished.

John Fleming still lives with Mr. Randall, but he does not seem to enjoy himself very well. I do not believe that Mr. Randall will live there longer than untill fall. There appears to be something about there that smells strongly of discontent & a longing for something better. Guilt will always overcome its votaries and make them miserable. Mrs. Randall has changed very much since I first knew her. She has lost her cheerful & ladylike demeaner & has got to [be] haughty & unkind in her ways. She has not much to be insolent about, for she does not occupy an enviable position. I would never have done as she has, that is if I still retained my reasoning faculties. I have come to the conclusion that she is guilty and that she is getting her punishment for her improper actions at this time.

Yesterday was Sunday, which I spent pleasantly & proffitably. I was at Chas. Cliftons nearly all day. . . . I was trying to teach the young idea how to shoot. I had the whole family spelling. We got along first rate. They appear to take an interest in these things, & I have always liked to teach willing schollars. It does me good to see people taking an interest in educational affairs. . . .

The Maine Liquor Law has at last passed in this state, & we will soon see the effects of that far famed law, whether it will be productive of good or evil. I think that it will be a good law & ought to be carried out to the fullest extent.

[Saturday] May 13th, A.D. 1854
. . . The news here is about after the old sort. Nothing new except that we have had a few weddings over in the woods. Miss Lydia Robinson is married, so report says, & it sometimes tells the truth. She married Mr. Joseph Jackson, who is a widower. His wife has been dead about a year. He owns a small farm out in the barrens. They say that he has crazy spells occasionally.

. . . Mr. Nichols & Miss Elisabeth Robinson were married last Tuesday evening at Miss Barbara Robinsons. Elisabeth is a pretty fair kind of a girl; a little tempery, but that makes no difference if one understands how to manage his p's and q's. I do not know much about Mr. Nichols. I guess that he drinks some. He used to own property in Jefferson but does not own any at this time. He is a grass widower. His wife ran away with a stage driver about five years ago. He is a butcher by trade & used to kill cattle for the Jeffersonites.

We have got along very well with our mill and will raise it in a couple of weeks. I think that milling will pay very well here, for lumber is in great demand & bears a good price. The same stuff that used to sell for 75 cents now brings a dollar. I am glad of it, for we need money and good times if anybody does.

Yesterday I went fishing with Mr. Garns. We had a first rate time of [it] and caught about three pecks of fish. Lazarus (Bently Burdet) went with us. We had him mad about half his time. He is certainly one of the biggest liars that I ever saw & the greatest fellow to gass around about what he can do & what he has done. He, for instance, said that he could swim like a fish, but when he came to be tried he was found wanting. He had to own up to the corn & knock under. He is a consumate lazy fellow & will not work if he can help it.

. . . I have been trying to teach Cliftons girls how to read. They have been making very good progress, & I think that by the time I get through here that they will know how to read some in the first reader. They all appear anxious to learn, & I am always willing to help those that will try to help themselves. I do not like to see people grow up in helpless & hopeless ignorance and will always try to teach anyone that wants to be taught or anyone that I can teach.

We have got our corn planted. We have in ten acres. I would like to raise a good crop this year, for corn will bear a good price this fall. It is worth 50 cents per bushel at this time. Flour is worth eight dollars & a half per barrel, and other things in proportion.

[Tuesday] May 16th, A.D. 1854

Today is an idle one and I feel like writing in this good old book. There is something that seems to make this journalism interesting. There is a charm about it that I like. I do not know that I can make any original ideas shine with more than common refulgence, yet I love to note down the little steps of everyday life. There is something great always attached to men and things, & I always want to keep all the good things in remembrance.

Nancy Porter is not expected to live. She is in the last stages of consumption. . . . Nancy has always been a fine girl, full of life, and appears to have been a goodhearted, generous, & amiable young woman. I recollect well when she and I were schoolmates together. That was a happy time, and I am sorely afraid that I will never see the like again. . . .

Mother and all the rest of the folks have gone to Oak Run & left Allen Anderson [and me] here to take care of ourselves the best way that we can. We are getting along very well. I have cooked two meals & Allen milked the cow twice. Bachelors Hall goes very well, & I do not know but what I will keep it up.

Mr. Hollar is still working at the mill frame. He will get it ready to raise sometime next week. We are not going to raise it untill after corn planting. He talks of renting the mill after we get her started. I do not know whether Mother will rent it to him or not. I expect to help him or someone else to tend it this winter.

James Morris & Co. have got their mill in operation at last. I heard that they have had a kind of a tearup amongst their machinery. . . . They have been building their mill for the last year or two, & it would be a real spite to have it run into the ground before they make anything of it.

I have written to a millwright to come and do our work for us. I have not received an answer yet but expect to get one in a day or two. I wrote to Mr. Standish Culver, the same man that put in the flutter wheel and old rigging that Father & Randall had put in the mill in the first place.

Mr. Randall has not been over to Columbus for some time, and I hear no more about his doctoring. I guess that it did not pay well enough, so he quit it. His wife still holds a high head. I think her nest will be upset one of these fine mornings, and she will find herself amongst the lowly once more. I see that Mr. Fleming has moved his washing. Now, some people will make a mares nest out of this. I myself think that this is a commencement of more trouble in the camp. . . .

I must have more system in my studies and in my manner of living. This thing of living in aimless, shiftless listlessness I do not like, and of course I must quit it. What is the use of ones dogging along just in the same singsong way, never thinking only about what he shall eat and drink? No! Man was never made for such ignoble purposes as these. He was made with a mind & heart as well as a back & stomach. He was never designed to be a meat house or a scarecrow. No! No! He was made to investigate & beautify nature. He was made to progress onward and upward untill at last he will come to be as nigh perfect as God intended in the beginning that he should be.

The creek is as high now as it has been this year and is still rising very fast. It is still raining. . . . There is no work to do nor no one to talk to but Allen, & he has got out of talk. The bottoms are all covered with water. So goodby fencing & corn.

James H. Roberts is getting along very well, I guess. He has got a school and is teaching at this time. He and some of the other youngsters up there tried to raise & keep up a grammar school. I do not know how they get along. I am anxious to hear.

[Wednesday] May 17th, A.D. 1854

. . . The rain has ceased & everything looks bright & pleasant this morning. The birds sing as gaily as ever, and the forest seems to be alive with them. I love to hear the wild birds sing. There is something enchanting in the songs of the wild birds early in the morning. The[y] seem to be returning thanks to pale Cynthia for her wa[t]chful & benevolent rays & a song of welcome to Old Sol.

I get up these days tolerably early, & it richly repays me for my trouble, for the great god of day makes a splendid appearance in his first appearance, and then the wild gush of musick that you hear from every tree & bush is something grand indeed. It is more touching to a sensitive mind than the grandest concert of musical instruments in the world. The mournful notes of the whipporwill mingling with the wild & merry notes of the mockingbird, these with the drumming of the pheasants and whistling of the partridge make a concert worth a mans while to look at and to hear.

These things are denied to the city dandy & the country slug-gard. . . . I never want to live in town amid the dust, crime, and smoke, where sociability is banished & selfishness reigns supreme. No, but give me country with its green fields, pure water, & pure hearts, where sociability & plenty reigns, where the true democracy dwells. This is the place for me. Here let me live & here let me die. . . .

[Wednesday] May 24th, 1854

. . . The greenness of the foliage is now the predominant feature of the landscape in this vicinity. But after all, death lurks in every bud and in every flower. It seems as though all things are passing away with an increased rapidity that is truly alarming.

Nancy Porter is dead. She has been sick for a long time, but at last tired nature had to succumb to the repeated & long continued attacks of the druggist and physician. Well, may the great and good Father of us all take her to where medicine is unknown.

It does seem to me as though we are all to be among the sheeted dead before long. It has been but a few months since I saw Nancy Porter at grammar school. She was not, however, in very good health at that time. In fact, she had to quit the school on account of bad health. I have known her ever since she was five years of age and have always found her to be a lively, agreeable girl & one that one could spend an hour or two with pleasure & proffit. . . .

I have been doing various kinds of work since I last wrote in this book. I am trying to get along with my work as fast as I can, but [it] seems as though the rain will not let me do much.

Wm. Orpet is here. He is working by the day. We are to give him 75 cts. per diem. He appears to be [the] same old chap that he always was. I do not know that he has improved any morally, physically, or intellectually for the last six years. He seems to have been created for a hewer of wood & drawer of water. He is, however, a goodhearted kind of a fellow & not prone to making mischief or fighting. He will get drunk, and that is the worst fault that I can find with him. His sister

Betsy it appears is in a bad way & lays the mischief on to Hamilton Wilsons shoulders. I was considerably diverted the other day at Bill. He was telling me about it, and after he got through he says to me, ["]Dont you think it was good for him?["] Well now, that kind o' took me, as the fellow said. He wanted to know if I thought "dat Bets waz to blame." Well, I never "seed the beat in my born days." But here I will let the subject "drap."

I was up at Oak Run last week. Henry is getting along very well up there, I think, from what he says & from what I can see myself. We went up there to help him with the milldam & race, which got broken by the last flood. We got it all fixed up in one day. Uncle James, Allen Anderson, Ryall Miller, Henry, & myself all worked at it.

Uncle Jim has got into a pretty good school up there. He has a lot of fine looking schollars. . . . Jim got a certificate for one year. He came out among the first at the board of examiners.

[Monday] May 29th, A.D. 1854
. . . I have quit chewing & smoking tobacco and intend to stay quit this time. Tobacco is an evil weed and ought to be banished from the land. It has something in it that lures its victims on untill it gets them fastened with the slavish chains of habit; and then it is impossible for them to get loose without great annoyance to their mental and physical appetites. It is thus that man is ever at war with his beastly propensities.

My health at this time is very good. . . . I believe that [sickness] can be avoided to a great extent if we would only follow up the principals of hydropathy. But this is almost a moral impossibility in this age of pork, coffee, & tobacco. I am afraid that all the hogs in America will have to be consumed before hydropathy will be universally adopted by the people.

Nancy Porter . . . was litterally medicated to death. I cant see for my life why people will still patronise the drug system when they have so many glaring facts staring them in the face. We know by daily experience that the drug system kills more than it cures. . . .

We intended to have raised the mill this week, but I guess that this rain will stop us, for this week anyhow.

There is a report out that the elephant, alias Lydia Robinson, is going to marry.

[Saturday] June 3d, 1854
Today is Saturday & I and Allen have taken a quarter of it for holiday. We have been working at various things this week. There has

not been much rain this week, so we have got along first rate with our work. I have got the mill pit cleaned out at last, but it was a very heavy job and took a great deal of work to get it done. . . .

Mother and the boys have gone up to Oak Run. They started this morning with Paddy and the buggy. Mother appears to be very anxious to go back to Oak Run to live again. As for me, I would just as leave live here as there.

This has got to be a very quiet place. . . . Mr. Burdet, however, is trying to raise a breeze occasionally. He appears to be a kind of a restless individual & wants to have all his neighbors lugging one another over the coals of discord and strife. He wants to make himself noticeable by some means, & he does not know how to do it any quicker than to take to manufacturing lies & peddling them around among his neighbors. He has gone up to Mr. Ryans to shear sheep. I do not believe that he will make much at it, for his wife says that he tried it once & made out to shear four. I think that a couple of days will convince his employer that he is shearing the money out of his pocket faster than the wool off of the sheeps backs.

We have not tried to raise this week but intend to make an effort towards it next week. Mr. Hollar went home last week & has not got back yet. He has two or three sticks to get out and frame yet.

[Monday] June 5th, A.D. 1854

Today I have idled away. I must . . . try & make up for it tomorrow. I will have to dance around pretty lively if I get all the work done up down here. Allen Anderson did not get up here untill it was too late to make a half day, so we concluded that we would rest & make up the time by working harder hereafter. . . . I feel considerably jaded at this time. . . . I suppose that it is the hard work that I have done this spring. I do not know what else. I acknowledge my laziness & inability to perform as much manuel labor as some of my acquaintances. Indeed, some of my friends think that I have that fell disease called consumption. I do not believe it but it may be so, & if it is I may not live very long in this busy world of ours. One man has prophesied that I will not live over five years longer . . . but I think that if I live up to the water cure doctrine that I will not die that soon. . . . I am bound to keep the saying of Mr. Link in my mind & see if I cannot avoid the consumption by living in strict obedience to the laws of hygiene. . . .

[Sunday] June 25th, [1854]

. . . I staid a week at Oak Run some time since. I still found everything going on in the same old way. The rich were getting richer &

the poor were getting poorer, that is in respect to the things of this world & in a sensual point. But as far as the moral & intellectual world is concerned, they were about on the same old track of nonprogressiveness, still keeping on in the old way that their fathers trod. . . .

I hear that John M. Allen has joined the church [of] the radicals. Whether it will make him more radical in his views I am unable to say. He is a fine, upright fellow, I know, & would be far from joining for the sake of popularity. I think that it is from the purest motives. He has always been actuated by that kind of principle, anyhow. . . .

[Tuesday] June 27th, 1854

. . . We have not got our sawmill raised yet, & I am afraid that we will not get it raised for some time to come yet, for Bill Hollars wife is still sick & he will not get to work untill she gets well. I do not like to lay on my oars this way, but I cant help it, so there is no use of grumbling.

Allen Anderson still stays with us. He has been working for us all spring & summer. . . . I expect that he will stay with us all summer & perhaps next winter if we can agree about the price. . . . Mother has gone to Oak Run today. She wants to see Mr. Hollar & try to get him to come down this week.

. . . I was at town on the 24th of this month & heard three trials under the new whiskey law. They had a great time of it amongst the grog bruisers. The first case that came up was O.H. Bliss versus the State of Ohio. The complaint was that Bliss had sold whiskey to one Henry Tillman, who was in the habit of getting drunk. They proved that Tillman went there with an empty quart bottle & came away with it full of corn whiskey, but the evidence was not strong enough to convict him, so they had to dismiss the case.

The next case was the selling of liquor to a minor by O.H. Bliss & Co. This was proven by a straitforward oath. Mr. Bliss tried hard to quash the indictment by counter evidence but did not succeed. He was bound over to court in the sum of one hundred dollars. I suspect that the jail had quite an alarming aspect to Mr. Bliss, & I think that he will be apt to pay the bail & get out of another suit at court if he can.

The next case that came up was Mr. Hancocks, who was indicted for selling liquor to a minor. He was also bound over to court in the sum of one hundred dollars. I suppose that he will pay the bond & not risk another trial. He appeared to be very much concerned about the matter.

I think that the whiskey trade will be very apt to decline a little in the town of West Jefferson if they keep on jerking them up for selling it. I was considerably tickled to see them squirming under the lash. . . .

They had about twenty witnesses summoned for the defendants. Bliss had every clerk sworn that was in his whole establishment. They turned out en masse, but all would not do. The poor widow & her son were heard and respected by the squire, who appeared to deal out with an even hand the merits of the case.

It appeared from the evidence that one Henry Tillman was in the habit of getting drunk and was altogether a trifling kind of a chap. He came to Jefferson sometime in [the] last month & purchased whiskey of the defendents, went home & got on a beat. He got down sick & sent to town by his son Eli for more of the beverage of pandemonium, who went there without an order. Well, it seems as though the two sold whiskey to the boy. When the old man at last had to give over & die, the direct cause of his death was whiskey & no mistake, although he had been drinking for the last twenty years. He died about a month ago.

There was another trial at Jefferson the same day. One Elias Bierly was convicted of drunkenness & fined five dollars & sent to jail for ten days. They had quite a time with him.

[Saturday] July 1st, A.D. 1854

. . . Miss Nancy Clifton & Barbara, her sister, are here. They have been working in the corn field. They are in fine spirits & appear to be enjoying themselves first rate. Nancy & I had a first rate time while Mother was up at Oak Run, but of that au revoir, more anon.

The mill at Oak Run is broken. The water wheel shaft is broken. It will take some time to fix it. We will have to leave here & go up & fix it. We are going up week after next. We have not engaged any millwright yet. We will have to pay considerable money to get all the mills fixed. We will have to jump around pretty spry if we get all of these things done in time.

I want to get everything fixed up so that I can go to school next year. . . . If everything else goes to rack & ruin, I must have an education. . . . Everything is getting to be more complicated & harder to analyze. Temperance & all other reforms need the fostering care of genius.

I see that the people of West Jefferson are awakening up to a sense of their duty in regard to the liquor traffick. They have been informing on several rich old soakers, who by the by are of the opinion that the law was not intended for them but was a mere machine to persecute the poor devils of the grog shop. They have taken up William Wilson for getting drunk in West Jefferson. How the case will go I know not. It is to be tried next Monday in London before the probate judge.

[Saturday] July 8th, 1854

. . . The corn here looks well . . . for the time of year. Old Charlie Clifton has the best piece I know of. It looks first [rate] & is beginning to tassel & silk. I think that we will have plenty of corn this fall. If anybody has any, we will, . . . for ours is in a prosperous condition at this time.

. . . Clark Garns went past here on the road to town. He appears to be kind of on the progressive order. I do now know how far he goes, but I believe that he is a Universalist & holds some pretty good sentiments in other particulars that go to make up a man of progress.

I wonder if I will ever be ashamed of the sentiments that I have expressed in this book. . . . I can have the book to look at & judge how far I have progressed or retrograded, as the case may be. They say that whatever a man is at eighteen he will be at forty five. Now, I will try & preserve this book untill I arrive at that age & see, for this book certainly has a stamp of the writers character in it.

I am now a believer in Universalism, hydropathy, democracy, & progression in everything. These are my sentiments & will [be] until something more potent is brought to bear upon my mind than has been heretofore.

I have had some insight into the effects of the liquor law lately. It was not, however, fairly tested. I am of the opinion that the corrupt parties gained the day. Money has a powerful influence in the courts of law in this country. I believe that it has as much influence as anything else. O.H. Bliss & Mr. Elijah Hancock have got clear of their liquor fine. It was not, however, because they were innocent that they got clear, but on account of the cloud [of] witnesses that they had summoned to controvert the oath of Eli Tilman, a witness for the state. I believe in my heart that they had all the anti temperance men in this end of the county summoned. I think that they will get caught yet if they do not look pretty sharp. I for one would be glad to see them trotted through. If the law is to stand, let them suffer the penalties thereof to the fullest extent, & if not, let them alone.

[Tuesday] July 11th, 1854

. . . I have got all my chores done up & intend to start to Oak Run tomorrow, although I have become so attached to Darby that I do not like to leave it. There is something attractive down here that I like, although the everyday humdrum of life is nearly the same here as it is everywhere else.

Barbara Clifton is washing for Mother today. She is a queer kind of an individual. She is a great talker & a great smoker. She loves to talk first rate but she loves to smoke better, so she loses some time in lighting her pipe.

I was considerably interested the other evening by Mrs. Clifton, who gave me a history of their sojourn in Indiana. It seems, according to her story, that about 15 years ago old Charlie took a notion that he would go to the West, so he packs up & starts to that land of promise. He got as far as White River & drove his stake. Well, so far so good, but no farther. It appears that they all took the ague soon after they landed. Well, they worked on for four years without bettering their condition in the least. They were never clear of the ague during the whole four years. They said that there was not the first child raised for more than ten years in that neighborhood on account of the ague & fevers.

Well, after they had staid there four years, old Charlie came back to Ohio to get a team. Well, he staid here four months & never sent word to them, so Mrs. Clifton hired a team & starts back. The driver took sick the next day after they started. All the rest were sick at the same time, and there was some six or seven of them in [the] family at that time. She had a babe six months old at that time & had to carry it & drive the oxen. She said that she would get up in the morning, feed & yoke the oxen, put the sick man into the wagon, fill her water bucket & hang it on the coupling pole of the wagon, & start. She would have to stop every few rods to give the sick children some water & tend to the sick man, who was unable to get up one moment. Well, she came all the way from White River in Indiana that very way. It took her eleven days to go through.

I think that that trip was a remarkable one for a woman to perform with no one to help or advize with. She must have been made of iron to stand the fatigue of an eleven days journey & have to stay up every night nearly to watch & tend to the sick man, who she expected would die every day, & would sometimes have to stop the wagon for hours to rest him while his nose was bleeding.

But this is the way the world goes. One half of the people revel in luxury whilst the other half grovel in abject misery. . . .

I am going to commence mowing day after tomorrow. How long it will take me I know not, but mow I must.

Lydia Robinson is not married yet, so I hear, nor is there any likelihood of her getting marr[i]ed. Well, I care not, I am sure, but I would like to see her do well if she does get married. . . .

I must try and replenish my purse one of these days, for it has had a protracted attack of the sweeny. Money, money is all the cry, & money makes the hobbyhorse, the public patronage, come right up to the trough. I would like to have that horse come up to my trough if I can by any legitimate way. But if he wont come by fair means, I will not employ any other. So I must try [and] see what I can do to raise the wind & make a little money. . . .

[Sunday] July 23d, 1854

. . . The news of the day is very spicy at this time & abounds in every variety of talk. The latest piece of news is that the United States intend to annex the whole of South America & introduce slavery into the new territory. I think that the undertaking is most too much for Uncle Sam at present, but no one knows what may be done by a few of the heads of the government. I do not think, however, that there is much danger to the republic so long as the native part of the citizens are in a posture of defense & are fully aware of the gigantic danger that is threatened by the powers that be. It is very plain to see that the old parties are fast tumbling to pieces & that in a few years they will have ceased to exist. But be that as it may, Roman Catholicism is bound to go down in this country before long.

This neighborhood has been furnished with a ten days talk by the elopment of Miss Martha Wilson & Mr. Jacob Shoemaker, both of Somerford, Madison Co., Ohio. Well, if Jacob has a mind to keep forever in the sight of Marthas beautiful physiognomy, I have no objections. Mr. Shoemaker, it seems, is a widower. His wife died some years since. He never had any family, I believe, & was considered a kind of a rake. I do not know that this was the case, but I have been told so. Miss Wilson is a daughter of Dr. Daniel Wilson, who by the way has two more fair girls. She is about as homely [a] creature as a person could find in a days ride & is but 15 years of age. She is at Midway at this time with Shoemaker.

[Saturday] July 29th, 1854

. . . I have been haying for the last ten days & have at last got done. I worked four days for Uncle James, who took some grass to cut on the shares. He got four stout stacks put up. Two of them he thinks will do his stock over winter. He intends to commence teaching his school next Monday. He talks of going west in about six weeks.

I am at a loss what to do. I do not like to leave home if I am needed & do not like to stay if I am not, so here is a quandary. I will be twenty one the 21st of next month, and according to the rules of the country I will be my own master & will then be held responsible for my doings. I have resolved to spend several years in acquiring an education. I must have one, let it cost what it may. I intend to work & lay by my money untill I get enough to carry me through one term at college, & after that is spent I will work for more & spend it in the same way. How I will get along with this undertaking time alone will determine.

Mothers business has at length come to a standstill. It is all outs & no ins, but I think that there will be a turn for the better soon. Mother has gone to see Wm. Hollar about the raising of the mill on Darby. I do not know what she has concluded to do yet. . . .

Henry went yesterday to hunt a millwright & has not got back yet. Millwrights have got to be a scarce article in these parts. It seems as though everybody is engaged at present. He talked of going to get Mr. James Hays, a man that used to work for Daniel Anderson in the carpentering business.

. . . Old Charlie Clifton was getting ready to burn a limekiln at the last account. I do not believe that he will make it pay very well. He has not enough stability of purpose about him to succeed very well at any kind of business. . . .

There is not much news in this part of the moral vineyard at present, although it appears that the temple of Janus is not to [be] closed yet for aw[h]ile over on Deer Creek. I hear that Wm. Hollar & young Valentine Wilson have had a combat. It commenced, I believe, about one of Tines children that Isaiah Wilson had taken to raise. It seems as though Tine wants to gather his family together again & his friends do not think that he is capable of raising them right. I am of the same opinion, for he has the tremors at this time & is raving mad—all the effects of rotgut.

[Tuesday] August 15th, 1854

. . . The Maine Liquor Law is still a dead letter. Some people think that this will be the last effort that the temperance people will make. I am of the opinion that this is only the commencement of the battle & that it will not be twenty years before whiskey drinking will be a dead letter. At least I hope so anyhow.

I was in London not long ago to a show there & saw more drunkenness than I ever saw before. Everybody seemed to be in liquor, or nearly so. Young men & old patriarchs whose feet were upon the very verge of the narrow house of death were to be seen in every stage of intoxication. . . .

When we were going to Darby the last time we met Miss Martha Wilson coming like the prodigal home to her fathers mansion. She appeared to be in fine spirits & said that she was united with her Jacob in "Lexicon," Kentuckey. She had quite a warm reception when she got home. They said that old Dr. Dan wanted to get to talk to her but was prevented by his folks. But . . . he accomplished his object at last & told his erring but ever attractive daughter that she might stay at home but must do better in future.

4

Man's Estate
August 21, 1854–June 8, 1855; July 30, 1857

*Now twenty-one and "a full citizen of the United States," John
Roberts goes in for "pure Americanism" as a Know-Nothing, a mistake
he confesses in print years later in attacks on the anti-Catholic crusade
of the American Protective Association (London* Madison County
Democrat, *December 19, 1894, January 16, February 13, 1895).*

*Back on Darby, the family finally gets the sawmill raised and
operating, but John complains of his prosaic life there and the fading of
his hopes of going to college. He does continue his preparation for
teaching, however, by studying algebra at an academy in Jefferson. At
Uncle Jim's school he observes pupils' pranks, and he recites humorous
pieces at a school exhibition. He fails to live up to his repeated vows to
quit smoking and chewing tobacco. While he lacks intellectual
excitement, he finds sensual pleasure across the creek at the Cliftons and
worries that he may have ruined all his dreams by his intimacy with
Nancy.*

*A camp meeting, an apple cutting, debates, a Christmas Day
shooting party, and a New Year's Eve hoedown where whiskey drinking
leads to wrestling over a pistol, all help dispel the ennui John often
complains about. He thinks about moving to Nebraska and muses about
marriage, but not seriously about either.*

*An entry in the nature of a backward look two years later finally
fills the last page of the big book. It hints of regretted acts but also shows
that John has gained a more mature understanding of himself.*

[Monday] August 21st, A.D. 1854
　　Today is my birthday & I am now a full citizen of the United States.
. . . My past career has not been of very great importance to myself or to
the world, but I hope that my future may prove more beneficial to all. I
have not [at] this time any definite occupation in view. The fact is, I have
let things take their course in a very natural manner & may do so
hereafter. . . .

I was at camp meeting last Saturday & Sunday and had a great time, take it all in all. I never was at one before & had a curiosity to go & see how such things were carried on by the Methodists, or confusionists; either name could be applied to their methodical mania. They preached the strongest kind of doctrine. They held forth the idea that out of the pale of the church there is no salvation, which is a pretty hard doctrine for me to believe. They had very good order on the campground while I was there. They had a lot of fancy women there, which made quite a stir amongst the country boys. All of them wanted to get to see them & talk to them. There was about a dozen of them on the ground. Whiskey went off like hot cakes, and some that I saw there were a little kind of intoxicated from what I could see of them. . . .

[Wednesday] Aug. 30th, A.D. 1854

. . . Mother is getting the mill in order at this time. She has three hands hired to do the millwright work. Their names are John, Joseph, & Robert Hamilton. They are working by the day & will get done in a week or such a matter. They are good workmen & nice men as far as I know. They came from Warren Co., O[hio].

The Know Nothings are all the rage in these parts at this time. They appear to be getting very strong all over the United States, & I hope that they will still increase, for awhile to come yet anyhow, for the Catholics are getting to be very saucy & want to put the native party under their feet. But I think that they have made a stand a little too soon. I see that they have undertaken to keep the American voters away from the polls in different places but have not succeeded in their nefarious attempts as yet, & I hope that they never will. I go in for the American party head & ears. Three cheers for America & her common schools!

Somerford has again been thrown into a commotion by the late tragicomedy at old Doct. Wilsons. It seems that the tailor, Mr. Clingan, left his wifes bed & tried [to] get in with Nancy Wilson, but she was not acquainted with his design untill after he made the trial, & then she had the imprudence to cry out.

[Monday] September 4th, 1854

. . . The chief topic now is about the d[r]ought, which is very severe all over the whole Union. I never saw things look so bad in all my life. Everything seems to be litterally scorched to death. The ground is like an oven. The hot air steams up into ones face & nearly suffocates every animal that has to draw burdens or do any kind of work. On the highway the roads are from three to five inches deep in dust, & the thermometer up to 115 in the sun & not a breath to stir a leaf. The trees have a withered & decaying look. I never saw a sand pile look any browner than the pastures do at this time. It will soon be so that we will have to feed our stock just as much as we would if it were winter. We are praying for an easy winter, for if the weather should happen to be very bad, we will have no feed for our stock.

I do not hear much of the grammarians any more. They all seem to have taken a backset since the dry weather set in. I have not heard of Dr. H. Simmerman for some time. He has been badly remiss in his promises of late. It may be that unavoidable circumstances have overtaken him. He was to have had a school in Lafayette but never came on, so the thing failed.

I was at an apple cutting last Friday evening at Eli Wilsons. We had a tolerably good time of it, take it all together, although the young lady of the house rather bluffed me out. But that makes no difference to me. I care little for her & she seems to have the [same] opinion of me. . . .

[Saturday] Sept. 9th, 1854

. . . There has been some very exciting themes among the people since I last wrote in my book.

I was an eyewitness to a scene that will never fade from my memory till death shall close my eyes. Eli Bradley was found dead this week near the graveyard at Somerford. He had lain till he was litterly rotten. He had a quart bottle lieing beside him with some whiskey in it. He was full of maggots. My God! What will this world come to if it keeps on the way that it has done! I was shocked to see some of the boys a little drunk that buried Eli Bradley. They are certainly far gone when such a sight as that will not keep them from drink.

I am bound not to drink, for God only knows what may be the consequences. . . . I would like to have had all the eloquence of a Demosthenes & then had all the liquor dealers in the state around Eli Bradleys corpse; & then to have let loose upon them all the reasoning, both human & divine, would have been glorious.

There is a new order called the Know Nothings which is doing much to purify the American government. They are anti Catholic in sentiment & go in for pure Americanism. I say, God speed the day when these things will be accomplished. . . .

[Thursday] October 5th, 1854

. . . The news in this part of the country is getting very stale. I do not hear anything worth recording without it is the marriages that have taken place of late. . . . We have had five within the last three weeks. . . . The last one was Mr. David Williamson to Miss Mary Ann

Wilson. Mr. Williamson is from Midway. He appears to be a very fine kind of a man in every respect. I do really wish that Mary Ann may have some peace this time, for she has had some very [bad] luck in getting husbands. . . .

I have heard some sad tales about some of my old playmates & neighbors that are in the West. Richard Hull used to live over between this place & Somerford. He has always been poor & had to live from hand to mouth. He moved away from here about three years ago with his family. He has not been doing very well out there. His children have all turned out badly. Isaac Hull, his eldest son, is accused of perpetrating one of the most horrid deeds that we have ever heard of. He is accused of no less a crime than incest with his own sister, whose guilty offspring was put out of existence by Mrs. Hull, so the report says. I have not heard anything for a long time that has surprised me more than this story of the Hull family. They have indeed sunk low in morality to [be] guilty of the like, but I guess that I will drop the disgusting theme & try & find something more pleasing in the items of the day to chronicle in this book.

In another week or two Jim's school will be out. He is going to teach this winter in our district, I guess. He has done pretty tolerably well this summer by teaching school. He is now making a short quarter & gets a dollar a day. . . .

[Wednesday] October 25th, A.D. 1854
. . . One of our neighbors daughters died today of milk sickness. . . .

I have been doing various things since I came here, but the most has been done about the mill, which Mother wants to get running as soon as possible. I think we will get her going this winter if we have no bad luck. Grandfather is here. He is going to oversee the work & show us how to do it. He is pretty tolerably healthy & still enjoys a good joke.

I was at London last Saturday. I went in the wagon along with Henry, Allen & Bill Anderson, & Elias Clifton. We had a first rate time. Valentine Wilson went along with us. He wants to teach school & was going to get a certificate. I went in along with him, not expecting an examination, but the boys insisted that I should & I yielded. I got along first rate & got a certificate for five months. . . . Valentine, Jr., did not succeed.

[Sunday] Oct. 29th, [1854]
. . . Peter Clifton is very sick at this time with the dropsey. He is very much swelled. I went up . . . this last week in the wagon with the Clifton family to see him die, but were agreeably disappointed to find

him a great deal better than he had been for some time back. He is a very ignorant kind of a man & does not know much about the nature of religion or anything of that kind. I staid there part of two nights & a day. The family were considerably affected by his apparently nigh death. He is the old lady's favorite, & she will be very apt to take his death very hard.

Pete lives up amongst a very hard set of individuals. They are perfect ignoramuses & do nothing but clear up ground, smoke, & swear. They are fit subjects for a new country and ought to go to one, for they could take every thing as it come[s]. They have some redeeming traits, however. They are generally cheerful & hospitable to strangers or neighbors. But when that is said, all is said.

Allen Anderson worked for us yesterday. He is going to do our hewing. He has some corn to husk & one thing and another to do at home, but I guess that he will get off for the forepart of the week anyhow. We got out two posts yesterday an[d] a stick for the carriage.

Henry & Doc went up to Oak Run this morning. They are going to bring down the rest of the family & a couple of cows.

[Friday] November 3d, A.D. 1854

. . . I was up to Father Fullers last night & had quite a refreshing time in talk. We talked untill near midnight on the immortality of the soul & its final destination. He gave me some new ideas in regard to some of the most intricate passages of Scripture. He understands the Scriptures to a T. . . .

[Thursday] November 23d, 1854

. . . We are engaged at the mill & will be for some time to come, I am thinking. We have got a great part of the work done. The carriage & wheel are finished. The rag wheel & gig are to make yet. I do hope that we will soon get done.

Allen Anderson still stays with us. He quit work today to go to a frolic at Mr. Sidners. They are going to have a brush cutting there today. . . .

I am nearly killed off here for the want of intellectual food, somebody to talk to & [who] can appreciate a sentiment. Mr. Garns is one of that kind but is rather inclined to be egotistical, I think. Perhaps I am mistaken. I hope that I am. He has been talking some about having a debating school in this neighborhood. I do hope that he will get up something to stir ones blood, for I really cant stand it much longer. I must have some place to vent off my steam or I shall burst.

[Saturday] November 25th, A.D. 1854

. . . I have been working at the mill all the time. We are getting along very well. Grandfather still stays with us. He is tolerably healthy at this time.

I was up to Mr. Sidners the other evening. I heard that they were going to have a frolick there, but it turned out to be a fizzle. I, however, got all the cider that I could drink and some rotten apples to eat. But it was not the fault of mine host that I did not fare better.

I have been over at Charlies all day pretty near. Well, I begin to feel kind of tired of the place. I long for something better. There is a void somehow that I want to have filled with something better than slang talk & hard phrases. I have not been enough amongst white people lately to know how they do act or how they look.

I have run down lately to almost nothing. I must try & do better & raise myself out of the mire of dont-care-ativeness, or I will never get out of that lamentable state. I must attend church more regularly & mix with the ton, the big bugs, even if pride & deceit are their main motives to action. There is still some good traits in the higher class, & I must try to court their favor, or some of them.

Meeting is still going on in Jefferson. They seem to be bound for the Kingdom & want everyone to go there too. . . .

I have often made many promises to reform, & I will make another now, which I intend to keep if there is enough of stability about me to do so. I have often said that I would abstain from the use of ardent spirits entirely. Although I have not taken more than three drams in six months . . . that was three drams too many, & I will not take any more if my firmness is sufficient [to] carry me through. I am bound not to touch another drop of liquor that will intoxicate or any poison of any kind.

I have been in the habit of using tobacco for some time past, but if it is possible for me to quit, I will do so. I am bound to do it, & I here make a vow that I will never use tobacco in any shape or form. I will neither smoke, snuff, or chew any more of the vile stuff. If I do, I wish that I may puke a week for each & every time that I break through this vow. I am bound to throw off the shackles that bind me, & I mean to be a slave no longer. . . . I am going to call to mind the text of Scripture that says "Tempt me not" every time I want to smoke, chew, or snuff.

[Thursday] Nov. 30th, 1854

. . . We are still working at the sawmill & will be for some time to come. We finished the rag wheel today & got it into the mill. We have the carriage on the mill ready to be put together. I think that we will get through by Christmas if we have luck. I want to see the thing going, for it has been a long time. We certainly ought to make money on it after we get it to going, for there is a set of fellows above Jefferson who have bought the timber off of 1500 acres at nine dollars per acre. They intend to run two saws & rush things right through. They are going to have some awful roads in the winter. If they can make money at those licks, we certainly ought to do something here where we have our own timber to saw & our own time to do it in. If people can make money on a steam mill, a water mill certainly ought to pay pretty well.

I have lived up to my vow first rate. I have been tempted some by the sight of flaming pipes & expansive plugs. Still, I said to myself "Tempt me not" & have desisted from the weed & feel much better by it. I am quits & I intend to stay so if my firmness is not all gone. But this book will be a witness for or against me. So mote it be. [The sheet containing pages 160 and 161 in Roberts's book has been torn out.]

[Sunday] December 24th, 1854, continued
Last Friday evening I was at a debate over at the Archer schoolhouse. We had a tolerably good time but would have had a better one if there only had been a few more there. Mr. Clark Garns & his brother were there, & Mr. Noah Garrison, the schoolteacher, Mr. Durflinger, Allen Anderson, & myself were all that were there. The question was, Resolved that pride & fashion has been a greater curse than intemperance. James Garns and myself were on the affirmative; Clark Garns, Wesley Durflinger, & Allen Anderson were on the negative; Messrs. Garrison & Wright, judges. The affirmative gained the question.

I was a little deceived in Mr. C. Garns. I thought that he was a little extra, but I find that he is nothing more than ordinary. He is a little too much on the gassy order. James Garns is a tolerably good speaker if he would only let his ideas come out. Wesley Durflinger is a pretty shrewd kind of a young man & I have a pretty good opinion of him.

I have made some promises lately . . . some of which have been broken by me. I have made a vow not to touch tobacco nor taste it. But I have smoked some segars, which are not very detrimental, but I must not let that get to be my master. I am bound not to be a slave. . . .

[Tuesday] Dec. 26th, A.D. 1854
Last night there was a party at Mr. Shepherds. We had a very good time of it. . . . We had four girls from old Charlies & there were three of the Shepherds girls. Everything passed off about right. Nobody was drunk nor no quarrellings. . . .

[I also] went to the shooting match at Ben Hoe's. They had a pretty lively time of it over there. I did not see but two drunken men on the ground & they kept pretty civil until I went away. There was considerable of card playing done there. I saw several dollars change hands. I spent about forty cents myself in raffleing & won nothing. Not one red cent did I get in return for my investment, but I came away a little wiser than I was anyhow.

Wm. Watsons sister ran away with John Orcutt about a week ago & was not back the last time I heard from there. . . .

I have my mind crowded with old memories & it is not yet bedtime, so I guess I will while away an hour in writing them down.

I recollect well my former schoolmates up at the Chrisman schoolhouse. Many the happy day have I spent within its unpolished walls. . . . Let me see. There is the Peterman boys who were known by their dingy linen. They have all left this state & now live in Illinois. They will never rise above the common level. Dave is still in this country. He is rather too fond of low company. And then there was Susan Peterman, who was another dingy looking specimen of the Darbyites when we came here. She is in the West married to a man by the name of Young. Then there was the Richardson family, all very tidy & nice in their nicely made homespun toggery. They were interesting & well behaved. The fact is, they are about the first ones that I ever gallanted, and of course I am a little prejudiced in their favor. I recollect well one night when I gallanted Miss Rachel home. The roads, oh Jemima, were awful, but we waded through & I came home & that is all there was of it. And there was Mary, who was always full of her jokes, but I hear that she is in bad luck. She married a man by the name of Smith in the West who lived but six weeks, so she is now a widow.

[Wednesday] January 3d, A.D. 1855

. . . I have been to several dances within the last two weeks. I was at Mr. Shepherds some time since to a hoedown & had a good lot of fun. I was at one at John Helterbrans on New Years evening. . . . Jac. Wilson was there pretty well corned. He got into some difficulty with Eli Williams & John Helterbran which might have ended seriously. Jac. got to making a noise & wanted more whiskey than he was entitled to. Well, that raised old man Williams' spunk, & he collared Jake & was for administering a good threshing to the lad. When Helterbran pitched in & was going to help him, Jake drew a pistol & would have made sad work of it if Joe Reed had not wrested the pistol from Jake. But they all coiled down at last, so the dance went on & we had quite a time. We danced till two o'clock, & then I started for Darby along with V.C. Wilson & Mr. Orpet in a buggy & led my horse home.

[Friday] January 5th, 1855

. . . Old Uncle Valentine Wilson is about to die. He is getting to be very frail & must soon go the way his forefathers went. He must soon relinquish his right to the many broad acres that he now has in his possession. . . . I verily believe he has not been as happy as some much poorer men than he is. . . .

Wm. Orpet is working for us. He is going to work a half month. Wm. is a pretty fine kind of a fellow, a little "non compos mentis," however, which is natural.

There is a ball at Shepherds tonight. Whether bright eyed beauty will be there I know not. Neither do I care. I am not going. . . .

[Monday] January 8th, 1855

. . . I have been doing a little of everything since I last wrote in this book. We have got the sawmill . . . going at last, & it has been quite a job, I tell you. I think it is going to do very well. It seems to cut right along through a log.

Grandfather is still with us. He is going home the last of this week. He is [in] pretty good health & in fine spirits. We will be very lonesome after he goes away, for he has many a quaint story to tell & sometimes a song to sing. He is, however, getting very frail, not half the man that he was ten years ago. . . .

Miss Lydia Robinson is working for us at this time. She is going home tomorrow evening. There is going to be an oyster supper at Mr. Shepherds which is going to come off tomorrow night. I am on a stand whether to go or not. I have a notion not to go. . . . Lydia is going to go with Owen McShane, I believe, if report says aright. Well, I am sure I care not. I must not get out with Lydia, for she is going to be my cook for a few days. Mother talks of going to Oak Run next Saturday, so I must lay low & keep dark.

[Thursday] January 18th, 1855

. . . I was up on Oak Run a few days ago. Jim still keeps school up there. I think, however, he sometimes loses his temper, although Job himself would be very apt to grumble if he had to teach school. Jim has a pretty merry set of scholars sometimes. I saw a little of their merriment while I was up there. They, however, paid for their fun before they got through with it. . . . I suppose this is what people might call the spice of life.

The scrape up yonder was about some ink that some of the scholars manufactured out of some unmentionable liquids, & it seems as though the boys must send some over to the girls & they must make some of theirs & send it back. Well then, there must be some letters written, which unluckily fell into Jims hands, & of course he would have to notice the affair, which he disposed of in a very nice & complete way. He made them get up & acknowledge to the corn and ask pardon of the school and teacher. Better believe the girls hated it right bad. I felt sorry myself for them, but it had to be done. . . .

We have at last got the mill fairly started. She cuts very nice & strong, but the saw varies a little in the log. I think she will do prime business if she is attended to properly. Henry is such a blower that I expect that he will smash her all up yet before he leaves.

I had a strong notion of leaving myself this last week & I did make a start, but Mother said that she could not get along without me, so I came back again after staying away a week or a little better. The fact is, Henry is a little too overbearing to suit me exactly, so I thought I had better go & keep out of trouble. He has gone to meeting tonight along with Shepherds boys & old Charlies girls. I think that they will have a grand time, for it is as dark as pitch & no moon to be seen in this part of the moral vineyard. . . .

[Sunday] January 28th, 1855

. . . We have a grand sleighing snow on hands & it is still increasing.

. . . Jim still presides as chief pedagogue in the Oak Run temple of knowledge. He gets along finely, I hear. He has a speaking school two nights in every week. He is going to have a grand exhibition on the last day of his school. I must go up by all means. If I can get [i.e., memorize] a piece, I will.

. . . I find that this book will condemn me if I am not more careful. I have said that tobacco & I will be friends no more. And how has it been? I must confess guilty and own up to the corn & promise to do better if I can.

. . . Val C. Wilson is not getting along with his school the best in the world. He is a little too fond of Blue Lizzard. He is going to teach over by Columbus somewhere on the river. Well, may luck attend him.

[Friday] February 2d, 1855

. . . The weather is very cold at this time & the snow lies very deep on the ground. . . . Sleighing is all the rage now. Everybody seems to be bent on going at the rates of two forty on a sled.

Old man Shepherd is cutting wood on our place. He gets the wood for the clearing up of the brush. I guess that the wood trade does not pay more than two hundred per cent anyhow, for they only get [$]1.50 per cord for dry wood.

. . . Gam Saunders has got into a hopple, I hear. He and Sarah Tingley have been a little too intimate, & she has sung him out of four hundred an[d] fifty dollars. Gam was not up to snits or he might have got along without any trouble, but wisdom is not always on hands to admo[n]ish & restrain earths children. Well, it is a kind of a dampener on Gam, but I cant help it, and there is an old adage which says that they that dance must pay the piper. . . .

Sunday, February 11th, 1855

. . . I have been in the habit of using tobacco lately, and I know that it is injurious. Why do I use it then? To kill time, aye, but time will not die. What then? To enjoy the good feelings of the present moment? No, not that, for I do not feel near as well when I use it as when I do not. . . . I still keep on & still keep sinning and still keep making good resolutions and breaking them as soon as the tempter comes in my path. I have condemned myself in this book. These pages speak of my shame, yet I still continue in my old road.

. . . The news here is stale and uninteresting. I have not heard of anything going on that is good for either the physical or the mental part of man. Every[one] seems intent on gouging & cheating. . . .

Henry & Mother have gone to Oak Run. They went up last Friday in a two horse sled and left Allen, Lydia Robinson, & my unlucky self to take care of things. Lydia got into a huff and went away yesterday evening and has left Allen & I in the suds. Lydia may be kind and clever, but she is far from being decent. . . .

James Hall & Wm. Anderson were at Cliftons last night. They were both drunk, and Bill raised a fuss with one of the girls (Nancy); when she fell to and give him a cursing and then turned right around & fondled upon him with a baseness that was truly despicable. He will sting some of them yet, for he is a most notorious villian.

Wm. Anderson is a perfect bloat. He has got among a set of as hard men as anyone could scare up. He has not, however, crossed my path for more than a year, and it is well for him that he has not, for I owe him an old grudge and I would not be backward in paying him off if he come in my way. He has all the appearance of a drunkard at this time and is on the highroad to the penitentiary. He told a lie on Allen last night which made him pretty wrothy. He was for jumping upon the Shepherd boys. If he had, I do not know but what I should have had a finger in the pie

myself. Cliftons are a pretty hard set, I believe, or they would not permit
him to come about their house. Barbara is kind of half stuck after him, I
think. . . .

Elias Clifton staid all night here last Friday evening & sparked
Lydia. He is kind of stuck in there, I think. Well, goodness knows I have
nothing to say against it, but let her tell any more lies on me & I will
give her a setter by telling the truth on her. . . .

Allen is not here yet. He said that he would be here today
sometime, but white man is very uncertain, so I must not look too strong
for him. He is a first rate fellow and I like him. He is quite different from
his brother, Bill, who is a bad bill & ought not to pass.

Friday, Feb. 16th, 1855
. . . I was up at Mr. Fullers last night & had quite a talk with him.
He is pretty much of a theologian, and his remarks, though quaint they
may be, are sometimes quite interesting. He is firm believer in the tenets
of the Scripture. . . .

I have at last found myself in an awkward position in regard to a
certain affair which may terminate in a way that will knock all my
dreams to the earth at one fell blow. But let things come as they may,
what is done is done and cant be helped, although there might be some
amendment made.

I set up last night untill two o'clock & I, John, do not feel very well
today, so I guess that work & I will not trouble one another, this day
anyhow.

Allen Anderson still continues to work for Mother. I like him very
well & think that he can keep a secret. At any rate I have put some of my
secrets into his keeping that I would be sorry to have published at this
very time. But if he betrays me once, why shame for him; if twice,
shame for me.

Sunday, Feb. 25th, 1855
. . . We have no news here of any importance. Trade is very dull &
money is extremely scarce. I have not been up to Oak Run for some
time. Jim still holds out faithful in the temple of knowledge.

The weather is very cold at this time, and we are doing nothing at
all of any consequence. The sawmill is frozen up, and I am thinking it
will remain so for some time to come if the weather does not calm down.
We have been hauling logs all along & have got in upwards of ninety.

Pete Clifton is on a visit to old Charlies. He is a perfect hair brained
fellow, as wild & reckless as the waves of the ocean. Henry & Jack
Clifton had a quarrel this morning which liked to have terminated in a

fight, although there would not have been a very tall one if they had fought. Jack is a real trifling lazy fellow, fond of smoking & joking. I have got along pretty smoothly with old Charlies, & it may be that I have got into a snap, but be that as it may, "The cat will mew & dog will have his day."

The widow Anderson had her horse shot the other night. He was in someone's corn field at the time, I suppose. They judge old man Fuller for doing or having it done. It was a mean trick, let who will or has done it.

Allen Anderson still works for Mother. He is a first rate hand to work, although his education is very much limited. He & Henry talk of going to Nebraska next summer. I do not think that they will get off. I must try and leave in the spring if I can, for I am rather retrograding here and I want to go forward if I can by any means do so.

They are going to build a new schoolhouse in this district, & some of the people want it placed where the old one now stands. I for one would strongly object to that measure, for it is to[o] outrageously far for any small scholars to go. And who knows but what I might want to live here myself with some cozy little _____ [sic]? Bah! Nonsense in the highest! Who would have me, I wonder, or who is there that I would have? Echo answers, who?

Wm. Romigh still holds forth in the Deer Creek temple of knowledge. I have not heard how Bill gets along. . . . V.C. Wilson holds forth up at Dublin, Franklin Co. . . .

I was at a meeting of "Uncle Sams" the other night & found things getting along very well. I guess politics is about done for in this country. I sincerely hope so anyhow.

The snow is not all off of the ground yet, & the jingle of bells can still be heard on some of the roads yet.

Mr. Mathew Bonner is going to Nebraska in the spring. I would like to if I had a good enough education.

[Thursday] March 1st, 1855
. . . I hear that there is going to be an exhibition down at the Clover schoolhouse. I would like to be there if I could, but I am tied here, as it were, to Darby. I have one piece committed to memory called An Address to the Ocean, by Byron.

We have been hauling logs today and yesterday, but we do not make much headway at it on account of the bad roads. The oxen can hardly stand up in a great many cases on account of the ice.

Wm. Orpet was here yesterday. He is still keeping up his old occupation of loafing. He is still the same cypher that he always was. I do not see of what use he is to the community at large. . . . He is dirty & full of vermin, which he says is conducive to good health. Oh, what an idea!

Henry & Allen are over to the old place, Charlies. They have a natural tendency over that way, & so have I sometimes, but not always.

Big Lid [Lydia Robinson] was down today.

[Thursday] March 8th, 1855

. . . I have used an uncommon sight of that noxious weed called tobacco of late, & I suppose that that is one of the reasons why I feel like a pile of misery. Well, . . . I have no one to blame but myself. But then where, oh where are my good resolutions? . . .

I have been working at the mill today. We have at last got it to running, & I hope that there will be no more stoppages, for awhile anyhow.

I got a regular sett down this morning by old Aunt Sally about running her hogs into the creek. Well, but dident they swim magnificently & then dident the old woman cuss a few when they got tangled in the brush on the other side about ten feet from the bank. Well, it kind [of] excited [me] and that is what I like. The fact is, I got upon a cake of ice today at the dam & floated down to the mill just for the excitement, & I got throwed off too in the creek & got wet. Yes, excitement is what I want or I will die of ennui.

The creek is up pretty high at this time, & I hope to see a good run of water, some more than we have had this winter. I want a change anyhow, if it is even from bad to worse, anything but monotony.

I sometimes think about getting married just to get up a little excitement. But that wont pay. It would soon get to be an awful drag. It [would] do well enough at first. The squalls are what I am contemplating. It would all be well enough for a fellow to get up & take some pretty girl by the right hand & promise to cherish & support [her] through her natural life & then to have her kissed all around & praised by all your friends and to hear from all sides the general remark of, ["]O[h], what an excellent choice you have made,["] & then to fix up of a Sunday & go off to church with your wife smiling at your side. That is the sunny side; & what of the other side of the picture? Why, five dirty children all squalling around in less than that many years; & when a fellow wants to go to meeting he must hitch up the two horse wagon & drive along as slow as the seven years itch for fear of hurting the baby; & then to hear the people say, ["]Why, law!, how Mrs. Roberts has broke in the last five years["]; & then perhaps to have a wife that gets lonesome, has the toothache & thinks smoking would help her & smoke she will. From such a fate preserve me, ye gods!

[Sunday] March 18th, 1855

. . . Uncle James school is at last out & he is once more free from business and care. . . . I was up at his exhibition the last day of his school & had a good time of it, take it all in all. He had some first rate declamations & dialogues spoken. He has managed the school very well, I think, & I will long remember the pleasant time I had there. I myself spoke three pieces of indifferent merit. One was called An Address to the Ocean, which is quite sentimental. The other was The Exile of Erin & the last, though not least, was The Loafers Soliloquy, a very appropriate one for me to speak, for I kind o' lean that way myself. I spoke another piece, which I had almost forgotten to mention, called Hen Linden, a parody on Hohenlinden.

Poetry is all the rage up among the scholars. James composed a very nice ode & set it to music, which was sung at the close of the exercises in the daytime. John M. Allen is quite a poet. Some of his poetry will compare with the best of the sons of Parnassus. I wish I were only half as good. He & Uncle James came down with me last Sunday from Oak Run. We had a great time of it too. We all walked down & carried pieces of wood just for amusement.

Eliza Rafferty is dead. She died some three or four days since. She left a very small child, only three weeks old. The husband, Jac. Rafferty, is a kind of worthless piece of humanity, I guess, from what I can learn. Well, she is better off now than if she were here in this little cauldron of sin & misery. She has been pretty wild in her days but was never vicious or wilfully wicked, that is to the injury of others. Well, peace to her ashes.

Henry & Allen are over at old Charlies as usual tonight. I have got kind of weaned off from there lately. They went over in a boat that we made yesterday. It goes first rate. We made it in about an hour & a half. Uncle Jim put oars to it.

The creek is pretty high at this time. It has done the headrace some damage, broke it in two places, I believe. We have not sawed much lately on account of the high water. Jim talks some of tending her this summer. John M. Allen, James, and myself talk of going to Nebraska next spring to survey land for the United States, that is if we can get a job of that kind to do. Uncle Jas. & I went up to Mathew Bonners to get in with him, as we heard that he was surveyor general over the territory, but it turned out to be a hoax, like a great many other things that one hears nowadays. He (Math Bonner) is going but not to survey at all as was reported by some of the wiseacres.

I have heard a pretty hard tale on one of old Charlies girls. I do not know whether to credit it or not. It is on Nancy Clifton. I have the story in a roundabout way & it may not be so. However, there are some little "suckumstances" that I know that makes me kind of think that it is so. I have been intimate with her for some time & thought that she was pretty tolerably honest. But to my story: I hear that herself & father were in town some time since and that they were in O.H. Bliss'es depot, when one of the clerks took the old man to one side while O.H. Bliss talked to Nancy & invited her upstairs; when a customer happened to go up there without knowing he was up there & caught her & Mr. B. in a very suspicious position. I do not know how true it is, but such is the story that I heard & I have it pretty strait. . . . I am going to find out if I can. I came near to getting into a snapp some time since with Miss Nancy, & if she draws the wool over my eyes, she will have to rise very early in the morning, I assure her. She may be decent & she may not. I am rather inclined to think the latter, but I may be wrong & hope that I have ungrounded suspicions. . . .

Easter Sunday, April the 8th, 1855

. . . I was over to Mr. Thos. Jacksons today along with Mrs. & Miss Clifton. We had quite a time going and coming from there. Old Tommy is quite a piece. He is a great believer in witches & spirits. I do not know of anyone that is stronger in the faith than he is. He is, in fact, a monomaniac on that subject. He can talk on no other subject, & it is quite laughable to hear him talk of Washington & Jackson just as though he was well acquainted with them. He says that he sees thousands of spirits daily & that they speak to him & tell him things. I have never in all my journeyings seen such a man.

We stopped at old Kate Doanes as we went & also as we came back. Old Katie is one of them & no mistake. She can beat anything blackguarding that I ever was acquainted with, although the old [lady] is hospitable & obliging, I think, & may be honest for aught I know. However, that is her business, not mine. She tells a pretty hard story on Lydia Robinson. She says that Lydia [is] getting in a bad way & one that most girls would rather be excused from if they were unwed. I do not, however, believe that this is so.

. . . Henry & Allen [are] out sparking tonight at old Chas. Cliftons. . . . Charlie Clifton has moved off of our place. He lives on O.H. Bliss'es farm. He is pretty hard up at this time for the necessaries of life. He sold his hogs the other day to a man that lives below Georgesville. He got twenty dollars for them & is now living on the money. Charlies folks are rough, but they are hospitable & free hearted with what they have. . . .

Mr. Gifford preached in town today. I did not get to go, but I should have liked to went first rate. He is a very smart preacher & has such a nice & pleasant delivery that I love to hear him preach. Old John Hunter from Jefferson came here especially to tell me about it. Mr. Hunter is quite an enthusiast in the faith. He is a pretty smart old man & has a great deal of useful information in that old cranium of his. I like to hear the old gentleman talk. . . .

The township election went off last Monday here at Jefferson. Everything went off right. [Uncle] Sam [the Know-Nothings] was on hand as usual, working away silently & effectually. All the officers were the right stripe. I hear that the elections in Cincinnati did not go off very smoothly. The Dutch kicked up a rumpus down there and played hob with the ballot boxes. I hear that they had to call out the military to put down the riot. The Roman Catholic portion of the citizens of that town are noted for their unruly behavior. But there is a good time coming.

[Thursday] April 26th, [18]55

. . . It seems as though all my liesure moments are idled away and that I never improve. . . . I am afraid that I was born to be a clown or something of as little force. . . .

There is not much doing in our town since Charlies have moved away. Everything seems to be kind of on the deadhead order. They were the lives of the place. Grandfathers folks have moved into the Clifton place and have just about got the place cleaned up.

Uncle James has got back from the West and is sick with ague. He got back today. He left his goods at Cincinnati. They are to come up on the railroad. Wages are good in the West and everything is flourishing, so he says. . . .

[Monday] May 28th, [1855]

It has been some time since I last wrote in this book. I expected to be in Cincinnati long before this, but I have been disappointed in getting money. That is my luck, always in want of the one thing needful.

I am going to school in West Jefferson at this time to Mr. J.H. Drew, who is teaching at the academy. I have took but one study since I started and that is algebra. I am studying Rays Algebra, part first. I think that Mr. Drew is a first [rate] teacher. He takes pains to instruct his pupils, although some of them are not progressing very fast. We only have about twenty below stairs. Mrs. Drew teaches the small fry that are wont to congregate upstairs. She is a red faced, stout looking lady & I expect a good teacher. She teaches music to the small scholars. I think she teaches instrumental music too, but I think that that is a private concern.

I am anxious to go to some high school or college this fall. The teacher is going to go [to] London to teach after he gets through with the Jefferson school. . . .

I have not made much progress in my algebra yet. I have, however, got into fractions, which are very complex and hard to understand. Some of the scholars are getting pretty well through their algebras. We have some pretty tall compositions on Fridays. Some of them are right good & some of them are poor enough.

There are four or five scholars from the country. Miss Priscilla Hambleton is the largest of the young ladies. She is about seventeen years of age & is tolerably homely in my estimation. She is, however, a very amiable & pleasant girl & of course is esteemed by all that are in the school.

[Friday] June 8th, A.D. 1855
. . . Here I have been on Darby for the last year, threatening to leave every month. Yet here I am and here I am likely to remain for some time to come if some luckey star does not come along and pick me up. I am tired of the dull, prosaic round that I have to trudge. I want a little more excitement. This thing of living without any incident worth mentioning is enough to give one the blues.

I had an adventure . . . Sunday [before last] that had a little life in it. . . . I ran some risk in it, I can tell you. It was an adventure with Nancy Clifton near the brick schoolhouse. I shall never forget it as long as I live & keep my memory. Miss Nancy is working in town at this time for a man by the name of Adams. She is working at sewing & light housewifery.

Henry and Allen started from here about the fourth of June. They went over to Columbus & immediately got a berth to take cattle east. The[y] started away determined to stick to each other through thick & thin, but mark the very first thing they done. One started for New York & the [other] for Illinois—a pretty good beginning for them to make in sticking close to one another. Henry, he went to Illinois & Allen went to New York. They are to get thirteen dollars per month and found. I rather guess that they will get enough of car riding before they get through with their present trip. I hope that they may do well in enterprises, for they are just cutting their eyeteeth & this is their first voyage.

Jim has gone to Deer Creek, & the creek is to[o] high for me to get to Charlies. So dull is the day to me.

[Thursday] July 30th, A.D. 1857, Oak Run, Madison Co.

Many and strange things have happened since I last wrote in this old familiar book. June the 8th, 1855, is the last date I see in the book. Now this dates two years and nearly two months later.

Strange coincidents will sometimes happen. I am in now the same kind of a dilemma that I was in then: woman. . . . But there is a considerable difference between women, and this is a case in hand.

James H. Roberts is married and has one child. . . .

I commenced this book four years ago and have not made a finish of it yet, and I must now finish.

It seems as though the creek was too high for me to go to Charlies at the time I wrote in this book. Well, if it had [been] so all the time, I might have been some better off than what I am at this present time. No use, however, of talking about that now. It is all over now and I cannot recall it, even if I were ever so anxious to do so.

Henry & Allen never traveled together that summer at all. Henry went on to Illinois and Allen went with me. Henry did get into New York. Allen never did. Their eyeteeth were somewhat improved by the trip, but I am of the opinion that there is room for improvement yet in their occular grinders. . . .

> Old Book, goodbye, your leaves I've often turned;
> Much joy I've had, some grief, I wot, & much I've learned
> Since first I wrote on thy fair unspotted pages.
> Friends tried and true have died or grown colder,
> But some there are who have ne'er let their love smolder.
> Amid the wreck of matter in all its wandering stages,
> Camp meetings, funerals, frolics, and other lively matters
> Would ere this have escaped my mind or only left some tatters
> If it had not been for thee, Old Book.

By the sacred nine, I cant write poetry, and there is the end of it, as the Yankee said.

Well, this book has been a comfort to me anyhow. I am glad that I commenced it and went through with it, as it now gives my mind light on things that I must have entirely forgotten ere this had it not been for this book.

Old Book, never more again shall the pen and hand that glides over the[e] do so anymore. Thou art full. The blots on thy leaves must stay. The bad writing and spelling within, they must ever remain a monument to or of the ignorance of the author.

He is getting sentimental, Old Book. He buys his experience dear sometimes. He is not much more of a book scholar than he was when he first put a pen on one of thy fair pages. Yet he has learned much since that time. He has seen human nature. He has seen vice. He has been amongst many strange faces and has tasted of the bitter as well as the sweet in life. He has lived. He has been merry & he has also been sad. He has been happy, very happy at times, and can laugh yet at a good [joke] with a right hearty gusto.

Tis thus you end.

Finis

5

Itinerant Book Agent
March 17–April 26, 1857

*In the retrospective postscript that finished his "Old Book,"
John Roberts mentioned that while his brother Henry and Allen
Anderson failed to stick together in their journeys, he had traveled in
company with Allen. Whether with Allen or alone, John left home in
June 1855, not long after his "adventure with Nancy Clifton near the
brick schoolhouse," since in a later journal entry he recalls that he
had been near the mouth of the Ohio River at the end of that month.*

*In the spring of 1857 Roberts returns to his "journalism,"
recounting his travels as a book agent in Ohio counties to the west
and north of Madison. Using what appears to be a school
composition book, he again prudently wastes none of the available
space; when his travel account ends, and a brief one by his
bookselling companion, Turner Cobaugh, Roberts fills the remaining
pages by recording the events which will compose Chapter 6.*

He signs up few subscribers for the American Encyclopedia of
History, Biography, and Travel *among the farmers and villagers of
Wyandot, Hancock, and Marion counties; worse luck, in the end his
employers "come the Yankee" on him and Cobaugh and fail to pay
their expenses. Starting out with high hopes at Carey, Roberts soon
discovers there is little interest in "larnin" among the rural folk,
many of them recent German immigrants. While he likes the towns of
Findlay, Fostoria, and Delaware, the villages of Van Buren, Vanlue,
Mt. Victory, and Byhalia are ugly and depressing.*

*Walking the roads in cold, blustery weather causes John's nose
to run "like a fress tapped sugar tree." He shivers and his teeth
rattle at an exhibition where pretty girls in "airish geer" sing
familiar songs; he can only "stand back like a bound boy at a
husking" and envy their local beaus. The life of a traveling book
agent, he finds, is a lonely, unrewarding business.*

[Tuesday, March 17, 1857]

Journal of travel commenced by John M. Roberts, March 17th, A.D. 1857, in the town of Car[e]y, Wyandot County, Ohio, starting out as agent for Miller and Gilmore, canvassing for subscribers for a publication entitled American Encyclopedia of History, Biography, and Travel, at the rate of twenty five dollars per month, and expenses all paid.

Started from home on the 16th March inst. in company with W. T[urner] Cobaugh. Stayed all night in Columbus at the Exchange on the railroad. Started for Urbana on the nine o'clock train. Got into Urbana at half past eleven o'clock and from thence to Cary in the afternoon of this very day. I am very tired and hungry & will give the particulars at some other time, which will occupy several pages.

[Wednesday] March 18th, 1857

Tonight I find I am in good health and lodging in the house of a good old Pennsylvania farmer, three miles from Cary. We have had very good luck today. I got six good subscribers and talked to about fifty persons or more perhaps. Turner got about the same number that I did. The country around here is generally very level and is pretty wet in the winter. We stayed in Cary a day and a half. Tavern bill one dollar. I like this country pretty well, but I think that there are some pretty hard cases about Cary. They are all [John C.] Fremont men up here, I am told. They are in a great Kansas fever up here and a great many of them will be taken off by it. . . . I am tired tonight and shall add no more. I must try and write a page each day.

[Wednesday] April 1st, 1857

. . . I am now in Cass Township, Hancock Co., canvassing for subscribers. I have been pretty tolerably successful. . . . I have had a most an awful time today. The weather has been as rough as any winter weather could be. I had to go to four houses this evening before I could get to stay all night.

I have been at this business now nearly a half month, and I begin to like it pretty well. I have some fun sometimes, and sometimes I have pretty hard times. I stopped last Sunday with a man by the name of Sheets. He lives in or near a town called Arcadia. He is a first rate man. He took a book. . . .

W.T. Cobaugh is still with me. He is in pretty good spirits. I am with him about every other day. We take a township at a time. I am furnishing him with all of his cash expenses. Some of the folks down on Oak Run advised me not to let him have the money, as they were of the opinion that he would flicker out and go home. I am of the opinion that he will do the clean thing with me.

I was in Fostoria day before yesterday and was surprised to see so large a place. They have three churches and a college, two foundreys, & a mill.

[Sunday] April 5th, A.D. 1857

I am in Cass Township today, which by the way [is] Sunday and it is a raining at that. We have made pretty good success in this part of the moral vineyard. Vanburen is in this township. It is a very small place and a pretty hard town, I suspect. There is one tavern, two stores, and two groceries in it. They seem to be fond of whiskey in the place. J.R. Dye is the proprietor of the place. He has a store there. I rather sowed him up on the book business. I asked him to subscribe and told him that I would take it out in trade. He said he had some woolen comforts and set onions to sell. I just took him up as soon as he made the offer. It rather got the lad. He did not know what to do. He just mizzled and was among the missing in less than two minutes.

I came across a man yesterday that said that he intended to kick the next book agent that offered to sell him a book. He did not, however, try that giraffe on us. He went off muttering. . . .

The weather has been very bad since I last wrote. It has snowed and blowed great guns since I last jotted down the incidents and accidents by flood & field.

I am in good spirits at this time. I will not have more than 70 subscribers on my list at the end of the month.

Easter Sunday, April 12th, A.D. 1857

I am today along with W.T. Cobaugh stopping with a man by the name of Bolin. By the way, he is a Methodist, a Fremont man, and a well to do farmer.

Turner has caught up with me in the book business. Last week was an infernal week for travelling, and I almost gave up in despair. I cleaned up Marion Township that I had been engaged in when I first made a start in this county. I have been to Findlay several times since I last wrote in this book. The town is a pretty nice kind of a place, I think, & it contains somewhere near 1500 inhabitants. They have a pretty large kind of a courthouse and some fine buildings. We have not canvassed in the town yet. . . .

How I wish that some of my old associates were here. I could enjoy myself prodigiously. There is Semp Saunders, Doc Truitt, & others. I do wonder what the boys are doing today, perhaps having a good time with the girls. . . . I got a letter from Semp and Doc the other day. They were in fine spirits and everything was as it should be. They are worth their weight in gold. Gamaliel Saunders has been sick. I hope he may get well, for we cant spare him yet nohow. . . .

I bought me a German grammar yesterday in Findlay. I gave a dollar for it. I want to learn the German language if I can do so. There are any amount of Dutch in this country, and they just gabble away at me as if I understood it. I stopped with a man by the name of Haly on last Thursday evening that had family worship in Dutch. It sounded very Dutchy to me. There was a Yankee schoolmaster there that I had quite a chat with. His name was Beardsley. He is just fresh from York State & is as sharp as a needle. He has been engaged in getting subscribers for a map. He charged seven dollars & a half per map & must have made it pay well. . . .

Semp Saunders has a letter from Gov. [John W.] Geary, an ex gov. [of Kansas Territory] now, however. The gov. says that Kansas is as peaceable a place as any other and that there will not be the least danger in going there at this time. Semp, I suppose, has shown up the letter good. I hope he may always have as punctual a reply as the governor gave him. . . .

There has been some Egyptians [Gypsies] in this part of the county lately. I do wonder if it is the same ones that bamboozled Bill Wilson out of his 3000 dollars. Well, there are a great many people that start out to make their living and fail for the want of capital, but these folks will never fail for that reason, I am thinking.

This business brightens a man up more than anything else that he can go at. I have learned more of the ways of the world since I have been engaged in this business than I ever knew before. I have come across some most consummate dummies, & I have also come across some that had traveled in their time and were as sharp as a steel trap. The most of the people here treat me with respect, and I have not had any difficulty. One man last week was rather inclined to be pugnacious, yet he did not go very far. I could see him begin to make grimaces about his sons signing or subscribing, but he did not say much about the matter & I left him. His name was Elliott.

[Thursday] April 16th, A.D. 1857

Hancock County, Liberty Township, Ohio. My meanderings have brought me to this place and I am almost sick at heart. I have been very unsuccessful this week and I am getting in favor of quitting the business.

The weather is intensely cold. . . . It has snowed and blowed incessantly all this week and bids fair to continue on in the way of evil doing.

. . . I am stopping with a man by the name of George Mullen. He is a very common sort of a man with a very common sort of a woman. Nothing very attractive about either of them. They have a hired girl by the name of Ramsay who is sort of a merry piece, fond of fun, I guess, not overly well stocked in superfine knowledge; a good sort of girl, however, I guess. Make some man a miserable cub or happy rascal one of these days.

I was up at an exhibition last Monday night. They had a middling tall time of it. They had it in a barn and charged a five strikes [cents?] admittance. Women went in free. They had some good pieces and some that were rather indifferent, so I thought. The girls took more than an equal part in the performances. The young ladies at the exhibition were rather extra in intellect. They sung some very good songs, Ten O'Clock, Silver Moon, and several other songs that are pretty old but good and appropriate. They outstripped anything that I have come across lately. They nearly all wore white dresses cut low in the neck, arms bare to the shoulders, and pretty short in the skirt. I just shivered in my boots. My teeth came near being done for on account of the cold. Yet these tender females could come out in such airish geer. Well, they will do so anyhow, so I will dismiss them from my thoughts & dreams for the present. Of course, there was some of them had beaus. I, however, had to stand back like a bound boy at a husking.

I have been here every night this week and intend to stay until Monday if possible, when we expect a letter from Miller & Company with our months wages and cash expenses. I have written some dozen letters home and have not received answers from them all.

This is a flat, uninteresting country, full of big red barns and Dutch. I think Germany must have taken a puke into this part of the moral vineyard. Fried mush and homemade molasses is my chief diet at this time. I have made a water haul today. I have been amongst a lot of Mynheer Dutch Dunkerds, perfect clodheads that know enough to drive the plow and eat sour krout. Heaven deliver me from the Dutch and all their kin. . . .

Home, how sweet the sound! Friends, how dear the name! House homeless wandering is the life of a book agent, but they have their seasons of enjoyment as well as their times of depression. Once in a while he gets hold of a green one that wants to show off his sharpness. A few well timed remarks lays the individual out and does him up brown. Soft sawder and human nature are essential to do a good business. A stiff upper lip, an oily and ready tongue must be ever ready. An easy, affable demeanor must be practiced even if you feel like blowing a man up & giving him fits.

I have a decided hankering after Blanchard River. It is not a very large stream but has a very fine settlement. The most of my subscribers are denizens of this stream. The roads in this country are sometimes pretty bad; only on the ridges where they are always pretty good. These ridges are peculiar—long, regular swells in the otherwise totally level country running for many miles paralel to each other . . . with a swamp between them. They are covered with beech and sugar trees with some few white & red oaks mixed in. There is also considerable yellow poplar in these regions, but it is fast disappearing before the ax of the sturdy woodsman. Improvement is the order of the day here. . . .

I do wonder what Turner is doing today, trading books, I suppose, for baby cradles. [Turner Cobaugh's journal relates that a "poor booby" trying to kid him offered to trade a baby cradle for a book; Turner agreed, to the amusement of the man's companions.] . . .

Morgan horses, Shanghai chickens, and other fine stock are as popular in this country as most anything else. Some of the people here are the allfiredest wooden heads that I ever saw. They cant inscribe; they haint no larnin; never went to school in their lives; in debt; building barns; got more books than they can read. I am inclined to believe some of them when they make the latter assertion. By Saint Jimeny, some of them are so longheaded that it takes an idea about three weeks to get behind their ears. That is so, by thunder. I would like to catch some of them down in Madison Co. Wouldent I talk to them though! Yessiree, horse & buggy! Id make their hair stand on end, I know. . . .

The Lord said unto Moses, let us cut off our noses. I am thinking it would leave poor Mose in a bad old row of stumps if he had taken His advice. And furthermore he would not have been able to smell a rat. I find my smeller is not up to snuff yet, and I am afraid that the first thing I know it will be stuck into somebody's business affairs. It keeps so cold that I am nearly all the time using my pocket rag. It runs like a fres[h] tapped sugar tree. . . .

[Sunday] April 26th, A.D. 1857. At Home

I am once more at home, and there is a good prospect of my remaining. I have quit the book business, & I rather suspect that I have quit it forever.

This day one week ago I was in Vanlue, Hancock Co., Ohio, at Dr. J. Stoffers tavern living on J. & H. Millers expenses. I left there on Monday morning for Cary District, seven miles from Vanlue. I got there and lounged around with W.T. Cobaugh until the 11 oclock freight train came in from the east, when I got aboard of it and started for Kenton, Hardin Co., distant 28 miles from Cary. Got there at two oclock, or half past one. Got shaved there and got my daguerreotype taken in the town by an artist that was there. W.T. had his taken also.

We started from Kenton at half past two oclock p.m. for Mt. Victory in Union County, distant 16 miles. Kenton is a pretty smart kind of a town, not noted, however, for its beauty. It is pretty scattering and has a large public square of several acres. The buildings around it, however, are not very imposing or grand, so the square has not much effect on the beauty of the place.

We arrived at Mt. Victory at about sundown and put up with a man by the name of Jno. Blue. Had tolerably poor grub but paid a reasonable bill in the morning. . . .

The town is a very ordinary kind of a country village, not having more than fifty houses in it & ordinary ones at that. W.T. Cobaugh was almost afraid to venture into the town on account of some petty little debts that he had contracted in the place some two years since. He, however, went up manfully and gave his notes for the sums due and thereby got through without being checkmated by any of them. . . .

We started from Mt. Victory Tuesday morning for Newton in Union County, which is some 15 miles from Victory. We went through two very small places. The first was Bythalia. It contains two houses and a barn and store where we stayed and rested an hour or more. The storekeeper there was a clever kind of a fellow not overburdened with good sense. He had a few notions and some very bad whiskey. W.T. said so & he ought to know, as he took a pretty good taste of it. The next place was called Somerville, with about 14 houses in it & those of not a very extra quality. We stopped here and got some very ancient cheese. . . . W.T.C. told some of his choicest tales here to a gaping crowd who seemed to think that he must have seen it all and a little more. He told them that he was just from Kansas and showed his hand that he got burned with powder in W[esley] A[llen']s watermelon patch as evidence of his having been shot by the border ruffians in a fight that he had had with them. W.T. is a trump and no mistake. He will get along if anyone can.

We started from this place after we had regaled the citizens with fish stories as much as we thought consistent with prudence. We were now bound for the residence of Benjamin Glasgoe some eight or ten miles distant on Mill Creek. We got there in the afternoon, Tuesday, 21st of April, and soon made ourselves at home with Mrs. Glasgoe and her family. Benjamin was out plowing. He has a nice farm up there, which by the way he has nearly paid for. He has some two hundred acres, I believe.

Here I left W.T.C. and I am sure I left a very clever kind of a boy. He is passionate and hasty and is capable of doing well if he applies himself. He is the greatest enemy to himself. He is rather too fond of bad whiskey; but he will not be apt to indulge too freely unless he gets into a crowd that are in the habit of indulging too freely. He is a boy of more than ordinary capacity, and if he meets with encouragement, he will make a mark in the world. . . .

He and I have made a bargain with one another that the one that marries first must board the other three months. . . .

W.T.C. gave me his prospectus and told me to go to Columbus and see the publishers and settle them. They did not send us any money for to bear our cash expenses, which was a direct violation of the contract between us and them. They rather came the Yankee over me in the long run. They asked me to let them look at the prospectuses and then locked them up, a sharp trick in them. Well, I'll know better next time. I. Miller also told me that he was only an agent acting under brother and brotherinlaw, and that he understood them to say that we were not to have our cash expenses only at the end of the four months. Well, I have learned something by this operation.

. . . I left Benj. Glasgows Wednesday morning, Apr. 22d, for Columbus. I walked to Marysville, the county seat of Union County. The county by the way is very thinly settled. There are mile after mile of nothing but dense forest, principally beech timber, & the surface is generally very level and . . . very wet. I do not like the country at all. It is too wet and too many big woods for me.

I arrived at Marysville at 9 oclock on Wednesday morning. The town is a very ordinary kind of a place. There are some good houses in it but not anything remarkable about the place. I did not stay long in the place, but I saw enough to convince me that the place was not much of a town. I found an empty purse as I was going into Marysville. That was ominous of my entry into the town.

I took the cars for Delaware and arrived there at noon or near that time. I looked around the town and am rather in favor of it than otherwise. The college there is quite a building. It looks tolerable old and dingy. There are many, very many loafers in the place. I saw several hard cases in the place, one in particular, a poor, miserable man that had no home or no friends. He told me that he had been a student at the Delaware College. He was sitting in the depot when he & I got into a conversation, in which he asked me [to] give him a dime to buy some bread as he was very hungry. I asked him if he wanted a dram. He told me no. I went to a grocery & bought him some cakes. He thanked me kindly. I asked him why he did not go home to his friends. He said he had none. He said this with such a desponding tone that my heart bled for him. He said that he had but one friend in the world and that was his mother, and that he was ashamed to go to her. He had some shame left. What a picture he presented, a miserable picture to that fond mother whose very soul may have been centered in him. How it must harrow up her soul to see her son in this condition. He was a young man and would have been a very personable looking man if he had not been made a beast of by ardent spirits. This is what I fear may be my awful end. I hope not, however, as it is truly awful. May the Good Being always keep me sober & from ever becoming a sot.

I went from Delaware to Columbus, where I got on Wednesday morning and went to Miller & Co.'s office on Town Street & made a fruitless thing of it. I do not know what W.T.C. will think about the way I have managed the business. He will be mad enough, as he is pretty fiery. I hate it like thunder to do the way I did. . . .

6

An Aimless Drifter
May 2–August 20, 1857

At home on Oak Run, Roberts describes himself as "an aimless, viewless person, not making any provision or looking out to any future." He still wants to move to Uncle Cary's to go to school, but he makes no plans to. Although his "head has been turned by a woman," he makes no mention of courtship and marriage for himself, except through the words of a Gypsy fortuneteller.

An approaching comet gives Roberts a chance to engage in one of his favorite diversions: ridiculing superstitious beliefs and fears. The company of his male friends provides his chief pleasure, though one night's revel in London causes him to swear off wine. He works on the township roads for Gam Saunders and escapes his own required road work by parading with the Madison Guards. His Guards outfit of white pantaloons and military coat is expensive, but John earns some money mowing hay for Joshua Rankin and helping his brother Henry and Allen Anderson on a summer job of carpentry.

The high point of John's summer comes when he attends a camp meeting. The omnibus rides to and from the site, the drinking, fighting, and gambling on the fringes of the campground, and the diverse assortment of people among "the host of Israel" inspire a rhapsodic burst from his pen.

[Saturday] May 2d, 1857

Time, the enemy of mankind, still keeps on the move and leaves poor dilatory man on expenses. I am totally out of a job and see no opening to make anything out of as yet. School keeping, I am not in a very good row of stumps. I have almost made up my mind to go to farming.

What is this little world coming to? I guess it [will] come to a focus soon. The comet has made its appearance, and folks are beginning to quake with fear and trembling. Well, let them quake. It will be good for their consciences & the good of their souls and other mens pockets.

123

Everyone here is intent on the loaves & fishes as though they were never going to die. . . .

No news yet from W.T. Cobaugh. I do wonder what he has found to do. Perhaps he has some grubbing or rail mauling or wood chopping to do. I hope he may get into a good job. I have been doing absolutely nothing this week, and the prospect seems favorable for a continuation of the same blessing. Markleys want to rent me a small piece of ground, some ten acres or somewhere in that neighborhood. I may pitch in and tend it yet. Mother says she will let me have the horses if I can get feed for them.

Someone has stolen twenty five bushels of corn from Handy Truitt, an everlasting mean trick in my opinion, because he is a sick man and not able to do anything to help himself. That is what I call meanness whittled down to a point. Men who will steal from anyone should always . . . steal from persons who are able to lose it without any inconvenience. Some men in this neighborhood never work any, and of course they must do something for a livelihood. . . .

I was over on Deer Creek night before last and saw some of my old chums. Stayed all night with Uncle James Roberts, who is working in the matrimonial harness just as sage as any of the old stagers that have been sailing on the good old way for years. Jas. H. has a wife & a home and I suppose can sit back in his easy chair and take his ease when his days work is done. His wife looks pretty well at this time. . . .

I have some notion of going to Cincinnati this spring to live with my Uncle Cary. He has a good school there and I may make something yet, who knows? . . . I am an aimless, viewless person, not making any provision or looking out to any future. . . .

My head has nearly been turned lately by- by- by- a—shall I venture to say the word? Must I make the assertion? Can I stand the laugh of withering scorn that will follow the avowal? Yes, I must, I can, & I will if it is necessary. So here goes. Now, do not all laugh at once. Have patience & you shall hear the awful, never to be forgotten word that I am about to utter, that may perhaps set me down in your estimation as a fool. Yes, my head has been turned by a woman. Mirabile dictu. You have all [heard it] now and I have nothing for my pains. Dear reader, whoever you may happen to be, do not laugh at my calamity or mock at me for my fears. The word has went forth & it is true.

I once thought I was sharp and knew how to judge human nature, but I believe there are some of the feminine gender [who] have a little more cuteness than I have. I must not, however, go into particulars in this book, as it may fall into the hands of some of my friends. I must make as good a case out as possible in this volume.

I read Hot Corn over at Mr. Allens last night and this morning. There are some things in it that are very good. It gives the darkest shades of life in the most degraded parts of Gods vineyard & does it up strong and effectively. Some of the life scenes are truly affecting, & I suppose that the most of them are true. I have seen some of the scenes therein depicted. May I never be called on to be the chief actor in such scenes.

They say that V.C. Wilson is a bloat and that he is going down the broad road in a gallop. He has lost all personal respect for himself and does not seem to look forward to anything but idleness and dissipation. This is a sad sight, and a woeful picture to look upon, a young man of pretty fair talents hiding them under a bushel, or worse, making a beast of himself, a curse . . . to all his friends and a burden to himself. I do pity Valentine and hope that the news I hear from him may be exaggerated, and that . . . he may be able to get back to the shores of respectability and usefulness. I have not seen him for a long time. . . .

G.W. Saunders, my early friend and playmate, has just recovered from a long spell of sickness. He says that God has spoken peace to his soul and that religion will hereafter be one of his main objects. He views life through a gloomy veil and thinks that all amusement is vain. Dancing and all other kinds of merrymaking he considers as vanity and worse than vanity. He denies the infinite wisdom of God and believes in a dreadful future punishment. I hope he may be wrong in both of his suppositions. Time will tell the tale.

[Tuesday] June 9th, A.D. 1857. Oak Run, Ohio
. . . Ellen Todd is dead. She died on the twenty sixth of May. She had been sick for a long time and had suffered a great deal. She was buried in the Turner graveyard. She was an old schoolmate and friend of mine. She was of a lively temperament and shed a glow of happiness all around her. A Methodist in principle, she lived up to the requirements of that strait sect as nigh as the members thereof were in the habit of doing. It made me feel sad to follow her to her long home, as she is one of quite a number of my old playmates that have left the scenes of mortality for those of another and a better country. She makes nine or ten that have left us since I went to school to George Bowery. . . .

Mother is very sick at this time. I am doubtful if she ever recovers again. Dr. N.S. Darling is the physician. He does not say she will not get well, but he is rather in some doubt about it. Dr. Daniel Wilson will be here this afternoon to counsel with Dr. Darling. I do not like the plan of having two Drs. at once, but the folks want it to be done and I must acquiesce in that, as it is the will of all the rest and I am only one in the case. . . . Aunt Nancy Wilson & Grandmother are here at this time waiting on Mother.

Valentine C. Wilson has made a kind of a bad nest of it up in Delaware. He has a child sworn to him up there by a girl by the name of Cone. She is worth some 8000 dollars in her own right and lays a very heavy damage for breach of promise and seduction also. I guess V.C. will get a [marriage?] license for the future, as he will not more than be able to fit up the bill as it now stands. If he promised to marry the girl, he ought of course to do it & not desert her so shamefully. Women have rights and they ought to be respected in them. So say I. V.C. will not do any better than this if he tries ever so hard, and the best and most honorable course for him to pursue is to marry the girl and heal up the wound.

The comet has alarmed a great many folks here and elsewhere. I am of the candid opinion that it will not make any difference in our domestic arrangements or economy. . . .

G.W. Saunders has sold his interest out in the National Road farm, for two thousand dollars if he loses it and three thousand if he gains it, so he will make a very big pile out of his chance anyhow. . . .

I received a letter from W.T. Cobaugh the other day. He is up in Union County at Benj. Glasgoes at work on a farm. He gives Miller & Company fits in his letter. I wrote him a letter and posted it last week. I put in the Parody on Animals that I got of J.M. Allen. It is a rich thing in its way, and there are few things in the poetry line that I ever saw that can begin to come up with it.

I wrote an epistle to John Peterman last week. I directed it as follows:

> I am now a correspondent,
> On the mail I am dependent.
> This is for a neighbor boy,
> A comrade now in Illinois.
> John Peterman we call his name,
> Town Urbana, county is Champaign.

This is the direction, and now I wish to see if it will go through. . . .

Allen and Henry are making rails for G.W. & S. Saunders. They are going to make two thousand, I believe. They said at first that they did not know as they could make them for less than 75 cents [per hundred].

. . . Henry has lost one of his horses, a mare that he bought of G.W. & S. Saunders. He will lose somewhere in the neighborhood of 50 dollars by the operation. He is now at home and will continue to be until Mother gets better, I suppose.

People are starving to death in Michigan, I understand. Times are hard here but not quite so hard as all that comes to.

The immigration to this country is immense. There is no end to the raw Irish.

[Wednesday] June 10th, A.D. 1857

The time must roll around when we must all leave this earthly tabernacle for the new scenes of another existence. I do not think that I fear the change. Still, there is a cold feeling will creep over one when they investigate the subject of death closely. To think that the hand that now guides this pen must one day be pulseless and still, food for worms, that it must be in a few years that we must sink as it were into oblivion and forgetfulness, become as though we were not, or as though we had never been sojourners here on this variously checkered life scene. But there is a rest for the weary and a respite to the distressed where we hear the low, murmuring sound of the autumn wind, which seems to say: In the grave, beneath the soil, there it is that we shall find rest from all that can trouble or distress the mind of the rude or the more refined. . . .

Jas. Garrard was here last night, or evening rather. He made a very eloquent prayer at Mothers request. The words seemed to come from the heart. He is a Baptist, but I think he is a Christian. He believes that the will of God is always done. I am of the same opinion myself and think that all the wisdom of the world cannot thwart it or turn it aside. . . .

I have sometimes tried to write poetry, but I find my talent does not run that way. Below I give a specimen of an effort made:

> Once fondly loved and still remembered, dear,
> Accept this mark of friendship, warm, sincere.
> Friendship? Nay, call it by a stronger name.
> Without it the world is lost. It is a chain
> That binds the heart & wraps the human mind
> In one pure mantle of love & truth refined.
> Though through many climes he yet may rove,
> His heart no other heart will seek, nor find another love.
> Think of his hopes, a wreck on lifes rugged shore;
> One sigh for him he asks of thee, no more.
> In after years when present things thy mind must fill,
> Think of the one that loved thee then as one that loves thee still.
> May loved ones stand, ever cheer thee on thy way,
> May evil ne'er come o'er thee, or darkness cloud thy day.

I guess I will not write any more in that strain. It seems as though I cannot do anything in the poetic line.

I must go to town and get me a pair of white pantaloons to parade in. Captain Phillips has posted up an order for the Madison Guards to appear on the 20th inst. in London to parade and elect a major general for the division. I suppose that Captain Phillips will be the man. I am going to put in a ticket for him anyhow. I hope he may be elected. He would make a very good general, I think. I get clear of working the roads this season by belonging to the military company & I am bound to see the thing through if possible. . . .

The comet is to appear now in a few days & everybody is on the qui vive to get a peep at it. They say it can be seen at night at twelve or three oclock in the northwest or southwest. It is not yet determined . . . precisely which point, but it is one of the two places. I have not yet got a glimpse of the fiery monster of the upper deep. I am of the opinion that we are safe, yet anyhow, and we know that sufficient unto the day is the evil thereof, so it is of no use fretting about the catastrophe if it does come. We are all in a pile here, and it will make a clean sweep of all, both great and small.

[Monday] June 15th, A.D. 1857

. . . According to the wiseacres this is the last day of the worlds existence. The comet is to strike tomorrow at precisely ten oclock. Well, everything looks well, up to this period of time anyhow, and I see no signs of approaching disaster and ruin. The birds sing as merry as usual. The frogs still keep up their din & everyone seems to be busy.

I was in London and put in three dollars for cloth to make a coat—a military one by the way. London is getting to be quite patriotic. They have two companies there now. The Dutch have raised a company of artillerymen there. They will number some forty members. How they and the Madison Guards will hitch on I am unable to say. I suppose, however, they will agree well enough. I hope so at least, as I do not want to have any rows with the Dutch nor anyone else. We have to elect a major general for the division on next Saturday, and also we want to put in a days drill on the same day. We have three or four days drilling to do through the year, and Saturday will be one of them. The 4th of July I presume will be another. Captain Phillips talks of going to Springfield on the 4th. I do not much like the idea of going there on that day, but if the crowd does go, I of course will not flinch from the hot weather and dust that will have to be endured by the patriotic military of London. . . .

G.W. & S. Saunders have not yet got their corn planted and I suppose will not for a day or two at least. A little to[o] slow on trigger for the season, I am thinking. Maybe not, however. . . .

Mother is still very sick and gains but slowly. The physicians, however, think that she may recover yet, and I am of the opinion that she will myself. Some of the members of the church were here today from Somerford—Mrs. Wm. Allen, Mrs. G. Prugh, and Mrs. Palmer.

The night is stealing along and I must close for want of more light. How pleasant it is to the mind to sit and see the day slowly fading away in the west. Everything seems to wear a kind of dreamlike appearance. I love the closing scenes of the closing day. It refreshes me and makes me feel thankful to the giver of good for His bounty.

[Sunday] June 28th, A.D. 1857

This day two years ago I was on the swift rolling waters of La Belle Riv[i]ere, or Ohio, near its mouth. . . .

I am not in much of a sweat at this time. My little troubles are not more than enough to keep my mind right and my digestion good. The girls are nothing in my way anymore, & I am going to try and keep them at arms length in future if I can possibly do so. . . . These girls are a set of jilts, I am inclined to think. Perhaps they may one day see their error and mend their ways. I hope so at least.

Henry & Allen are going into the carpenter business this summer. They want me to work with them. I guess I shall do so if possible, as it is far easier than working in the harvest field. They say that they have nearly three hundred dollars worth of work to do this summer. I hope they have and that I can do one third at least.

Semp Saunders and Henry went to Darby yesterday. They are going to Samuel R. Stevenson, the man that boarded Henry & Allen whilst they were working at the old Cross Bow sawmill. They will have a rich time, I am thinking. I would be glad myself to take some sport amongst some of the girls down there. Yet I do not know but what I am better where I am than there, as I will not be running into dissipation here, and if I were there I would be sure to.

I want to go over to the Williams Chapel today to meeting. The blind preacher Musgrove preaches there today. I like him pretty well. He is quite original sometimes & makes some quaint remarks. . . . The meeting is to be at 3 o'clock in the afternoon.

There are some strange young ladies over there that I would like to get acquainted with. They are not pretty, but some of them appear to be quite intelligent and have a good smart look. . . . There are going to be a lot of old maids in this country the first thing we know. Well, they that marry do well, but those that dont do better. Pretty well said for you, old Paul, & I guess that I will follow your advice, in that anyhow.

I worked the roads yesterday and the day before for G.W. Saunders. He never would work the roads, so he gives the supervisor a chance to sue him & make more cost than there otherwise would be, or nearly twice as much as he would have to pay if he had paid it in in the first place. G.W. owes me about [$]31.00 for work and money borrowed. I owe nearly enough to take half of the money that he owes me. Clothing costs more than anything else in this country. I have spent upwards of thirty dollars for clothes this summer and have not got anything very fine yet. I am getting me a military suit made at this time which will cost me fifteen dollars at least. I think some of going to the western countries this fall to try my luck there.

. . . The London chaps are going to have a dinner on the fourth of July next and various other chicken fixings. A. Driesbach and others are going to head the procession with an eagle that they have there in a cage at the cowling house on the railroad. J.R. Montgomery is to make the oration, George Bowen to read the Declaration. I suppose that they will have a good time, take it all in all. The Dutch artillery are going to be out in full dress on the 4th. They think that they will have their cannon there by that time. They number some 40 members in all in the German artillery. . . .

Last Sunday I and S.D. Truitt were in company. We went to nearly every house in the neighborhood. We were at Tingleys, Prughs, Cornwells, Wilsons, & Allens. We stopped at Tingleys & took dinner. Wm. Tingley, by the way, is in a weakly state of health. He has the liver complaint. He look[s] like death in the primer. The girls were all there when we went there—Suse, Sarah, Minerva, & Elisabeth. The next place we went to was S. Prughs. The girls were not at home, so we did not stop there. We, however, met them between Prughs & Cornwells in company with about a half dozen others. Sein Markley was along with them. Sein is just in from Missouri. He has been there upwards of two years at this time. He is going to live there, I understand. Old Mr. Markley is going to move there too. . . .

Wesley Allen is going into the strawberry business strong this year. He has sold sixteen dollars worth already, and I suppose he will sell twice as many more before the season is through. London is a good market for him. He sells a great deal of garden stuff there in the course of a year. He sells potatoes, cabbage, beets, turnips, and onions. I believe that the raising of small vegetables & fruits is as good a business as a man can go at. There will be a greater demand for fruit every year, and those that turn their attention to it will make it pay richly.

There is a species of bug that is eating up the leaves of the oak trees which kills the trees.

The Urbana chaps have elected their major general, I understand. His name is Fife. He is a West Point graduate, I understand. The election, however, is going to be contested by H.W. Smith of London, who was an opposing candidate in the election. I am in hopes that we may get the general here or in Clark County so we will not have to leave the county to drill at any time. We will have some forty members in full uniform on the 4th, which will make quite a company.

They are going to have a camp meeting down near Newport this fall. I must be on hands and see what I can see. Camp meetings are a pretty good institution. There is, however, about as much harm as good done generally at camp meetings.

[Thursday] July 30th, A.D. 1857

. . . Jas. Melvin has enlisted in the United States army. They say he was very loth to go after he enlisted. Someone said that they tied him before they could take him. He is now at the Jefferson Barracks in Missouri. . . . He must go for five years.

Henry and Allen have got a job on the Glade of a Mrs. Gregg, who is an elderly widow woman. Her son Thomas lives with her and a girl they call "Minny," who came from the poorhouse, I understand. She has the scald head, I know, and is not good looking other ways.

I heard from W.T. Cobaugh the other day. He is up in Union County working for Ben Glascoe. They say that he has taken to drink pretty hard, and of course he is not doing much good if that be the case. . . .

I have been working for Henry and Allen at 20 dollars per month. They paid me up the other day for the work that I done for them over a half month. They are going to devote their time to the carpenter business hereafter, they say. They talk some of going to Illinois this fall. . . . I rather think they will not get off.

[Sunday] August 9th, A.D. 1857

. . . I have been mowing for the last week for Joshua Rankin. S.D. Truitt and myself have a small job over there of sixteen acres of light grass. We are to get eighty five cts. per acre for cutting it, board in the bargain. We cut about three acres and three quarters each day. Joshua is a fine sort of a man and . . . has a very fine kind of a wife, as lively as a cricket, but she is in poor health at this time. There is one Mag Heath there at this time who is a regular captain. She can squeal equal to a locomotive and is as full of devilment as an egg is of meat. She has been throwing out some of her bait for S.D., and I am of the opinion that he will bite at it yet. Her virtue may be of a solid kind, yet I am inclined to doubt it a little. Allen Anderson says that he is acquainted with her and that she is not overscrupulous in her virtue. I will not say, however, that she is actually an intrigueing vestal of Venus but let her pass. . . .

Henry and Allen have finished the widow Greggs house and have received nearly all the money for the same. They are up here at this time and also out of a job. . . .

Our neighborhood has been in a state of mental excitement only equalled by the comet, all on account of some Egyptian fortunetellers. They have told several persons fate, past, present, and to come. S. Saunders, Wm. B. Todd, and all the rest of the boys that were in the neighborhood have had their fortunes told. They [the Gypsies] have left for parts unknown. . . .

The Madison Guards had a drill on the 1st of this month. We had quite a time. We shot at a target. A man by the name of Acton made the best shots on the board. We also elected a first lieutenant. Dick Florence got that office and only came out two votes ahead, not much to brag of, sure. There were quite a number of corporals, adjutants, etc. elected. . . .

Camp meeting is going to be held on Darby to commence next week. I want to go if possible just to see the lions and have a kind of a spree.

I had a most an infernal time last night in London along with S.D. Truitt, Cyrus Hornbeck, and Pat Divine. I never drink anything stronger than wine and rarely that. I am therefore weak in the head when it comes to drinking any kind of wine whatever. Cyrus Hornbeck was as blue as an indigo bag. I drank three glass of wine, not thinking that it would do me any harm, but the first thing I knew I got my dose. I got into Divines buggy and went home with him and stayed until morning. Doc lost his horse and was in a fair way to pass the night in the woods when some of the folks found him and hauled him home. I am heartily ashamed of the part that I acted in last nights scenes, and I do hope that I may never be caught in the same fix again, and I do think that I will not. I do despise anyone that will make a beast of themselves. Still, I find it hard to withstand temptation. Some of the wine that I drank must have been mixed, as it was not the quantity that made me feel it, I am sure. I was most infernal sick all the time until I got to bed, & then I immediately felt better.

Experience teaches a dear school, but fools will learn in no other. I am henceforth done with wine and will try and keep the debasing stuff out of my mouth hereafter.

The weather is awful warm since the rain. I am sitting upstairs writing at a window, and I am sweating like a horse, or worse than a horse. The road is flooded with water.

S. Saunders was here this morning. He went to Somerford to see about a wagon that he has a man making for him there. The Gipsies told Semp that he was to be married twice & that he was to have six children & that he was to pull up stakes and go west before 17 months & that he was to be wealthy and all good things were to attend him. Bill Todd sold his horse to them. He got about 18 dollars for him. There was something the matter with his back. He would sink right down in the middle of the road with no load on his back.

[Thursday] August 20th, A.D. 1857
. . . This is the last day of another year of my life. Tomorrow I will be twenty four years of age. I have been an aimless creature; nearly one fourth of a century gone and nothing done. Still, the morning shines as gloriously & all nature looks as smilingly as when I first opened my eyes to the light of this world.

I have got through harvesting and I am glad of it.

Camp meeting has came and went since I last wrote in this book. I went down with Nat. Norris & Henry. We had some pretty especial times down there. There were more gamblers than preachers, more whiskey than religion, more rowdyism than shouting, more swearing than praying, more drunkenness than psalms, more fighting than kissing, more hard names given than good thoughts spoken, and more hearts pained than sinners awakened at this very same camp meeting.

We went to London in the morning and stayed until near one o'clock, when we got into the omnibus owned by G.W. Lock. Fare, fifty cents. Passengers: Nat. Norris, Mr. Bell, Geo. O'Brien, Mrs. Sutton & son, a Methodist minister, Henry, & myself. The preacher told some pretty stiff yarns. Mrs. Sutton descanted some upon the scenery. Mr. Bell & myself had a good time generally. We arrived at the camp meeting without any serious accident. The boys upon the top were rather inclined to be merry. We upon the inside were more disposed to be grave. Nat Norris & Henry danced some on the steps behind just as we went into the camp, which was not much relished by the preacher.

After arriving upon the ground we hunted up our acquaintances and inquired after their healths and where the best sight for fun was to be had. Nat soon found "Sorrel" and made a draw upon her. In fact he drew particularly heavy upon that venerable animal. She kicked him so hard that he had to lay down, overcome by his spiritual feelings. He heaved up his accounts most wonderfully. Well, he was not alone in that line.

Dan Wilson and a host of others were, even in the midst of the host of Israel, doing the same thing. Nat & Dan Wilson had a few words but not any fight. Henry kept them apart and made peace. Henry and someone else had a quarrel & Nat helped him out of that. Dan Wilson got into a muss and got a bran splinter new coat all tore to mash.

Sunday morning came in pretty gloomy. It rained on Saturday evening and we had an awful time to get to sleep. They had a union tent for strangers to sleep in. They said it was intended to & built for nice young men to sleep in. Instead of that nearly [all] those that were in there were drunk and noisey. There was one chap that made more noise than all the rest. He just sung and swore and blackguarded his very best until midnight. His name was Hann. I saw him stretched next morning on a brush heap. Nat was amon[g]st the slain next morning. There was a chap named Henry Nigh that got very much spiritualized & lost his money, consisting of some twenty two dollars. He was taken to a union tent where he just cursed and raved until all the preachers got around and pacified him. They sent him off, when we had some peace. Nigh got his money next day.

There were some gamblers on the ground who were throwing chuck-a-luck. I made some bets, and of course I lost. Well, sometimes I won but the losses overballanced the gains. Semp pitched into the chucker luck and lost two dollars. Nat Norris was more luckey. He made two dollars and jumped the game.

. . . We stayed until Sunday at the camp untill we had exhausted all our physical powers. We saw "Sorrel," fought the "Tiger," laid on straw, lived on bologna and chicken and crackers. We saw the flaunting city belle & the homespun country girl with rosy cheeks and happy faces. We saw the roue & the class leader, the dramseller & the deacon, the beardless boy and the hoary headed sire, the aging matron and the romping girl. All, all there: the painted smirk of a long face & the stupid, stolid look of the drunkard; the horn of the preacher mingling with that of the "buss" driver. The painted prostitute flaunts past the innocent country girl. The jaded country boy lays down by the side of the city blackleg. Life is there seen in all its phases. I live and learn every day in such a place.

We left the camp ground on Sunday night at the hour of ten. A merrier set never got into an omnibus than what we were. Song after song was sung and one after another treated to a kick from Sorrel. We got to Jeff[erson] near the hour of eleven. Some of the boys went to the haymow. Nat, Henry, & I went to B. Mantles hotel and got a bed. . . . Nat & I stayed until twelve o'clock, when we came up on the train. . . . I am at home from camp meeting minus nine dollars. . . .

I had my fortune told some time since by one of those godforsaken people called Gypsies.

Scene: big road.

Time: after night.

Actors: a woman with young child, two dozen other humans seated around a fire cooking.

Scenery: four wagons, eight or ten very lean horses, fence covered with sheets newly washed; dogs, pans, and various other kitchen utensils filled out the picture.

Country boy in ragged pants approaches.

Boy: Good evening, folks.

Old man: Good evening, sir.

Boy: Traveling, I see.

O[ld] Man: Yes, sir.

Woman: Would you like to have your fortune told?

Boy hesitates, says he dont know but what he would. Preliminaries settled, goes out to one side of the road. Woman takes the boy by the hand, asks for his knife; tells him not to be afraid, she wont cut his throat.

Woman commences telling his fortune after going over some Hebrew or other gibberish unknown to anyone now living. She commenced as:

Woman: Young man, you have some enemies and some friends. You have been in the West & was sick. Your first love was a greater evil to you than good. You were more vexed than pleased with her. You have thought some of going west. Bad fortune will follow you if you go there. You have two enemies, John & Bill; & Henry. You will be rich. Your dark days are over. You will be married twice, have 6 children. You can marry your present sweetheart if you wish. She has been much persuaded against you by her friends. She has dark hair. You are not long from your sweetheart. You are to marry against Christmas. Your days of trouble are over. Your good days are to come. You have two girls in your mind at this time. One has light hair. You can marry either of them if you wish.

Goodby, book. This is the last scratch I can make in thee. I must here close thy lids. I must here make my last crow track.

Finesse. The end. John M. Roberts.

7

Bachelor Teacher in the Brush
August 21-November 18, 1858

The chapter begins on John Roberts's twenty-fifth birthday. He has bought a big journal that he says will require "herculean" efforts to fill, and he will spend the next half century and more writing in its pages. After the events and thoughts that comprise this chapter and the next, the journal consists mainly of birthday annals in which he reflects on the past year and lists his acquaintances who have "joined the great silent majority." During the three months covered in this chapter, Roberts opens an account of his principal occupation for the next quarter century. He had supplemented his intermittent schooling by attending a short teacher-training course in Lebanon, Ohio, in one of the "normal" schools that Horace Mann had crusaded for.

"Keeping bach"—living as a bachelor—with young James McCabe, and later with his brother Henry, in an abandoned school-house, Roberts tells of their adventures with local girls, and of his more serious interest in Emarine Truitt on his weekend visits to Oak Run. The "hearty buxom lasses" of the Brush attract him, but he shows his annoyance at their "tittle tattle" about him, some of which reaches the ears of his "inamorata" back on Oak Run.

Roberts's "scholars" in the schoolroom, the rustic folk of the "A[r]cadian bowers of simplicity" around the villages of Mount Sterling and Palestine, and his companions in Brush Club debates, give him an excellent opportunity to engage in his pastime of studying human nature.

[Saturday] August 21st, A.D. 1858

Today I must pass another milestone on the great road of life. I am twenty five years of age today and have not yet filled my mission in life.

. . . I find that the most of my air castles are gone and gone forever, but the pleasure they have afforded me has more than ballanced the disappointment caused by their fall. I have just as good prospects before me now as I ever had in my life. I have six months work engaged at pretty good wages, and my health is good enough. I am out of debt in a measure, and I think that my life is in a fair way to glide smoothly and peacefully along for some time to come. As for love scrapes & amours, I am about as free as anyone else and perhaps more so. But there is no telling how long this boasted freedom may last. Perhaps a few short weeks may find me a worshiper at the shrine of Venus.

My head is getting to be a little on the bald order, but then a wig can make up that deficiency, and then old age is honorable, or should be so. My teeth are good yet, so there is still some bite about me yet. . . .

I have been idling my time away for some time past, but I have engaged to teach a school in the southeastern part of the county about three miles from Palestine and five miles from Mt. Sterling. . . . I am to get twenty five dollars per month and board myself. It is a little too low but I must either do this or do nothing. I am going to keep bach along with G.W. Saunders & Jas. McCabe. I have rented an old schoolhouse to set up in. It is a pretty snug kind of a house, and we will have a good time in it. I am to teach sixty days for a quarter, which is a shorter time than I have been used to and will make the wage more than if I taught 13 weeks.

Jas. H. Roberts is at Lebanon attending the short session of the Normal. . . . Uncle Jas. H. has been studying shorthand phonography this term. I wish that I understood the science. I am going to study it some this winter and see if I cant make more progress than I did last winter. I will have an excellent chance to study this winter, as I will be by myself and have no one to bother me. I am going to lay off my study hours in a regular order & have my programme posted up in my room. I am going to school next summer if I possibly can do so, as I want to be so that I shall not be anyways alarmed about getting a certificate to teach any kind of school whatever.

I have come to the conclusion that tobacco is hurting me and enfeebling my mental and physical powers more than any other thing. I am pretty sure that I have pains in my breast on account of chewing, & I think that I might as well declare my independence today. . . . I have made so many promises about tobacco that I am almost afraid to promise myself or make any more vows concerning the vile weed. I will, however, make one more trial and see the results. I will not take into my mouth another chew of tobacco for the next year unless compelled to do so for the toothache or cankered mouth or some serious matter of that kind, and I moreover promise that I will not make a practice of smoking a pipe or cigar, and that my pocket shall not be polluted with tobacco bought for my own private use, and that I will not smoke more than three pipes per week nor more than three cigars during the same time; & that even this shall only be when in company, & I do most solemnly promise that if I should smoke more than the above mentioned number

Journal August 21st A.D. 1858

To day I must pass another milestone on the great road of Life, I am twenty five years of age to day and have not yet filled my mission in life, I do not feel very well to day. I have been about half sick for more than a week, I find that the most of my air castles are gone and gone forever, but the pleasure they have afforded me has more than ballanced the disappointment caused by their fall, I have just as good prospects before me now as I ever had in my life I have six mon= s work engaged at pretty good wages, and my health is good enough, I am out of debt in a measure and I think that my life is in a fair way to glide smoothly and peacefully along for some time to come As for love scrapes & amours; I am about as free as any one else and perhaps more so ", but there is no telling how long this boa= ted freedom may last perhaps a few short weeks may find me a worshiper at the Shrine of Venus, My head is getting to be a little on the bald order but then a wig can make up that deficiency and then old age is honorable or should be so, My teeth are good yet so there is still some bite about me yet I do not know what may become of me yet still I hope for the best and twill try and bear my blushing honors mee kly if I should be fortunate enough to merit any, & if disgrace should be my lot I will try and cultivate a patient & humble spirit; I must however still keep my head above water and make the most of my privileges, be they what they may

Writing with unusual care, John Roberts begins his second big book on his twenty-fifth birthday. [Saturday] August 21st, A.D. 1858.

of pipes or segars in one week that I will desist entirely from the practice for three weeks, and if I break over after the 3d time, I will quit forever and aye under a solemn oath.

Jacob Davis has rented the mill & seems to think that he is the best miller that ever was in a mill since mills came into fashion. He is, however, like some other men that seem to know more than everyone else that have preceeded them in the same business. I begin to hear of a great many bad baches [batches] of flour that he has made here of late.

. . . Uncle Jake is a queer kind of a genius. He is terribly set in his way, in temporal as well as spiritual matters. He never has had any children, and of course as a man begins to get as old as he is, he is not as clear brained about everything that pertains to business as a man that has had the management of children & knows more of human nature.

Aunt Betsy is more of an oddity than Uncle Jake. She talks as much like a Guinea negro as any white person can talk & is as ignorant as a horse and most wofully superstitious. She is as blunt in her speech as a Billingsgate fish woman and is as insulting an old creature at times as anyone could find in any country. She has a dog that she thinks more of than anything else. She has a big round pair of shoulders, gimlet eyes, and a wabbling walk, and a tongue ready to take up any slander. . . .

The crops have went beyond everyones expectations, especially the corn crop. I think that we will have more corn this year than we had last, that is, more good sound corn. Charlies corn looks very well for the season & the ground. He may raise some 15 bushels to the acre. I did not think when he planted it that he would raise any corn at all on it. The melon crop is not quite as good this year as it was last. Wesley Allen has a patch, but it has not done very well, not half as well as it done last year. S. Saunders has a good patch and will have as many melons as anyone that I know of around here. They have a large patch of two or 3 acres.

. . . Somerford has been pretty well governed for some time past. T. Paice has been put in durance vile and also bailed out again. His case will come off in the fall term of the common pleas court. Liquor selling was his crime & it was well proven against him. He has acted very decent since that time & will not sell any more liquor, I suppose, until after court anyhow. A.J. Clingan has a grocery over there. He has liquors and keeps a wet grocery. He may get snatched over the coals yet some of these days for his misdemeanors. . . .

I was at a camp meeting on the sixth of this month & stayed several days. I went on Friday and come home on the next Monday following. There was considerable excitement on the ground, mental, moral, & physical. As far as the church was concerned, I heard of no one joining but saw some shouting in the camp and heard some very long prayers from some of the brethren & sisters in the camp. As far as whiskey was concerned, I saw an innumerable host of bottles and runners to and from the same. Every tree in the woods seemed to be haunted by some spirit. The most of these spirits were under the guardianship of some Greeks who passed the cup containing the same to the denizens of the camp, who thirsted for the spirit & were bitten at the rate of 5 cts. a pop. I saw more men drunk there than I had seen during the year. . . .

Venus, too, had quite an immense number of devotees, quite as many as Bacchus & perhaps a few more. She was well supplied with priestesses, who devoted themselves to the sacrifices with a zeal worthy of a better cause. The woods were lined with shameless courtezans, who made more money than anyone else on the ground. Gambling was practiced some but not as much as in former years. The whiskey and the women seemed to be the chief attraction.

I do not know whether there will be any camp meetings there next season. . . . If so I must go again & see what the play will be on the next occasion. I like to go to camp meetings to study human nature.

I intend to keep this book always on hand so that I can record all my transactions in it, with such reflections as may strike my mind from time to time. . . . This is the largest blank book that I have ever attempted to fill, & it looks like a herculean task to try to do so now; yet if I am left in this unfriendly world for the space of another year, I shall have it pretty well filled up, I think. I have a small pocket diary that I intend to keep a daily record of my wanderings in until it becomes full. I will thus be able to have the dates of all my transactions at hand for reference at any time.

Henry & William Anderson are working for Lancisco Peck building a kitchen and barn for him. Bill has been at C. Cliftons all summer, and of course he is not rich nor indeed can he be if he stays there. Henry had his tool chest brought up from Darby by Charlie, who was there yesterday. . . .

Miss Ree Wallace has been teaching the Oak Run school this summer & will teach two mos. this fall commencing on the last Monday of this month. She gets fourteen dollars a month and boards amongst the scholars. She makes a very good teacher, and I suppose she would make just as good a wife for some man. If I thought I was good looking enough, I do not know but what I might pitch in myself & see how my ticket stood with her. But as for me, I have given up all idea of marriage and must fight the battle of life alone, I think, unless I see some good chance to make an advantageous settlement in life. I am of the opinion, however, that Oak Run will furnish as many old maids and old bachelors as any other neck of woods the same size in the county.

Miss E[marine] Truitt will soon be upon the stage of action again, full of life and tales of western scenes. I have wondered why it was that she did not marry in the West. It was perhaps because she could not do as well as she wished. I understand that Handy [Truitt] started for Ohio on the 13th inst., and if this is the case he will be here next week sometime. The folks try to nig [tease?] me over her new advent, but I am thinking that her triumph will not come up to their expectations, although the heart of man is changeable and full of notions. But I shall not forestall the events. Let the worst come. I am armed to suffer & will meet the enemy with a bold front and a valiant heart. I understand that she said that I should have shed quite a quantity of tears over her departure and made many sorrowful prophecies for the future. Well, deception is womans name & may be mine too. Who knows?

Aug. 30th, 1858—Monday

Today I find myself in a schoolroom and doing business. I have but a very few pupils to commence with and will have a dull day of it, I am afraid. Still, I intend to go on & do the best I can for my charge, and perhaps I may be rewarded by seeing a decided improvement in the minds of my pupils. I like the looks of this place very well. There seems to be a very good spirit prevailing here, and I am sure that there is not much pride or aristocracy here, which is a thing that just suits me and will make my stay here agreeable and pleasant, more so than if there was a contrary spirit manifested by the people here.

I had a visitor a little while ago, Miss Stone. She is a very lively girl . . . and pretty intelligent, I should think. . . .

I wrote a letter to Semp Saunders today which I must put into the P.O. at Palestine tonight or have it done tomorrow if possible. . . .

Mr. Oglesbee gave me my orders this morning along with the key to the temple. He wants no night schools of any kind without it is an arithmetic school. He is down on spelling schools and meetings of every sort being held in the schoolhouse, and I am of the opinion that he is about right, on that point anyhow.

Tuesday, Aug. 31st, [1858]

. . . We have no broom to sweep the house nor bucket to carry water in, but I think we shall have both of these necessary articles before long. I hope so at least, as I am not in favor of sitting down in the dirt and dust.

I was at Palestine yesterday evening after school. It was a pretty long walk for me. Still, I made the distance in about 2-1/4 hours. I did not stay long in the village, as I could not see or hear anything to interest a man in it. The town is a poor excuse, I understand, and the country around would not miss it much if it were entirely shut up and banished from the neighborhood. They have two or three doggeries in it that are doing a great deal of mischief to the citizens and inhabitants. . . .

The folks here are very busy getting out timber for a new meeting house which they are going to build this fall and winter. Gould of London is the builder.

Wednesday, September 1st, 1858

I am decidedly out of sorts today and feel as much like a stewed witch as can be. I had a severe spell of the cholera morbus last night which makes me feel lank today. I heaved up an awful quantity of bilious matter and could not sleep much, so I feel weak and sleepy both today. I ate no breakfast this morning and but a very few bites of dinner. My stomach has been very tender all day, and I may have another siege of puking tonight.

I was at a prayer meeting at the Murphey schoolhouse last night. There was quite a crowd of the feminine gender there. This place is great for the number of its girls. All sorts, sizes, kind, & characters can be found in these brush, so I understand.

I have not many pupils as yet. One Miss Ree J. Thornton is here today or was here this forenoon. Miss Mary J. Stone was here awhile ago. She looks like a very clever kind of a girl. She looks somewhat careworn & seems to be kind of restless, as though she had something weighing upon her mind. I like her looks as well as any girl that I have seen in the brush. . . .

Thursday, Sept. 2d, 1858

. . . I have about fifteen pupils today. I am somewhat afraid that there is not a very regular attendance here in this district. I must try and remedy this if I can, as I am sure that it is one of the worst things we as teachers have to contend with. People never know the trials of temper & patience that teachers have to undergo on this account. Irregular attendance is a very prevalent thing everywhere, and I would be glad if someone would suggest a remedy for the evil that could be enforced by the teacher.

Mr. Smith was up at London yesterday with a load of wheat. He says that wheat is down to 80 cents per bushel. He got me some chalk pencils for marking on the blackboard. . . . I am in want of a broom & a bucket. I had to borrow a bucket every day this week.

I think that I shall go up home tomorrow and come down again on Saturday with my kit of bed clothes & traps to set up with.

The school hours are getting to go off more pleasantly than they did at first. If I only had about 25 scholars I should like it much better. . . .

Friday, Sept. 3d, 1858

. . . I was at the Douglas schoolhouse to a singing school last night and had quite a good time. They succeeded in getting up a class to be held for 13 Sundays, which will reach beyond my time of sojourn here in the brush. There were a great many young ladies in attendance. They appeared to be very mute & silent. I have not got acquainted with many of them yet. I like the appearance of some of them very well. They appear to have the rose tint of health and the bounding step of youth.

I was also to see a new married couple at a Mr. Lanes. . . . I understand that some of the boys cut the bed cord whilst I was there. If so, they must have come down upon the floor before morning. . . .

Monday, Sept. 6th, A.D. 1858

. . . I moved down on Saturday evening. I had an awful time going up home on last Friday evening. The roads were very slippery & bad on account of the rain that had fallen in the forenoon & also that fell in the afternoon. I, however, reached Saunders plantation just ten minutes before sundown. I stayed in London about a half an hour, which set me back some. . . .

Handy Truitt is again in the Buckeye state. He came back on last Thursday & had been about 11 days on the road. I saw none of them except Miss Emarine & Miss Caroline, who were at Mr. L. Pecks washing. They seemed to be enjoying themselves & looked just about like they always have; a little of the Illinois bleach, however, is perceptable. I think some of going up there next Saturday week.

G.W. Saunders has backed clear down the grade & will not come [here] at all. Jas. McCabe is with me, however, so I am not alone amidst the jeers of an inconstant world. Jas. McCabe is setting to rights today about the house and will not be to school until tomorrow. I think that we will have a good time of it here. We did not get here until nearly 11 o'clock on Saturday night. . . . C.C. Roberts brought us down in Mothers buggy, Mother not being willing to let her team come down. C.C. is sowing wheat & breaking up ground at this time.

Tuesday, Sept. 7th, A.D. 1858

. . . We are getting along amazingly well keeping "bach." I was at Miss Oglesbee's this morning to see about getting a couple of sacks made to hold our meal & flour & also to see if we could not prevail on them to bake some light bread. They are a couple of old maids that seem to be everybodies aunts, good, clever, old fashioned, hard working folks of the old school who are streaks of sunshine in any neighborhood & do a vast amount of good to the world in their peculiar way. . . .

James & I went on a pilgrimage to Palestine, not upon a religious mission but for something to enlighten our dwelling and also a vessel to hold water. This Palestine is not the Holy Land we read about, but there is enough of the spirit of *Darkness* there to make it the opposite of a Holy Land. Intemperance is an evil of no small magnitude at that place.

Wednesday, Sept. 8th, A.D. 1858

. . . I begin to feel more at home now than I did when I first entered this part of the moral heritage. I am getting more into the hang of the customs of the people. Some of them are very clever, and in fact I have met with nothing but kindness since I have been here. I have got acquainted with two schoolmasters since I have been here: one by the name of Horrel and the other by the name of Brily. Mr. Horrel is not a teacher at this time but formerly was engaged in the business. He is a man about 30 years of age and also a bachelor. Mr. Briley is a young tyro in the business. His first efforts were in this district last winter. He is of a religious disposition and takes quite an active part in their prayer meetings at the Murphey schoolhouse, where he is teaching at this time. I was over there last night to a prayer meeting & saw several of the folks. One chap drew my hat over my eyes in a very abrupt manner, but he apologized by saying that he mistook me for another person. I did not relish the proceeding very well.

Mr. King proposed that we should have a debate at my house on next Friday evening. Mr. Horrel said that he would come and bring two or three others, so I guess that we will have a little bit of a spout on that night if nothing happens.

Thursday, Sept. 9th, A.D. 1858

I feel a little nervous this morning oweing to the influence of that vile narcotic called tobacco. It seems curious that a man will persist in a practice that he knows is injurious to him, but so it is & so it will continue to be until the end of time, I suppose, as I have seen men drink whiskey and curse it at the same time.

The world still wags here as usual, some marrying and some are separating. However, the separating process seems to be in the ascendant here at this time. . . . One case of separation was that of a Mr. Chan Tuttle & his cara sposa. They have not been married more than 6 months. His madame was not a very strict adherent to the conventionalities of unmarried life before she was united to Tuttle, as she had four or five children outside the pale of matrimony. The other case was that of a Mr. Riddle and his wife. The quarrel originated about two pairs of shoes and some calico that Madame Riddle purchased without the consent of her *caro*. The shoes were for another person. She went upon tick so long that it came at last to striking. Grass widows will be a plentiful commodity if they keep on at this rate. . . .

Friday, Sept. 10th, A.D. 1858

My school still grows more and more interesting every day, and I am getting to like the place better & better. Mr. Oglesbee was here this morning. He brought me a new pail and tin cup. The broom, however, is not on hand as yet, and I am afraid that it will not be. I am of the opinion that they do not take an interest in their school here that they ought. . . .

Jim wants to go home tomorrow to buy him a new tile, as the headgear that he now has is getting to be a little on the fragmentary order. He is getting along finely and will make this quarters schooling pay him very well, I think, as he seems to enter upon his studies with a will & a vigor equal to the emergency. I hope sincerely that he may make it pay, as he is now at the turning point in life and will make either a hard case or a good citizen. He is a person of good principles and a kindly, generous nature and has a bright future before him if he will only take hold of it and use it right. . . .

I must take more pains with the grammatical part of my composition in this book, as I find that there are some very broad mistakes & glaring errors in it that I overlooked while I was writing. . . .

Tuesday, Sept. 14th, A.D. 1858

. . . I was down below Palestine on Saturday with Wm. Anderson. We had a special good time, long to be remembered by those that participated in it.

James McCabe went up to Saunders & brought down their bell, which comes in very good play. He also brought down a small toilet glass, a thing that we needed very much, as we were in danger of forgetting how our mugs looked and could not tell whether we were presentable or not.

I had four or five new pupils yesterday, two Miss Douglas'es, Aaron Oglesbee, & Marion Douglas. I got my daily register straightened up yesterday. They had promised to furnish me with a book but did not do so, and so I had to furnish one myself to keep my register upon. . . .

Saunders boys have sold one load of melons in London. They got nineteen dollars for it. They will have about fourteen hundred melons.

Those at 10 cts. apiece will bring in a good pile of money. Theodore Smith is at work for them at this time, and I suppose he will work for them until winter sets in. I think that I shall try and get a room in their house this summer to board myself in. There are a great many things in this system of self boarding that I like. . . .

Wednesday, Sept. 15th, A.D. 1858
    . . . My days are passing smoothly and pleasantly down the stream of life. I feel pretty well in physical health, and my mind is not troubled with far off fears or flattered by delusive hopes. My amours are all in a favorable situation, but why should a man trust his happiness to the capricious fancy of a woman, whose mind will turn like the tide? Still, the love of a constant, pure, and faithful woman is something that is of very great importance to mankind, and I think that there are some of that description left in the world, and when I meet with one of this description I will pitch in. I must, however, be fully convinced that I have found the genuine article. Still, we must not expect to find perfection in earth born mortals here below the skies.
    There is a considerable amount of sickness here in this neighborhood at this time. One of my smallest scholars had to leave this morning on account of the sickness of his mother, who has something like the flux.
    Tonight some of the boys are coming to my house to have a debate. The question to be debated is that of intemperance and African slavery. I hope that we may make some headway at the organizing of a debating club, as there is a good deal to be learned from this kind of an organization. There are not very many good speakers in this part of the country.

Thursday, Sept. 16th, A.D. 1858
    I have almost run out of something to write, as all the neighborhood topics have been exhausted and there is no chance to hear from any other part of the moral vineyard, as the communication between this and every other place is very irregular & uncertain, kept up by the folks that go to the mill and the grocery. I would not like to have to live here the remainder of my days. There is not enough excitement here. . . . Still, there are some features in this place that I like. There is a simplicity & a frankness about the manners of the people that I always did like. . . . There are no family quarrels to excite the minds of the peaceful inhabitants, no drunken Irishmen & Dutchmen to fight, nor gamblers to strip the young sprouts of their spare change. So the times are dull.

Friday, Sept. 17th, A.D. 1858

. . . I had about 22 pupils all told yesterday besides a visitor, Miss Mary Stone, who stayed here from the morning till noon. She is a pretty good reader and has a pretty good intellect, with a robust constitution, a model of perfect health. There is a kind of wild abandon and artless naivette about her that rather pleases me. Always give me a country romp in preference to a town flirt. These artificial women I do not like. There is too much stiffness about them. They have too much starch and crinoline to suit me.

I understand that Miss Hannah Smith has changed her name to Brown. . . . I heard a lot of bells & horns down there last night which were making night hideous with their din.

I am going to be in the shades of Oak Run tonight ere the clock shall tell the hour of twelve, and then tomorrow I must see Miss E.T. But that is all the good it will do, I am thinking. I suppose people will soon have it that I am going to make a benedict of myself. Well, let them talk. . . .

Monday, Sept. 20th, A.D. 1858

. . . I had a very pleasant time up at home during Saturday, Sunday, & part of Friday night. The hours flew by on lightning wings, the smiles of friends were propitious, and good health and good cheer seemed to be everywhere prevailing; and long may it continue to be so is my earnest wish and prayer.

I paid H. Truitts a visit. They all seemed to be in pretty good spirits and seemed to be the same kind of folks that they always were. They have found that all is not gold that glitters and that distance lends enchantment to the West. They thought that I was exaggerating when I told them about the western prairies, but now they are convinced that these tales are painful realities. I could curse those wide spreading prairies heartily and sincerely, & I am sure that there are thousands of poor mortals who are suffering out their three score years with quaking and burning of fevers & the twinging of the rheumatizm who could heartily curse the day that they were first tempted to leave a comfortable country for those delusive prairies that delude a man with the prospects of ease and plenty.

I am not prepared to say whether my future prospects in the hymeneal line are to be, but I still live in hopes that my ticket will turn out O.K. . . .

Tuesday, Sept. 21st, A.D. 1858

. . . My school is progressing finely at this time & is getting to be a little interesting to me, more so than I at first anticipated. The recitations are not, however, as thorough as I could wish. Still, however, they are improving rapidly. I have some fun sometimes. Last night I had two or three of my large spelling class upon the floor studying a poorly recited lesson. Amongst the number was Jas. McCabe. I thought that it bored him somewhat.

We went up to Mr. Wm. Stones last night with some washing and met with a very kind reception from the old lady. . . .

I saw Uncle Jas. H. when I was up at home. He has engaged a winter school of six months at the Turkey Run schoolhouse 8 miles east of London. He talks of teaching six months at 30 dollars per month. He is going to move there this fall if he teaches that long.

Wednesday, Sept. 22d, A.D. 1858

. . . Last night I was at the Murphey schoolhouse to a prayer meeting. There was not a very large congregation there, and the chief actors and workers were the last to appear. I saw Mr. Jas. Horrel & Mr. B. Brily. Mr. Horrel is a teacher of the ancient regime who has made his cake at teaching & has retired from the profession. . . . There is a fund of good, practical, sound common sense about him that I like. He is not too forward nor too unassuming. Briley is a young hand at the bellows and seems to be a clever, good natured soul with not quite enough moral & mental force to make a thorough teacher. He will never follow the business long.

I saw Miss Mary Stone at Mrs. Tuttles last evening along with the two Miss Douglases. I must study her character some, as I think she is a good subject to investigate; she has one of those mercurial dispositions that seem to infuse a new life into the surrounding company, a vivacity, a bounding of the blood that creates a smile of pleasure upon the face of the most confirmed hypochondriac. I am afraid that I am getting to be enthusiastic on this subject, but who does not feel a glow when he comes in contact with a gleam of sunshine? . . .

Thursday, Sept. 23d, A.D. 1858

. . . We had quite a debate last night at our house. Messrs. Horrel, Jones, Briley, King, Davidson, & myself were engaged in the discussion question, Resolved that the intemperate use of ardent spirits has been & is a greater evil than African slavery. Messrs. Davidson, Jones, & myself on the affirmative; Messrs. Briley, Horrel, and King on the negative; Messrs. King, Jun., P. Long, & Brown judges. Decision in favor of the affirmative. After moving to have the society organized and a question adopted for the next evening, the society adjourned to meet on next Wednesday evening. Question for the next discussion, Resolved that

Christopher Columbus deserves more praise for discovering America than George Washington for defending it.

I do not think that the speakers here are anything extra, not any better much than myself. . . . I think that when we once get fairly installed up in the Garrard schoolhouse that we will have a good time with our debates, as we have quite a number of boys up there that will pitch in. . . .

I got acquainted with one of the teachers in an adjoining district last night, Mr. Davidson by name. He is a good, clever, sober kind of an individual & I think that I shall like him very well. We had some visitors yesterday evening, Miss Stone and Miss Douglas. . . .

Friday, Sept. 24th, A.D. 1858

The morning is dark and gloomy. The wind whistles through the branches with a melancholy sound as though it were whistling requiems to departed hopes. The melancholy days have come, the season of sad musings and pensive wanderings. Still, there is a great serenity about the aspect of things that makes a sweet sadness steal over the heart and that drives the mind back over the bright scenes of other days.

I am about ready to take a violent fit of the blues. . . .

Monday, Sept. 27th, A.D. 1858

. . . Jas. & I went to Mt. Sterling and Palestine on last Saturday. They are a set of deadheads in both of those places. I could not find a solitary powder flask in either of those places.

We had a meeting here on Saturday, preaching by Mr. Reading. He is a Christian preacher, and I think he is a genuine Christian in character as well as in profession. I like his preaching very well. He preaches right along without making any hesitation, and what he says is generally to the point. However, he does not stick as close to the text as he might.

We had about 20 visitors on Sunday last & more perhaps than we shall have again on the same day. They were a jovial, rollicking set of chaps that take things as easy and good natured as the law will allow. I am getting to be most too well acquainted. I am not in favor of getting to[o] familiar, as I think that familiarity breeds contempt. . . .

Jas. McCabe is getting to have the sulks. He has been mad for the last 3 days. I do not know hardly what it is about, but I suppose that the storm will blow over without doing any damage or leaving any lasting effects. . . .

Tuesday, Sept. 28th, A.D. 1858

. . . My school is progressing finely. Some of the pupils are making a decided improvement, and I hope to see them come out more than conquerors on the good road up the hill of science. Some of my smaller pupils are taking quite an interest in their studies. I have offered no rewards of merit this term, and in fact I do not know as I shall ever adopt that plan again, as I think if a teacher can infuse the right kind of spirit into his pupils he will succeed better without rewards of merit.

Jas. McCabe is making slow but sure progress. He finds considerable difficulty in getting his spelling lesson. I think, however, that he will soon be able to comprehend the sounds of the letters so that he will be able to learn his lesson without much difficulty.

I had a couple of visitors last night, Mr. Jas. Horrel & Mr. Ben Briley. We got up a kind of a constitution for our lyceum. It is to be called the Brush Club. That is the name we settled upon as one that would be pertinent, short, and easy to understand. We had considerable chimney corner talk and kept it up untill about 1/4 past 9 o'clock. I found both of the . . . gentlemen to possess a considerable fund of useful knowledge & altogether quite interesting & instructive. We are to have our discussion on Thursday evening instead of on Wednesday as we intended. . . .

Wednesday, Sept. 29th, A.D. 1858

I do not feel overly well this morning. My nerves are a little unsteady, and my head is not as clear as it might be. I still indulge in tobacco and still feel the effects of it upon my system.

I was up at Mr. Stones last night and saw Miss Mary. She is sick with the chill and fever at this time. I got a novel of her to read called Mary Moreton, or The Broken Promise, by T.S. Arthur. It has been some time since I read any novels of any account, & I am in favor of breaking the monotony of ones course of reading by a perusal of some of the light literature of the day. But I am not in favor of an overdose of this kind of reading, as it blunts a mans appetite for the plainer but more solid reading of history & philosophy.

I find that even here in A[r]cadian bowers of simplicity the tongue of the slanderer is not altogether dormant and that the petty rivalries of an obscure neighborhood are very bitter and much more lasting than in those places where the communication with the great mass is much easier & quicker. The reasons for this are that the little family jars and jealous fits of a large place are lost in the bustle, hurry, and confusion of business & new objects so that the minds of the community are not able to hold them all at once. But in a smaller circle the case is different. The mind there has leisure to brood over and magnify such things, and they are brooded over by the people with a vengeance sometimes, as the whole neighborhood is at times in a perfect ferment about a mere trifle that ought not to have interested more than two persons.

Thursday, Sept. 30th, A.D. 1858
. . . My school is getting to be more interesting to me every day. . . . I think that I am winning the love of my pupils and that I shall have a kindly regard for me implanted in their young hearts. I do sincerely hope that it may be the case, as my heart always yearns for the friendship of youth. This is one reason why I love the teachers profession. I love to see the minds of children expanding, growing, & refining in the country, and although I am not as well qualified to give them the right kind of ideas as I should be, yet I feel like devoting my one talent to that noblest of professions, the training of the immortal mind.

There was a prayer meeting at the McKendree Chapel. Mr. Lane lead the meeting. He is a man of the old school and has been once engaged in teaching. He gave us quite an exhortation on the subject of religion. There was but a very meager attendance. One lady by the name of Kyle offered up a very sensible & appropriate prayer. There is an eloquence in prayer that I always love. The independence of the Supreme Architect is there manifested and shown by the attitude and the humble language generally adopted by the suppliant. Prayer is a healing balm to the weary soul & I think is the best evidence of Christianity that can be found.

Friday, October 1st, A.D. 1858
. . . We had a debate at our establishment last night. The question discussed was, Resolved that George Washington deserves more praise for defending America than Christopher Columbus for discovering it. Messrs. Robison & Brily on the affirmative & Mr. Horrell & myself on the negative. There being no judges chosen to make a decision, the sentiments of the house were taken. The affirmative seemed to have the good opinion of the majority. We also adopted a constitution. The name given to the society was the Brush Club. The society adjourned to meet at the Murphey schoolhouse on next Thursday evening at early candle lighting. The question to be discussed upon the next evening is, Resolved that there should be laws enacted for the prohibition of the sale of intoxicating liquors. Mr. Robison is the leading disputant on the affirmative & myself on the negative.

There was about 30 individuals out at the debate on last night, but a very few persons were willing to pitch in and go into the merits of the case & make speeches of their own. I gassed some myself upon the utility of such institutions, but not feeling in very good speaking order, my effort was not a very protracted or brilliant one nor very potent. . . .

Monday, October 4th, A.D. 1858
. . . I was at Mt. Sterling on Saturday and was also at Palestine. The business of both those towns is not very extensive. Forty or fifty thousand dollars ought to buy out both of those towns and fit them up a great deal better than they are at present. I was also at C.C. C[lifton's] and had a very good time as usual. . . .

I [was] down at Mr. Timmons'es yesterday and got acquainted with the folks somewhat. There are two very fine young ladies there, Miss Harriet & Amanda. Miss Harriet is a very intellectual looking girl, full [of] religious enthusiasm and fervor. She is the best looking girl that I have ever seen since I have been here and has a pair of sparkling eyes that illuminate and brighten her countenance with a fire that is truly refreshing. I must cultivate a close acquaintance with her, as she is a good subject for investigation.

There was two meetings here yesterday, but I was at neither one. I must try and go to the next one. . . .

Tuesday, October 5th, A.D. 1858
. . . Yesterday I had two new pupils that had not been here before, Miss Ruhamah A. Ward an[d] Louis Timmons. I also had three gentlemen visitors to see my school, Mr. E. Stone, Oglesbee, & Kittener. The last named gentleman is a stranger in this country. He is a kind of an exhorter and is a Pennsylvania Dutchman. Miss Ward is eighteen years of age and is rather handsome than otherwise. She is below the common size [and] of the nervous, sanguine temperament. She seems to take Jas. Mc's fancy. Nothing serious will result from the fancy of the young gent. Miss Thornton is here today. She has not been here before for more than a month.

I have nearly ran out of something to write about. There is nothing here to excite a mans mind. . . .

Wednesday, October 6th, A.D. 1858
This is the fall of the year, and all things are dropping sadly and silently on the ground. The farmers are all busily engaged in sowing wheat. The recent showers have moistened the ground so that they can plough. The ague, however, is shaking the handles of the plows from some of their hands. I am sometimes afraid that I may get it, but I am in hopes that I may escape it, as I am anxious to put in every moment of

time so that I can get out of debt and swim clear once more. I believe that my wages at this time would nearly clear me of debt, as I will have 37-1/2 dollars coming to me at the end of this week.

I was up to Mr. Stones last night along with Jas. Mc. We stayed untill eight o'clock and had quite a long chat with the folks. I must visit more around amongst the neighbors and get to be more acquainted with them, as I have met with a kind reception wherever I have been.

The scholars are getting along very well here at this time, and I am sorry that I must quit the place so soon, but the money call is stronger other places than here, and I must obey the call so that I can keep pace with the times, as money is the sinews of war. [R.C.] Messenger, my old chum at Lebanon, is getting $38-1/3 per month this winter for teaching in Preble County. I must strike for higher wages myself, as . . . I have been teaching entirely too cheap. However, I will teach too cheap rather than not to teach at all. My time will be out in 6 weeks from this week & then hio for home, there to stay.

Thursday, October 7th, A.D. 1858
. . . Miss Mary Stone was here yesterday. . . . She is of a very merry disposition, I think, but she must also be subject to the blues, terribly addicted to them, I should think.

I must try to make my passage through this quarter as smooth as possible, although I do not expect to see the place ever again . . . although I think that it is a pleasant place and that pleasant folks are in it. The most of the folks here are descendants of Marylanders, & therefore they have the red & white heads peculiar to the Swedes and Finns. The Swedes are a different people from the English. They are not so brave or so haughty as the Johnny Bulls, and they generally are devoid of the obesity of the Englishman. There is generally a vein of coarse humor in the Swede that is kind of refreshing, & the women are not very slow to crack a smutty joke now and then.

Tom Corwin spoke in Sterling yesterday.

Friday, October 8th, A.D. 1858
. . . Last night the Brush Club met at the Murphey schoolhouse. The society organized and elected officers. I was chosen president, J.M. Horrell secretary, J. Robison vice president, Jas. Anderson treasurer. We then went into a discussion on the question . . . , Resolved that a liquor law for the restriction of the sale of intoxicating liquors as a beverage is right and expedient. . . . Decision in favor of the affirmative. Question for the next discussion is, Resolved that it is expedient to annex Cuba to the United States. Society adjourned to meet at Utopian Hall on Tuesday

evening at early candle lighting. Jas. McCabe and I got home at half past 10 o'clock and we were tired enough. . . .

Jas. McCabe & myself are going up home this afternoon. We will have a good long walk of it & will be tired, sleepy, & hungry when we get there.

Monday, October 11th, A.D. 1858
. . . I had a good time up at home at this trip. I was at Saunders, Truitts, Somerford, & home. They are carrying on a singing school at the Garrard schoolhouse, D.J. Cartzdafner teacher. There was a large attendance, both of boys and girls. Miss E.T. was not home. I walked to & from the singing school with her sister, Miss Eliza.

Jas. McCabe came down on Saturday. He wants to find out the goodly fair of this neighborhood. He is getting to be quite a favorite among the fair sex. . . . He escorted Miss R.A. Ward from church last night. . . .

Uncle Jas. H. Roberts has moved down on Turkey Run. He is to teach five months at the Ray[?] s[chool]house at $30 per month and board himself. He has a snug schoolhouse to teach in. R.T. Polk is teaching at $2.00 per diem along with Miss Julia Hadley, who gets $1.12-1/2 per diem.

I have heard from the rest of the old set of Normalites that were there when I was there. I must send down my name and have it registered in the teachers exchange in the Normal.

Henry will finish Lance Pecks job this week. He then talks some of coming down here to school. . . .

Tuesday, October 12th, A.D. 1858
. . . I am getting tired of the tittle tattle of the talebearers of this part of the moral vineyard. They seem bound to draw Jas. Mc. & myself into their quarrels. Miss Margaret King & Miss Harriet Timmons, also Miss Mary Stone, have been telling one another some things that I should have said about them. Miss Timmons told Miss King that I should have told her that Miss Kings hands were so black that I was ashamed of my own, & also that Miss Stone should have told me that she had given Marion Strain the mitten sack, or his dismissal. That is, Miss King said that Miss Timmons said that I said all these things. Now, all that I have to say is that the whole of the above talk said to have been said by me has not the remotest foundation in the truth, as I have never said, thought, or done anything about these things. Miss Stone is perfectly infatuated about this Marion Strain, and of course this set her angry passions in motion. She asked me about these things yesterday. I must

see Miss Timmons and ask about these, also Miss King. This is the only drawback I find in this neighborhood. The women will tattle a little too much. They are all clever, kind, and good for aught I know, but they will let their long tongues run away with their prudence.

Election today. I must go and vote against Tho. Corwin, who is running for Congress.

Wednesday, October 13th, Anno Domini 1858

. . . I was yesterday at Mt. Sterling and at Palestine. I voted the Democratic ticket all but for auditor. I voted for O.P. Crabb, who was upon the Republican ticket, for auditor. There was no excitement in Mt. Sterling. No one was drunk, so we had no fights or quarrels, no horse races, or gambling of any kind. . . .

The Brush Club met last night and had quite an animated discussion. 2 questions were discussed. The first was, Resolved that lawyers have been a greater evil than doctors. Five or six new speakers were engaged in this question, mostly boys. Affirmative gained the question. The other question was the everlasting Cuba question, Horrell & myself in favor of annexation, Messrs. Robison & Defebaugh on the negative. The negative gained the question. . . . The next question for discussion is, Resolved that circumstances make the man in opposition to the old adage that a man is architect of his own fortune.

. . . I feel miserable today. I have a small touch of the blues. I believe I am nervous and weak and rather inclined to be peevish. Last night, however, I had pleasant dreams, dreams of love and reciprocal attachment. But why should a man trouble his mind about love? What does it amount to? Life is filled nearly full of vain delusions & empty bubbles, & love is one of them. . . . I feel a little better this afternoon. . . . The scholars are having a good time generally playing black man. . . .

Thursday, October 14th, A.D. 1858

This morning my spirits are good. I had a good sleep last night and dreamed very pleasant dreams. I dreamed of fishing in a clear, nice stream & that I caught the most as well as the nicest fish that were caught. I also dreamed of the ladies and that they smiled propitiously upon me. I have at length got rid of the depression of spirits that had weighed me down. . . .

Yesterday I had a visitor at my school, Mr. Jacob Stone. He stayed an hour or two in the forenoon and seemed to inspect my mode of teaching pretty closely. He has taught here in this neighborhood himself but is not much of a scholar. He sometimes exhorts a little in the Methodist Church.

. . . I am looking for Henry & John Peck to come down today or tomorrow. We will have a good time if they come down.

Wm. Anderson talks of marrying his old flame, Barbara C[lifton]. . . . It is to go off next Saturday week. . . .

I have for some time past been studying upon last winters religious excitement. Has it done any good? Has it improved the morals and increased the benevolence of the masses? Has it stopped the mouths of the slanderer and defamer of public virtue? That is the question. I am of the opinion that it has not in this neighborhood nor in my own. The excitement has died away, and the people have fallen back and are as wicked at heart as ever. . . . There is too much selfishness, too much pride in the religious denominations of the present day for them to prosper. They are too hard upon an erring brother or a frail sister. They should have more charity. . . .

Still, there has been a great deal of charity. Where there has been so much smoke there will be some fire, and this revival of religion has made the rude, outbreaking sinner a reproach and an unfashionable personage, and they have become more circumspect in their walk and conversation. . . .

Friday, October 15th, A.D. 1858

. . . Jas. Mc. & I went to Peter Longs. He got Peter to cut his hair. It makes Jas. Mc. look boyish to have his hair bobbed off. We stayed till eight o'clock & cracked jokes and eat apples. They are a jovial, ranting [trio of] old bachelors that live all alone and tend a pretty smart farm. They have more old traps and hen houses than would supply a small village. They have about twenty peafowls and as many geese as would save a hundred Roman cities. They have about forty beehives. They have been living in this way for some time and have waxed rich by their labor. They are of a German extraction & talk somewhat broken.

There are three brothers of them, viz., John, Jacob, & Peter. John is the youngest and has a game leg. He does the cooking and the housekeeping. Jacob works upon the farm, & Peter does a little at the blacksmithing business and makes ax helves [and] ox bows and is a general tinker of all works. They are fond of fun and whiskey. They are of the old school of men. Modern vices are not extensively practiced by them. They have quite a fund of anecdote and story of the early times of this country. . . . They live about 3/4 of a mile from here, right in the most out of way place they could possibly have chosen, as there are no public roads nor any way to get there hardly from any other place.

I am learning more and more of human nature every day. . . . Even here I find some selfishness and animosity existing. Some even here are treacherous and unfold the secrets of bosom friends to the unfeeling scrutiny of an uncharitable & selfish world. Some of the male portion of this community are a little too apt to boast of their triumphs over the weakness of the other sex and to scatter abroad the tale of their laisons and debauches with them; but then the women themselves are somewhat to be blamed for this, as they do not discard and cast off these very persons who have made such declarations about them. They still countenance them; nay, seem to cling closer to them on this account. Frailty, thy name must be woman. . . .

Saturday, October 16th, A.D. 1858

Jas. McCabe has went fishing and I am left alone.

I moulded up all the lead we had into bullets and righted up the house and thought I might as well . . . pass away an hour or two before noon in writing in my journal. There is no scandal going now, I believe, so I am nearly sowed up for something to write.

I understand that a certain young woman told another certain young woman that I might have part of her bed this winter if I wished it. Well, that is strong talk if true. I must keep my eyes wide open here and my tongue inside of my mouth if I do not want to get into hot water, as the very trees have ears and *Stones* can understand. A smooth tongue and a smiling face, however, will do the business here, I think, and [a] good heavy coat of soft sawder well laid on. . . .

Last night the boys came in to have a debate. There were quite a number of them from the creek. They got up a couple of questions. 1st was, Resolved that intemperance is a greater evil than slavery. . . . Question decided in favor of the negative. The next question was, Resolved that money will go farther than love. I was appointed critic & Jas. Oglesbee judge in my place. No decision given in by the judges as it was so weighty that they could not agree.

There will be a meeting at the McKendree Chapel tonight, and I . . . must go and see the show and hear the fight. It will be a Methodist meeting, I suppose.

Jas. Mc. wants to pitch into the fair sex tonight, and I . . . may do so myself, as it is quite a relief to get to talk awhile to one of the Brush girls. They are very good company, and a person can pass away an hour or two with one of them very agreably.

There are some pretty hearty buxom lasses in here that if they were only polished up and set in some city parlor would make the eyes of the city bucks glisten. And why is it that the farming part of the community do not take more pains with their daughters? They do not cultivate them half as much as they do their corn fields. If the female portion of the community were only well informed and thoroughly roused up to a sense of their weight and influence in society, I am confident the state of society would soon be thoroughly revolutionized. But as it is, there is not more than one woman in every 10 in country that have a knowledge even of writing and grammar. They know nothing of rhetoric, logic, arithmetic, or any of those branches that are calculated to strengthen the mind and make it able to think. There should be ten dollars spent to where there is one in educating the female, and the same for the male.

Our board and expenses will come up to a half dollar per week. We live upon bread & butter and tea and sugar. We are now paying 1-1/4 cents per pound for baking our bread. We get our butter for 12-1/2 cents per pound and have nothing [to] pay for wood; that we get for the picking up. Our house is comfortable enough; only when it rains it then leaks some around the walls. We pay 10 cents for sugar and 18 cents per pound for candles. Flour is 5-1/4$ per barrel, meal 50 cts. per bushel. This I believe ends the chapter of prices. Jas. Mc. gets his washing done at Mr. Douglas'es, and I get mine done at Mr. Wm. Stones.

We have not studied as much at night as I could have wished. However, we have done something at it. Jas. Mc. is studying reading, writing, and arithmetic. He is ciphering in federal money at this time. He has read once through the fourth reader and is now learning the rules in the forepart of the book. He has made considerable improvement in his reading. It will take him some time, however, to make him a real good reader. He will make a very fair scribe if he practices penmanship. He talks some of going to school here this winter. I do not know but what he will do so, as he seems to be attached to the place and the folks treat him very kindly. He says that he will stay here if he can get boarded for a dollar per week. . . .

My classes are not very large and also are not very interesting. Still, [I] will notice a few of them. The fifth reader class numbers four. It recites four times per diem. Miss Ward, Miss Thornton, & Miss Stone are in it at this time. Jas. Mc. was in it, but he has went into the fourth. Mary J. Stone is a pretty fair reader. She has a strong voice and if she was trained would make a good reader. Miss R.A. Ward is a very smooth reader but does not understand principles. R.J. Thornton reads most too low but is generally correct. She does not understand principles. The fourth reader has about six in it when they are all here. There are some very poor readers in the fourth. I am drilling them upon principles at this time. They have made quite an improvement since they commenced. . . . A.L. Oglesbee is the best in the class, and he has a whining tone to his reading. The third reader has but one in that class, Albert Morrain. He reads fluently but has a drawling tone. Second reader is the largest class in school. The greatest fault in this class is faintness and indistinctness of utterance. . . . They have made a nice improvement. Still, there is room for a greater improvement yet.

Monday, October 18th, 1858

. . . Theo. Smith came down from home. He says that they are all right side up with care up there. He has quit working for S. Saunders because they would not give him wages enough. He offered to work for $12 per month. They only offered him $10, which is too cheap. He says that they have sued Isaac Evans for laming their ox so that he died by cutting him with an ax. . . .

There was an immense congregation of people here on Sunday to hear Mr. Reddin preach. The house was crammed so full that I could not get a seat, and there were more than fifty others that could not get in the house. He preached at night to a very large congregation. His text was "Behold he whom thou lovest is sick" and gave us quite a sermon upon Lazarus and his miraculous resurrection from the dead. Some of the young bloods came riding up very fast to the meetinghouse and made quite a racket. The minister gave them a pretty sharp lecture about it. I had about forty visitors who came and talked pretty free and pretty loud. I expected a lecture from some of the old steady churchgoers but did not hear anything said about it.

Tuesday, October 19th, A.D. 1858

. . . Theo. Smith stayed at our house last night. Jas. Mc. and him went coon hunting last night along with Jac. Oglesbee, J.R. Smith, and Longs boys. They caught 2 coons. They tell me that they caught one that never had any tail . . . not even have a stump of a tail.

Jas. Mc. did not get up this morning untill after I left the house, and I am not sure that he is up yet. He was out last night until near eleven o'clock, and he is sleepy and felt cross this morning. I ate a cold breakfast, nothing but cold corn pone and butter. Theo. Smith did the same. I must go down and leave the key at the house.

I have just come from the house this moment and found Jas. Mc. still in bed snoring away.

I will not have a very large school this morning, as Mary Stone will not be here and I do not know whether Thorntons girls will come or not. I am looking some for Henry and W. Anderson to come down. I wish that they would come down today, as we shall have a debate tonight at the Murphey schoolhouse.

I have not heard from Uncle Jas. H. since he commenced teaching up on Turkey Run. . . . He will have a long siege of it before he gets through five months or more.

I am getting to be nearly disgusted by the tittle tattle of this neighborhood. I am afraid that I shall be drawn into some of their disputes & petty quarrels. I must try, however, and keep as clear as possible of these things. It will keep me busy, as I never saw as artful a set to draw a man into a trap to get him to say something so that they can have a chance [to] come down on him.

Four weeks more after this week will finish my course here, and then hio for the fleshpots of Oak Run to luxuriate in their bounteousness.

. . . My health is not as good as I could wish. I am of the opinion that tobacco is one of the chief causes of my debilitude. We are now, however, out of a pipe, and I am not in favor of buying any more tobacco nor pipes.

I saw Caleb McPike at meeting. He says that the Madison Guards are about to be disbanded & that they have quit paying rent for their armory and have boxed up their guns and cartridge boxes. I am in favor of continuing the company if possible, but I cannot attend to it myself. It has cost me already more than it will ever profit me. I have spent nearly $15 on it, & now I must give it up and see it go down into oblivion. I believe that I will wear my uniform out this winter. Let me see. My coat cost me $4, my hat cost $3 more, pants cost $3-1/2, besides dues paid into their treasury to pay rent for armory and for lights. The Dutch are still kept up by the whole of the German population. They have a nice armory of their own. There are but few of them, yet each and every one pulls the same way. I must see the captain the next time I go up and see what they are going to do about the company.

The election has passed off and the Republicans have gained their points. They elected their sheriff and all their officers in this county, O.P. Crabb auditor, Wm. S. Shepherd sheriff, &c., &c. . . .

Wednesday, October 20th, A.D. 1858

I feel badly this morning, as I have such a severe cold that I can hardly speak. I must do something to arrest its progress or I shall have a bad time of it. I am afraid that my lungs are none of the strongest and that the consumption will be the cause of my dissolution. . . .

Why will men be so blind, so lost in ignorance and slothfulness as not to improve their immortal minds? What blindness in a man to neglect the culture of his finer faculties and to cast all things from him but the blind pursuit of wealth and sensual pleasure. There is a very decided pleasure in the exercise of a mans intellectual faculties. It is a feast that lasts forever and is ever an inexhaustable source of pleasure. And may the day speedily come that all persons, kindred, and tongues may be fully enlightened and civilized and be able to drink deep of the fountains of knowledge and happiness. . . .

Last night we had a debate at the Murphey s[chool]house. The question was, Resolved that circumstances make the man. . . . The decision was given in favor of the affirmative. The discussion was kept up until near ten o'clock. The next question for discussion is, Resolved that land monopolies are injurious and should be restrained by law. Mr. Horrel and myself are on the affirmative and Messrs. Robison & Waldo on the negative.

We had quite a large attendance out at the last discussion. Some of the boys, however, were out of doors engaged in wrestling, and finally two of them got to quarreling. There is a kind of rivalry between the Creek boys and the Brushites, as the boys term themselves in this neighborhood. . . .

There is another schoolteacher down on the creek by the name of Page that I must try and get acquainted with. He is an Oberlin student, and if he is like most of them, he is teaching for the money he gets. However, I am prejudging the man, a thing that I detest, and I must see the man ere I make any reflections upon him. . . .

There is going to be a prayer meeting at the McKendree Chapel tonight. I must try and attend. I do not know whether to pitch in and escort some of the young ladies or not. I might meet with a rebuff that would not be very flattering to my vanity. Still, I am not much afraid of it. I would like to have some conversation with Miss Mary E. Elmore, as I think a man could pass off a few words with her very pleasantly. She knows my antecedents, however, and knows me to be rather inclined to be fond of sensual gratification. Still, this does not make much difference in this country, as they are somewhat addicted to that practice themselves. I must try and get better acquainted with her, as she has a life and vivacity about her that pleases me, and I think she is a girl of good sense and native wit. She lives over on Opossum Run about two miles from here. . . .

Thursday, October 21st, A.D. 1858

. . . There was a prayer meeting at the McKendree meetinghouse last night. It was the dryest thing, however, that I have been to for a long time. Jac. Lane gave a kind of an exhortation that was as dead as a stone. He is a licensed Methodist exhorter, I understand. It would take him a long time to convert the world if he never did any better than he done last night. He preached not Christ & Him crucified but Hell & it full of brimstone. He read a chapter in St. John concerning the new birth and about Nicodemus the scribe.

There were only three ladies out, as the roads were too muddy for them to turn out. Their prayer meetings here are good on account of all denominations preaching in and praying within them. Some of the prayers that I have heard at some of these prayer meetings have been right good and possessed the right kind of fire that makes one feel good.

. . . My school has had a daily average of about 17-1/7 up to this date. I have 33 enrolled. This shows that they do not come half of the time. There is no teacher under heavens broad canopy that can do any great things for a set of pupils that attend school so irregularly. The parents of these pupils never take these things into consideration. They never think of the time lost by the pupils, and half the time the fault is with the parent, their neglect of their own little concerns until they are so much behind hand as to have to stop their children from school to help them up . . . to their business.

I am of the opinion that our ministers are a good deal to blame for not preaching about the sin of idleness and slothfulness. They might reach the hearts of their patrons much easier than the teacher, and it would be to the advantage of the church to have intelligent members to carry it on. One intelligent and sensible and well informed Christian is of more force and weight in the church than twenty blockheads and ignoramuses. Their influence would be much greater, and it is gratifying to see the churches taking as much interest in education as they do. If they would only devote about three fourths of the time to Sabbath schools and education generally, they would do much more good in the world; and I am in hopes that they will do so, as there are a great many colleges and seminaries springing up under the immediate supervision and fostering care of the churches, and they are doing an incalculable amount of good in the country. But we need more extended exertion on the part of the ministers.

Friday, October 22d, A.D. 1858

. . . Jas. Mc. broke our last pipe last night, and we have resolved not to buy any more pipes or smoking tobacco, so I am in a fair way to get rid of one bad practice.

Jas. Mc. got some fresh fish of Mr. Kings folks this morning. They caught them in Deer Creek yesterday evening. They were quite a treat for us, as we have not had any meat of any kind for a long time. They talk of going fishing today again with the sein. I never heard of people fishing in the fall of the year before in this country. However, the fish taste very well, and I believe that they are very healthy. . . .

I am almost entirely out of a subject to write upon, and if there continues to be such a dearth of news I will have to pitch into biography and miscellaneous composition. There is quite a field here for descriptive biography & scandal hoarding. . . .

I have been taking up school at half past eight. I believe that I will make it some later next week, say a 1/4 of nine o'clock. Then I can have more time to write. I have but very few pupils today, not more than 13, and they are generally small chaps that are not far enough advanced to keep a mans mind in exercise at all.

There is going to be a debate at the Murphey s[chool]house tonight carried on by the boys. I am not well and I do not think that I shall go down.

. . . If I only had a horse, I would go up home tonight and get me a pair of stockings and an undershirt, as I am dreadfully in need of both. . . . I am of the opinion that if I do not take more care of myself that I am bound for a siege of the ague. I hope, however, that by judicious management I can worry through without getting the shakes. I feel awfully like the chills just now, but I do hope I may not get as far along as a shiver. I have been sitting near the fire untill the perspiration had flowed freely from me, and I felt much better while the sweating process was going on, but it has ceased and I feel as bad as ever.

Our old shanty is a little too airish for comfort, and I must get at it and stop up a few of the largest ventilators and see if we cannot generate more caloric in there. . . .

Tuesday, October 26th, A.D. 1858

I find that debauchery and dissipation are not very conducive to happiness or health. I have been trying it on myself and find that there is no real pleasure in it. . . .

Henry talks of going to school here. If he does go, he will come down this week. We were down to C.C. C[lifton's]. I went down early on Saturday morning, leaving Jas. Mc. in bed snoring away. He and Theo. Smith had been up to Mr. Kings the night before to see his dearie, Miss R.A. Ward, but not having the grit to edge up to her closely, he let the opportunity slip past without squeezing her any. I got up early and had him make on a fire. He felt very sulky about it, but I guess he slept off the effects of it before he got up.

I got to my journeys end before seven o'clock. None of the boys were on hands and things looked dull. E[lias] C[lifton] & wife were in Ross Co. They, however, came home at night along with a sister to C.E.s [*sic*] wife, who is a grass widow. . . . She is one of them & no mistake and is as wild as a March hare and as lecherous as a monkey. C.P. came down on Saturday evening, so we were soon in a very good way for some fun.

Some of them went to church. There were about 20 persons there to see Wm. Anderson married. He, however, did not make his appearance on account of his having a very sore foot caused by his wearing a tight boot and being compelled to stay abed. His inamorata was extremely wroth about it. There was, however, another couple of hard nuts tacked together; Wm. Streets was the man and a girl by the name of Gaines[?], both hard nuts. This was upon Sunday night. . . .

Wednesday, October 27th, A.D. 1858

We had a debate at the Utopian last night & there was a prayer meeting at the Murphey s[chool]house. Mr. Robison and myself . . . made a speech or two on the land monopoly question, I affirming that it was wrong & he saying that it was right. . . . Decision in favor of the negative. The next question for discussion is, Resolved that there is more pleasure in pursuit than in possession. I take the affirmative of this and Robison the negative. . . .

Henry has got himself into business at last. His inamorata, Miss Margaret Stevens, has given birth to a fine boy which is now six months old. She has sworn it to him and sent the constable after him to West Jefferson, but as luck would have it, he was at home and A. Anderson told him [the constable] that he had went west, so he went back. Of course he must come up to the scratch someday. If he is not taken now he will be sometime or other. The[y] say the little one has a red head and is quite a lad. Well, there is one more of the breed in the world anyhow. I think that I must go down and see it as soon as my school is out, which will be the case in three more weeks.

I have set the no. of my pistol down here so that if any one should steal it I can swear to it—142260 V.M. . . .

I just now paid a boy 15 cents for a peck of walnuts, as I am in favor of having some of the luxuries of the season while they are to be had for money.

My system is very much prostrated and reduced by the severe cold that I have been laboring under for the last ten or twelve days. I am afraid almost that the cold has settled permanently upon my lungs. If so, I must go under in less than two years, as a quick consumption would be sure to follow. I still, however, live in hopes that it is not the case; but if it should be so, I must try and meet my fate like a man and go through the trying ordeal with firmness and composure. . . .

I must go up next Friday evening to Oak Run to see about moving my traps up home at the end of my time here. I do not know whether to keep bach this winter or not. I am almost afraid that my health will not permit it. I have some notion to go to Miss [Mrs.] Saunders to board if I cannot get boarding at home. I wish that I was up there now teaching. I would soon make myself more comfortable than what I am at this time. There is more intelligence in that part of the country than there is here, and I always feel more at home in such a place.

It is in fact my home. My heart and my treasure is there; it is there that my early joys and pleasures were most abundant; the forms of loved ones haunt the place and lighten up the scene. Early associations and friendships make the memory of the place dear to my heart of hearts. . . .

"The best laid sc[h]emes of mice and men gang aft agley" is a true bill, and I have found it so this fall myself; as I had laid a plan of study out that was a good one and would have benefitted me materially if I could have pursued it as I intended to have done. But not having the opportunity that I expected and [not] being in the right frame of mind to pursue my studies, I have sadly neglected them. Debates have been one hindrance to my studying, meetings have been another, and visitors another, and ill health another, & carelessness another, and so on to the end of the chapter. I had made a firm resolve to improve myself materially this term, but all these circumstances have conspired against that good resolution. I must, however, post up some this winter, as there will be some scholars that are pretty well posted who will come to my school, and they will be very apt to go through the arithmetic and perhaps through the grammar also. . . .

I am doing the clean thing here with the readers, as I am drilling the most of them critically on the rhetorical, grammatical, and poetical pauses. So I am posting myself in reading if I am doing nothing more. But I must wind this up as my time is out and I am now encroaching on the time of the district. No matter, however. They can stand it.

Thursday, October 28th, A.D. 1858

. . . The girls are all as merry as larks this morning, singing and looking as bright as a May morning. W.H. Roberts is here and will remain the rest of the term. He wants to post up and try teaching sometime or other. He came down with John Peck yesterday in a sulkey.

I am going up home on next Friday afternoon to get a pair of stockings and some other necessaries. W.H. will teach on the afternoon of Friday. It will be a good training for him.

The folks are all well up on Oak Run. Mother talks of going to Chillicothe along with Mrs. Peck in a buggy. Jno. Peck is going along as driver. He started for home this morning in the rain. He will have a juicy time of it . . . as he will be in the rain all the way. He has, however, a gum overcoat and another good one under it. . . .

Last night there was a prayer meeting at the McKendree Chapel, and there was a very good turn out, quite a congregation in fact. Mr. Lane gave an exhortation, and some of the brethren made very good prayers. Lane pitched into the rowdy part of the community hot and heavy. He gave them particular fits. None of the sisters were called upon to pray, so we did not have as fervent a time as we might have had if this had been the case.

Jas. Mc. escorted Miss R.A. Ward home, & if his eyes are any index to his feelings, he must have had a good time generally. I guess he sat her all night. Some of the boys caught him as he was going out of the meetinghouse. He made some remarks and went on his way rejoicing. He told them that they might get hurt if they did not watch.

I gallanted a gal myself, Miss Timmons, who by the way is not a bad talker. I got home at about half past nine o'clock and found J. Peck & Henry snoring away in bed. I routed them up and we made the bed down on the floor and snoozed away untill day spread her rosy wings in the eastern horizon.

I have a slim school this morning, not more than 13 pupils. Nine or ten of them are girls. . . .

I must wind [down] soon and have a recess, as Jas. Mc. will drop off to sleep and his girl too, as she is here too at this time. . . .

Miss Mary Stone & her caro are not yet joined by the bonds of wedlock as has all along been prophesied by the newsmongers of this part of the moral vineyard, and I am of the opinion that she will not be if some of the reports are true that are afloat concerning her and Mr. Marion Strain. He, I suppose, has kept her fed upon airblown promises for the sake of gratifying his sensual appetite; but as for pure, genuine love for her, I do not think he has a particle, or he would have married her long since. I do not have a very exalted opinion of Strain. . . .

Miss Stone is a person of a very good natural mind, but she has become soured by disappointment and is getting to be whimsical and fretful. If she never marries, she will make a tremendous cross old maid anyhow, and if she does marry and does not get the man of her choice, she will make this earth a bedlam to him and no mistake. I may be prejudging too strongly, but this is my candid opinion at this time. . . .

Friday, October 29th, A.D. 1858

. . . I suppose that the wedding went off over on the run last night, as I have heard quite a noise over there. Weddings are getting to be so common here that they are not much noticed any more.

I got up this morning at about four o'clock and put on a huge pone of cornbread and flew around and dusted things about in a tremendous manner.

Tonight the boys are going to have a debate at the Utopian, and I will not be there to pitch in with them. Henry will have to take charge of them and keep them strait. . . .

I must write a letter to A. Holbrook to let him know where I am and what I am doing. I want to have my name in the Teachers Exchange, as I am determined to follow it as a profession, it being the one that is more congenial to my disposition. I love the schoolroom and its appurtenances. It is indeed a glorious occupation and one that is not patronized as it should be by the community. The profession needs more sympathy & hearty support from the American public, but I think that there is a better day dawning. God speed the happy day!

Tuesday, November 2d, A.D. 1858

The rain comes straight down this morning and no mistake. I am of the opinion that my school will be rather slim this day. Well, I am perfectly willing that it should be so, as I will then have time to write some letters and do some tall scratching in my journal.

I started up home on last Friday afternoon and got to Uncle Jas. school on Turkey Run before his afternoon recess. He was putting them through on composition writing whilst I was there. He had Brookfields first book on composition and was putting them through in the right kind of style. He has a right nice kind of school, I should think, from their appearance. They are a great deal farther advanced than the scholars in this district.

I got up as far as Handy Truitts a little past sundown. Met Miss Emarine going to singing school and hitched on and went with her. We had a very good singing school. Not as large attendance as there had been; still, the house was full & a number of the fair sex were in attendance. They had a very good order as far as I could learn. . . .

After singing school was out Miss Emarine went home with me. When we arrived there we found the house full. . . . We had a regular built good time . . . as they all stayed untill nearly twelve o'clock. P.L. Roberts and Wm. Roberts [first cousins of JMR] stayed all night. . . . We played everything that we could think of, and then Wm. Roberts cornered Miss R.J. Cornwell & I Miss E. Truitt. Oh, the blissful moments from that time till 5 o'clock in the morning. P.L. Roberts stayed till morning. So did Wm. Roberts. Miss E. Truitt went home next day at 11 o'clock and I went with her. That ended the spree as far as the women were concerned. . . .

Semp Saunders and I went to town on the cars. I went to Dr. Brown to have him examine my tooth. He said that he could plug it so that it would be as good as new. I had no time, however, to get it done.

I got about a half dozen papers and four letters whilst I was up there. I must answer some of them this very day. I received a letter from Jos. A. Conard. He is teaching in Pilcher, Belcher Co., O[hio], & one from Hugh Andrews, who is teaching in Anna, Union Co., Illinois, and one from Jno. Peterman, who is going to school in Urbana, Champaign Co., Illinois, and one from my old friend Henry Peck, who is in Jackson, Amador Co., California, digging gold. Some of us are widely separated. Nevertheless, we will not let the chain of friendship rust between us. Henry Peck is doing pretty well now in Cal., but he has been sick for some time. . . .

I am getting behind the times in the way of news here in this out of the way place. I must try and get where there are some newspapers so that I can get some idea of how the great world wags. I have five papers that Uncle Jas. took from the London P.O. for me.

I must begin to look up my books here and have things in shape for going home. Jas. M. Horrell has my Masonic chart, & I suppose he will let B. Brily have it. I must keep track of it or I shall lose it.

Uncle Jas. H. lives on Oak Run and teaches in Turkey Run. He has a little cabin rented and will have a cosey time this winter; not much to bother him. I stayed all night Sunday night at his house. He says he may possibly come down here next Friday.

I understand that there is another grass widow in the Brush. Old Mr. Sam. Oglesbee & his wife have parted. The quarrel commenced over the cover on the bed, I understand, he saying that she was taking all the quilt and she denying the assertion. They must have had a coolness between them before this time, or this little exposure to the night air would not have shivered them apart. This old lady has been married 3 times, and I should think it was high time that she was getting up to married life so as to make it easy and comfortable without kicking up a shindy about a blanket. Mr. Oglesbee has been married once before, and he of course must be somewhat experienced in the management of the fair sex. . . .

Jas. Mc. has went to Mt. Sterling for some flour. It will take about 25 pounds to last us through the remainder of the term. We have settled up and I find Jas. Mc. about $1.42 behind hand. Our board will cost about $.75 per week counting the cost of setting up & all counted in the expenses. . . .

Jno. Peterman . . . is in Urbana, Illinois, going to school at a seminary there. I do not know what he intends to follow, but I suppose he wants to become a teacher. I am sure of one thing, however. He must be better than he is now to be worthy of the office.

Wednesday, November 3d, A.D. 1858

. . . The world still wags on as usual. The girls, God bless their eyes, are still forming a great part of my reveries. Woman, oh woman, we are prone to think of thee even though we know thou art frailty & inconstancy and softness. . . . What have I, a studious man, to do with woman? I am getting old & will soon be bald & perhaps toothless. I do not have much trouble now, and matrimony is a leap in the dark at best, and why should I venture what little peace I have in such a riskey scheme as matrimony? I might get bit and have no one to help me cry but my wife, & she might laugh at my calamity and mock when my fear would come. Better be called an old *bach* than be a henpecked husband, a pettycoat slave. I guess, however, that there is no danger of my getting my head into the halter soon, as there dont seem to be any for me to drop into just at this time.

I am getting the toothache.

I was up at the Murphey s[chool]house last night to a prayer meeting along with Jas. Mc. The night was as dark as a bog and the roads were very muddy. Not many of the fair sex were on hand. A few, however, had the nerve to appear and participate in the exercises. Bro. Brily pitched into some of them pretty freely for misbehavior during prayer. I was not in the house at the time, however, and did not see any of the misconduct. . . .

I was up at Mr. Stones this morning and took some washing there to be done. Miss Mary was still in bed when I arrived there. I got to talk more to her caro ami last night than I ever ever did before in my life. He told me considerable about his affairs. He stands with Miss Stone just as I expected he did from the reports of outsiders. . . .

I heard today that I had went up home to get married and that my bro[ther] came down to take Miss Timmons off of my hands. All stuff.

I have been keeping looser school here this quarter than I ever intend to again. I have made no rules whatever, but I have done some good, I think, here in this place and would continue to teach [here] if I had not made other arrangements that pay me better in a pecuniary point of view.

I am putting Henry through on teaching. He thinks some of going to teaching himself. He might get this school, I suppose, if he would apply for it & could get a certificate for the same. . . .

My school has been very noisy this afternoon, & I am afraid that I will lose my patience if [I] do not watch myself. No one knows the trials of the teacher untill they try the business themselves.

Tonight we have a prayer meeting at the McKendree Chapel, and I suppose the faithful will all be present, not so much to worship a God they love but one they fear. It is the fear of Hell that is their hangmans whip, what holds them in order. . . .

Thursday, November 4th, A.D. 1858

I stayed at home last night and by this means saved my credit, as I had a kind of appointment made with Miss Margaret King. I, however, did not make this appointment myself. It [was] done by Jas. Mc., who wanted me to take her up to Mrs. Wards and set her. But my stomach was a little too tender just at that particular time to go with her, and I am afraid that it will always remain so when she is brought in question.

I am almost getting to be disgusted with the girls of this place. They are continually lugging one another by the ears, or to speak plainer, they are continually fomenting quarrels amongst themselves. Tattling is so common here that I am almost falling into the practice myself, and it is a practice that I detest above every other vice that I know of. It is a mean, dirty, nasty, despicable, execrable, hell born, impious, nauseating thing, this thing called tattling. If I wanted to curse a neighborhood, all I would ask would be to send amongst them two or three whispering talebeare[r]s. . . . I would be sure that misery, jealousy, & every known crime would soon find its way into their midst. All the priests of all the churches in the universe could do nothing for such a place. In fact, I believe they could not long withstand the blighting influence of such a place themselves. And if I ever do become a confirmed tattler, may my tongue cease to articulate.

Jas. Mc. escorted his inamorata home from prayer meeting and set her up till half past 12 o'clock. He is getting to be more and more enamored every day. Well, let him bask in loves young dream, for it is a delightful sensation and makes one feel first rate while the fit lasts, but alas, the bubble soon bursts and leaves the astonished victim cold and heartless, almost soulless in fact. He then doubts all womankind and almost doubts his own feelings on the subject. Still, this is wrong. There are true and faithful hearts, warm and faithful, still to be found upon the face of Gods beautiful footstool, and when one does come across such a one he ought to pitch in.

I do not know whether Jas. Mc. has come across such a specimen of femininity. If so he is right, and if not, he is building a castle that will fall upon him and crush all his finer sensibilities and make a wreck of him, or of his heart rather. His rival, Bowers, is very wroth about the matter. He & some of the Californians came down to bluff Jas. Mc. off. They were prepared with firearms, but they did not make any demonstrations toward him, as they learned that he was armed ready for them. . . .

Monday, November 8th, [1858]

I was unable to fill out this page [Friday] on account of visitors and a press of business. Mr. Sam Oglesbee came in the morning and got me to write an article of agreement between himself and his wife about his estate and her separation from him. Now, here is an example of the ill effects of an ill assorted marriage, a difference of tempers, and the interference of outsiders. She is a harridan, I guess, and led him a bitter life of contention and strife.

I must look out if I marry for fear of falling into a snare myself. I must in the first place find out if she has reason and good sense at her command. If she has not, I must not pitch in, as a man could not possibly live with a woman not possessed of these very necessary qualifications. Such a life would indeed be a hell upon earth and no mistake. There is, I verily believe, more crime committed under this head than under any other—i.e., of marriage with a fool or one whose temper governs them at all times. . . . It is better to live in the corner of [a] housetop in peace than to have to live in a wide house with a brawling woman. So says Solomon, and he was a man of extensive experience, in the woman line anyhow.

They had an extensive time in Mt. Sterling on last Sunday dedicating their new church and also their quarterly meeting. The Methodists have a splendid new church there. It is [a] large, commodious, and imposing looking edifice and makes quite an imposing and fine addition to their town.

I had about a half dozen visitors on Friday afternoon, Mr. Strain and all the Morrain boys. We had a spelling school in the afternoon. Henry pronounced. Two of the little girls got the mule into them and were not going to spell. One pleaded headache; the other had no excuse. I had to send out for a stick before I could get them to come to terms. This is the first stick I have had in my school since I commenced this school, and I hope that it will be the last time that I may be called upon to send for one.

I am chewing tobacco at this time for the benefit of my tooth, as it growls sometimes; and I am going to have my tooth plugged as soon as I get through here, and I must keep it from aching as long as possible . . . .

I am getting to have the cold shoulder turned on me by the fair sex. . . . My old flame, or rather my old partner et amour, Miss N[ancy] C[lifton], is down on me for smiling on a grass widow; and my ideal, my intellectual inamorata et sposa, Miss E.T., is down on me for escorting Miss Harriet Timmons; and Miss Margaret King is down on me because I do not go with her. So at every corner [I am met] with a frown from those that once pretended to love me better than anyone else in the circle of their male acquaintances, all on account of jealousy.

I am glad that I am still free from this miserable passion called jealousy. It is more cruel than the grave, more lasting than life, and sharper than a two edged sword. The peevishness of the individuals above alluded to have almost set me against the whole sex and turned me into a downright woman hater. . . .

We had quite a good meeting down at the Murphey s[chool]house on Thursday evening. We had a new speaker, Mr. Young, who has a decided German accent but who is a very good speaker for all that. His logic is very good. The question we discussed was art or nature. I took the side of art and was beaten, of course, as usual. . . .

We have got up the tariff question [for next week]. It is stated in this style: Resolved that a high protective tariff is injurious to the community at large. Mr. Young & myself are on the affirmative, Mr. Horrell [and Mr. Robison] on the negative. . . . We are going to meet on next Wednesday evening at the Murphey s[chool]house. The switch [in meeting places] is because [we] met at the Utopian on last Friday night and had a big discussion on the [Negro] question. The Indians gained the question for once. I, however, hardly ever knew this to be the case. People are prone to side with the negroes. My candid opinion is that the Indians are the more oppressed & have the most to complain of the white man, as all of their sufferings are brought on by the white man, not from their own perverseness but from the cruel disposition of the white man. . . .

Tuesday, November 9th, A.D. 1858

I still live and I still learn. Thank my luckey stars for this blessed privilige & long may that time continue. I was—O, ye gods!—I was at a- a- a-punkin cutting last night at Mr. Stones and stayed till the late hour of eight o'clock & passed a most excruciatingly, enchantingly intellectual time. I live, I learn, and long may I continue to fall in with such a good place for mental, moral, & physical education & general information as the Brush!

I shall never forget the Brushites. They never talk about one another. They never quarrell. New York society is nothing to the refinement to be found here. Paris is thrown into the shade. And Lord Chesterfield could learn politeness if he was so fortunate as to be alive and here. St. Paul could learn religion here, as his vision on the road to Damascus is nothing to the visions of the people here; no, not even a circumstance. His Damascene vision ought not to be mentioned in the same day with the religious experience of some of the inhabitants of this enlightened part of the moral heritage. I drink in new life daily. My mind soars beyond the mortal ken almost, on account of the sublimity of the associations I am brought in contact [with] here in the Brush. But soon I must depart to the shades of Oak Run, there to brood over the happiness of my sojourn here and to improve by reflection what I have learned by inspection. . . .

Yesterday one of my smallest pupils was sever[el]y hurt by falling from a teeter or plank put across the fence, on which two of them were riding seesaw fashion. I must put a stop to this sport as it is dangerous. Her name is Miranda Douglas, a very pleasant, smart child. I felt very sorry for her. She seemed to be very patient and gentle under her affliction and did not murmur or fret any on account of being hurt. She is a gleam of sunshine to me and I shall miss her sadly. I hop[e], however, that nothing serious may result from the injury. . . .

The human mind is made for association and affection & also for sympathy. This is the reason why old maids are generally such cross, disagreeable persons. They are cut off from all sympathy from the opposite sex, and their hearts become withered, soured, & contracted on this very account. When we exercise our faculties they become stronger and more permanent. Still, there are some old maids that seem to be aunt to everybody. They appear to be ministering angels sent into a neighborhood for the benefit of the afflicted and the sorrowing. They seem to have a kindly smile for everyone, and their presence acts like a gleam of sunshine wherever they go. Such are the salt of the earth. There are two such characters in this neighborhood, the two Miss Oglesbees.

. . . I am going to Palestine this afternoon to buy some groceries and some candles for the benefit of the Utopian. We must have light of some kind down there, as our minds are not sufficiently luminous to lighten up the dark hall of a dark night so that we can see to eat and cook.

All my girls here are bound not to come on the last day of my school. Well, let em rip.

Wednesday, November 10th, A.D. 1858

The first snow of the season fell last night. It was only a light squall, however, and will all be gone again at noon, I think.

I was at Palestine yesterday afternoon and bought some sugar, candles, & paper, also some tobacco for Jas. Mc. There was nothing going on at Palestine. The town is perfectly dead in the shell, & I am of the opinion that it always will be, as there is no railroad nor good road of any kind coming into it.

These little country villages are a curse rather than a blessing to a community. It is a grand rendezvous for all the blackguards in the country & produces more vagabonds than anything else. We ought to have fewer towns and more farmers of the right kind. If people in the country would only band together and buy a wagon load of groceries and necessaries at a time, they could do much better than to patronize these one horse hamlets and sinkholes of iniquity. The merchants ride the people to death and keep them poor all their days with their infernal credit system. They sap away at a man year after year, and he never suspects the leak untill it is too late to turn back. I am going on the cash system if possible hereafter. Then I shall know exactly what I am worth.

I understand that A. Anderson was at a ball in California last week & also that he lost a $30 note, which I suppose must be the Saunders note that I wanted. I must see about the matter and make arrangements for getting it from Semp, as it is the only way that I can ever save myself on the Clingan note. I am afraid that Allen is not doing much for himself at this time, and I am afraid that I shall have to pay the whole of that Clingan note. I will know now who to go security for on a note of $50. I am down on this credit system. It does very badly for all parties and never has been of any benefit to anyone, if we except lawyers and judges & sheriffs. It lines their pockets and keeps bread in their mouths.

Jas. Mc. went after butter this morning and Henry is shooting, but what at I am unable to say; a mark, however, I suppose.

It will soon be half past 8, and only two pupils here. There will [not] be a very big turnout today, I am thinking. They do not care much here for schools. They are naturally shrewd enough without calling on any artificial helps or aids. Well, let em think so if they want to. . . .

The sun is shining brightly on the snow and the white mantle will soon disappear. I wish we would have a good snow. I do want to hear the merry jingle of the sleigh bells, and I love to wheel around to the hickory fire on the family hearth. There is some solid comfort in the very thought of the charming influence of the first made fire. I love to hear it sputter and sparkle, and there is such a quiet about the gradual dying away of a huge fire. The sticks seem to molder away so gradually. Once in a while a bright blaze will break forth from the ash covered logs that brightens up the room with a sudden brightness that almost makes one start up out of their chair in surprise. This starts a cheerful train of ideas, and one weaves bright scenes for the future. His paper drops from his hand. He sees an ideal cottage & wife & a little farm well tilled and his two children, just such ones as we read about, and a lovely wife moving about the house like some fairy diffusing a perfect halo of happiness around him. He sees himself growing old, to be sure, but getting more hale every year until he is finally called Uncle by everyone in the neighborhood, and he is finally elected squire by the almost unanimous voice of his own township.

Such is the bright side. Dont want to look at the dark side just now.

Thursday, November 11th, A.D. 1858

I was at a meeting of the Brush Club last night. The tariff protection business was warmly discussed. The affirmative were in favor of a high protective & the negative in favor of a revenue tariff. . . . The affirmative came off victorious as a matter of course. I got an introduction to a Mr. Condit, who is a teacher engaged across the creek near Sterling. I do not think he is a very great speaker. We picked another question, one that I proposed myself, Resolved that England has been a greater curse than blessing to the world. . . . I anticipate a good time at the next discussion as we have a broad field to work upon.

I will only meet with them another time. Then farewell forever to the Brush Club. Bro. Briley has entirely deserted the Brush Club. He has not been on hands for some time. He is fitting himself for a preacher, so I understand. It will be a long time before he will eclipse Henry Ward Beecher. He is a good, clever soul, however, and may be very much esteemed for his social qualities. . . .

Last night there was a prayer meeting at the McKendree Chapel. Henry and Jas. Mc. went to it. They had rather a dry time, I guess, from what the boys tell me this morning. Most of the feminine gender belonging to the Brush were out to the Dennison s[chool]house to hear a new preacher, a young man of the Methodist persuasion.

Jas. Mc. . . . escorted his inamorata from church and set her up till after the small hours. He got home at 1/2 past 2 o'clock. He is getting interested up there in that piece of dry goods. His attachment grows warmer and warmer at each interview. . . .

The girls around here are not going to appear at the end of the term for fear of being made fun of by the Oak Run folks. Well, this kind of gets me down. They must think that the Oak Run folks are paragons of perfection and that they will not be able to hoe their own row with them. Well, I cant help it, I am sure, and what is more I will curry no favors from them. . . .

My school today is very slim, not more than a dozen pupils, so I cannot do much for them. They do not take enough interest in their school. They just let their children come when they please and go when they please, and when this is the case there is not much to be lear[n]ed by the pupils. The teacher cannot then establish a strict discipline, for if he does he will soon find himself in an empty schoolroom, monarch of all he surveys. And if he does not keep good order, he is of no account. If he whips, he is too severe. If he does not, he is too lax. If he listens to the tales told by his pupils, he is partial; and if he dont, he is of no account. If he scolds a young woman for disobeying orders, he just does it to show off big. If he lets her go, he is partial. . . .

This is the gate all teachers have to travel through, no matter who he is or where he comes from. He must grin and bear all these things. But why do you follow such a profession? asks some person. Well, I like it for all this, and feel more at home in the school than anywhere else. So I love the profession even if there are drawbacks upon it. Yes, I love the schoolroom and its associations, and were there ten times as many vexations attached to it as there is, I would still attempt to teach. But I hope that there is a better day coming for teachers. God send it soon is my prayer.

Friday, November 12th, A.D. 1858

. . . Yesterday I had a good time . . . with my large spelling class. They took a dead set on the lesson and I drilled them about a half an hour. . . . Three or four words went entirely around the class. I then made them take their books and look over [the words] while I pronounced the lesson and had them pronounce it after me. I am of the opinion that they will have a better lesson for today; if not, I must try the same thing over again with them.

. . . I was up at Mr. Kings last night and talked some with Miss Margaret. She is afflicted some with envy and jealousy, I think. She is, however, getting old, and her mind is getting to be soured by disappointment. It is a bad case for a person to get old, and cross too. This is a double misfortune. One ought to try and keep their tempers even and sweet if they do grow old and homely. They will then be bearable and perhaps desirable companions. Miss King is 29 years of age, so she tells me. . . .

Wednesday, November 17th, A.D. 1858

. . . Saturday and Sunday last I spent at the Utopian cleaning up and setting things to rights. I washed up the towel & the dish cloths and carried a cart load of ashes out of the fireplace.

On Friday evening I was up to the Dennison schoolh[ouse] to a geography lesson taught by Mr. Davidson. He teaches it by singing, & I am of the opinion that it is a very good plan. He offered to teach very cheap. All he asked was for the pupils to pay him fifty cents per lesson & for them to find their own lights. The house was crowded full of spectators and pupils. Some of the Brush girls were there. I escorted Miss R.A. Ward home. Mr. Jesse Morrain went with Miss Ree J. Thornton. The other girls were without gallants. Jas. Mc. and Henry went to Mt. Sterling and Palestine. They also went to C.C. C[lifton']s and stayed all night. They did not get home until Saturday evening. . . .

Our Utopian Hall is getting to be pretty cool now of nights, and it begins to take a right good pile of wood to make it bearable during the night. If it was only tight and snug I would not mind it, but it unfortunately is not & we sometimes almost suffer with cold.

Jas. Mc. is not here this forenoon. He went to see the directors about his schooling. Some of them are for making him pay & some of them think that he should not. . . . If they demand it, I will have to pay it if Jas. Mc. will not, as I am bound to do so by a verbal contract.

I must be pretty busy this week, as I will have to make out my reports to the directors and the township clerk. I have my general register to make out to present to the directors. There is, however, plenty of time. . . .

Thursday, November 18th, A.D. 1858

. . . We had several visitors last night at the Utopian. . . . The most of them went to church at the McKendree Chapel. They had prayer meeting there last night. Henry R. & Jas. Mc. attended. Wm. H. R. came home immediately after church. Jas. Mc. escorted his inamorata home from church and did not make his appearance till this morning at the early hour of four o'clock a.m. He must [have] set her up strong. Well, sweet is loves young dream, and I have no objections, I am sure. He did talk some of going up to London today, but I am of the opinion that the bed is sweeter to him than the sight of a thousand Londons would be to him, today especially.

Briley staid last night till 11 o'clock. He is a great man to talk. I understand that he thinks some of going into the ministry. His school will be out on next Saturday at noon. . . .

8

Married Teacher at Home
December 8, 1858–July 28, 1859

Back on home ground, John Roberts teaches a three-months winter term, marries Emarine Truitt and builds a house, then teaches another three-months summer term. He occasionally helps Emarine's brother-in-law, William Godfrey, with his crops, and he contracts to take on a job of repairing the schoolhouse in his district. Weather, crops, and the health of livestock are constant concerns.

Married life and schoolteaching suit Roberts, and he no longer yearns for excitement, except intellectual pleasure, which he finds in debates and Masonry. A singing school is disrupted by boys from Clark County, but a diary entry of January 7, 1859, says that an apology and $25 settled the issue; still, Roberts continues to nurse a grudge against them.

Sure that his country is in the vanguard of a progressive age, he glories in Americans' mechanical genius and their republican form of government—but not the Republican party. It has succumbed to abolitionists, like the "Oberlin philanthropists" who defy the Fugitive Slave Law. He applauds the Londoners who beat a Columbus black and warn a local black daguerreotyper to leave town, and he shares the fear of many citizens of the lower Midwest of black migration to their region.

Wednesday, December 8th, A.D. 1858

Once more I find myself in the s[chool]room & full of business. I am here on my old stamping ground where I have played the schoolboy as well as filled the responsible office of teacher.

Things have changed very much since I last figured here. There are quite a number of new faces, and even the old ones are so much changed as to be hardly familiar. Amongst the boys the mustache & imperial is now to be seen, and their voices have lost the childish piping tones of youth. And amongst the feminine portion of the scholars there are greater changes. The mere infants of my last reign have come clear out of their short clothes & are now full grown women. . . .

179

I have about 33 pupils already enrolled, and the half are not here yet that are to come. I will be compelled to keep my hands out of my pockets this winter. This is the 3d day of my advent here. I am going to adopt the Lebanon [Normal] rules in my school. I have commenced already by adopting the self-reporting rule as they have it down there. . . .

Friday, December 17th, A.D. 1858
I am getting to be rather remiss about writing in my journal. My school is very heavy and throng[ed]. . . .

There are numerous night meetings here at this time. We have a debate here on Wednesday evenings, singing school on Friday evenings. The lyceum business wakened up with quite an energy. We have now about 30 members who have paid their fees and are all actively engaged in the good work. We also have a party once in awhile for a change in the drama.

There is a lyceum organized in Somerford at this time, also a phonography class. I have not been there for more than 10 days. I must try and get over there soon again, as I am getting behind the times over there. I am up every night at some kind of school or gathering. . . .

Thursday, December 21st, A.D. 1858
. . . I have got my money from Semp that was coming from Jas. McCabe ($5.50). Semp and I are good friends again.

They have organized a singing school here under the supervision of Giles James. We had quite a time here on last Friday evening. It was the understanding that we were not to have any spectators whatever. The boys soon made up enough money for the singing school in our own neighborhood. The Clark County boys then wanted to come in and sign. The class, however, made objections to their being any more signed, as there were already too many in the class. I was up at the table advocating the doctrine of no more signers when the Messrs. Wilson commenced a harangue about coming in. I told them they could not do so as we already had enough without them, and furthermore our own neighbor boys wanted to come, some of them, and we wanted to give them preference. They then swore roundly that they would come whether they signed or not, & if not permitted to sign they would break up the class. We finally had a vote taken on it and voted them out. They then said that the majority should not rule &c., &c.

Wednesday, December 22d, A.D. 1858
. . . I have about 46 pupils now every day, and they keep me busy all the while. My prospects are good in every particular now, I believe.

My health is good, my business is in a flourishing condition, and take it all in all, [I] am in a good situation. . . .

[JMR copies a long poem (by E.P. Ross?), given to him by Emarine Truitt, asking "Who'd be a bachelor?" and counseling the "lonely old bachelor" to take "a true hearted WIFE."]

Friday, December 24th, A.D. 1858

The holidays are almost on hand once more, and soon the firing of guns, the ringing of bells, and the pattering of feet on the floors of ballrooms will be heard throughout the length & breadth of the land. It is right that it should be so, as men & women ought not to be long faced always. They should relax from the high strain of business and be a little merry, for a day or two anyhow.

There is to be a ball in Lafayette tonight at the Wilson house. I have a strong invitation to attend, but I guess that I will not participate in the festivities there. I am going to be as quiet as possible tonight. Perhaps I may shoot some just for amusement.

I received a letter from Jas. McCabe yesterday. He got home safe and sound & met with a warm reception. The old sire has agreed to let him have money to go to school on. He will remain at home this winter. . . .

Friday, December 31st, Anno Domini 1858

. . . The year [1858] has been one of considerable variety to me. I have been engaged in teaching and in acquiring knowledge. I am now about even with the world as far as pecuniary matters are concerned. . . . I have enjoyed myself very well. My amours have all been fortunate. My speculations have all proven up to my expectations. My friends have not decreased in number or in efficacy. I have improved myself considerably over my last years stock. My health, however, has not been so good as I could have wished. Still, I have not been compelled to lie abed a day on account of sickness. I have not traveled much in foreign parts, but I have learned considerable about some of the institutions of my own neighborhood. Take it all in all, I have had a pleasant year of it. . . .

I feel languid and weak this afternoon on account of being up so much after night and also on account of using too much of the noxious weed called tobacco. New Years Day I must try and quit, for I am afraid that those two things will kill me dead.

I have 62 pupils enrolled on my books at this time, and the majority of them are pretty regular in their attendance. We have a lyceum and singing school every week besides other places to go to. Our singing school, however, has come very near being broken up by outsiders and rowdys from a distance.

Some time since, Mr. G.A. James from near Charleston in Clark Co., who is teaching school in the Botkin s[chool]house, proposed to teach a class in singing at this s[chool]house for the sum of $20 for 13 lessons. He came over about 3 weeks ago and we soon made up the money. There was an understanding, however, . . . that no spectators were to be admitted. Well, Messrs. Wilsons, Turners, & others from Clark County were very much put out about the matter. They came on the next evening after we had made up our class and wanted to sign. . . . These boys during recess swore that they would come in. . . . They went away swearing deadly vengeance against the singing school & its friends. . . .

On last Monday we had another sing, I being doorkeeper at the time. They had threatened to knock me down if I was at the door when they came. They had several of the class on their side of the question, and these came in before the class commenced singing and saw that the door was guarded. . . . These went out at recess and led the rest in. . . . I told them that they must go out, that they could not come in. They swore that they would come in & stay in and pushed myself, Jno. B. Garrard, & Henry back to the stove, they cursing & swearing they would stay in.

Tuesday, January 18th, A.D. 1859

. . . I have come to the conclusion to try married life. I am now under a solemn promise to be married to one that I have always loved, as dear as the apple of my eye. Miss Emarine Truitt has betrothed herself to me. I shall endeavor to make her happy & contented with her choice. She is young, but not too young to marry. Her only fortune is her own dear self. She is small, yet full of vivacity & natural shrewdness. She will suit me, I think, as a companion in the rough pathway of life.

My folks are perfectly willing that it should be so, and in fact they are in favor of the union. Some of her folks, however, are opposed to it. I do not care, however, if they are, as I am sure they have no right to interfere in a case that so nearly concerns her future welfare and happiness. I shall live for her & her alone, and I think that by economy and prudence we may never need any assistance from our present opposers.

I intend to try for this school next summer. If I succeed in getting it at a reasonable compensation, I shall teach here all summer.

I intend to try and get a room somewhere in this neighborhood and set up for myself as soon as I shall get married. I must begin to look around for a room to live in pretty soon. . . .

I expect that this affair will go off about the first of March. . . . I must try and get this school for another month and drive things right through.

Henry is still living at home. He still sticks to his first resolution about going to school for a year to come. I am glad that it is so, for he can make more money by a good education than by carpentering.

I was down on Darby with S.D. Truitt last Saturday. . . . Allen Anderson is working for Ashton Gregg, chopping wood and getting out ties for the railroad. . . . He talks some of going to Pikes Peak in the spring to dig gold. The yellow [gold] fever is getting to be prevalent here. . . .

Friday, January 21st, A.D. 1859
. . . I have never in my life seen so much wet weather as there has been this winter. Every hole, creek, and corner is full and overflowing, and the health of the community is very poor. . . . I am myself nearly dead with a severe cold, and I have not been clear of hoarseness this winter. . . .

My school will average nearly fifty this term. I am very busily engaged all day. I never rest a moment. Wm. H. Roberts helps me considerably. He hears four or five recitations each . . . afternoon. I have some very good readers in this school. . . . The greatest fault I have with the most of them is the extreme faintness of voice that some of them have acquired by going to female teachers. This is a fault that seems to be hardest to eradicate of any that I have to contend with.

I have been smoking a little too much lately, and I must quit it, as it is making me weak and nervous. . . .

Our Oak Run lyceum is still as interesting as it possibly can be. We had quite a good time on last Wednesday evening. The subject . . . was, Resolved that slavery should be abolished. . . . Decision in favor of the affirmative. The ladies were out in full force on the night of the debate. Kept it up till 11 o'clock, then adjourned.

Friday, February 11th, A.D. 1859
I feel nervous and weak this morning. I have used too much of that infernal tobacco.

The signs of the times indicate reviving time amongst the religious portion of the community. They are having a good time at the chapel. They have had over 50 meetings and have made 36 converts. They have quite a number of the boys up to the mourners bench every night. . . . I have promised myself to join in about six months. . . .

Religion, what is it? Is it long prayers, long faces, long consciences, long professions, or is it it pure love for God and man and a doing of good to all men? Is it being good to your family, to your neighbor, to your God, and to yourself? May God speedily open my eyes to a knowledge of the truth.

. . . Our singing school is in full blast at this time. Our teacher has joined church and got religion, so he says.

Wednesday, March 16th, A.D. 1859

. . . My school has been out for some time, and I have my money partly spent at this time.

I am going to get married today, no preventing Providence, to Miss Emarine Truitt. I shall be married in London at the residence of John Jones, Esqr., at about 3 o'clock p.m. All the arrangements are made . . . and I do not apprehend any failure. . . .

I saw Miss Emarine yesterday. She was fixing for her wedding & mine also. I must keep a watch out for the future now, as there will be more than ever depending on me hereafter. Everything seems to be propitious now. The day is fine as heart could wish. Not the first cloud is to be seen. The sky is as clear as a bell, and there is not a breath of air stirring to make it uncomfortable overhead, so I shall make a fair start at any rate.

I feel this morning as though I was doing right, and I feel hopeful for the future. I am sure my motives are pure and good, not envious or jealous, not for sensual or gross desires, not for ambition, not for pelf, but for something nobler, purer, better, sweeter, holier than all these, and that is love. This is what has prompted me to act in this as I have done and my wishes to be realized. Time alone will tell the tale. . . .

Sunday, March 27th, A.D. 1859

. . . I am married at this time. I am glad of it. Myself & wife are staying at Mothers [at] this time.

I have been getting out house logs for some time past. Allen Anderson has been helping me. We have only four more to hew & then we will be done.

Uncle James H. Roberts & his wife were here last night. P.L. Roberts was also here. Uncle Jas. H. talks of going to Missouri this spring to find some land to buy. He is coming back immediately. The rest of the family are still going to stay where they are at this time.

V.C. Wilson has come very near dying here lately from the effects of drinking whiskey. He is still alive, however, and may consume many more quarts of the beverage of hell ere his bloated carcass will be carried to the graveyard. He is a hopeless wreck and will soon pass away unregretted by any person. . . .

My wedding went off propitiously. Everything was as bright as could be. My wife stood up bravely and went through with the ceremony neatly and pleasantly. We were married at half past two o'clock p.m. at the residence of John Jones, Esqr. Wm. H. Roberts and Catharine M. Roberts accompanied us. We got home in time for an early supper and found Mrs. Peck, James Dillow, Theo. Smith, & Jno. E. Hornbeck there. John Hornbeck was a witness to the marriage ceremony. Sarah Tingley & Ree J. Cornwell were here also helping our folks. Jas. Bell & L. Dow Couples met us on the railway with a paddy.

There was a debate at the schoolhouse on this evening. The boys hearing of my wedding all gathered in & came down with bells and horns and gave a good decent belling, one of the old fashioned good ones. We gave them as much lemonade as they could drink and as many cakes as they could eat. I then thanked them kindly for their respect to me. They gave me three cheers & then started for Alvah Rushes, he having married the widow Porter on Tuesday in Springfield. . . . The belling party were not invited in at Rushes. They sung several negro songs that ruffled Rush somewhat.

Monday, May 9th, A.D. 1859

I am once more in the schoolroom and seated at the old table wielding the rod of the teacher & training the young ideas of this vicinity how to shoot.

Since I last wrote in this book I have entered fully upon the realities of life. I have built and moved into my house since then. I raised my house on the 6th day of April, 1859. I commenced housekeeping on the 25th of April, 1859. . . . I commenced teaching here on the 2d of May, 1859, & have made a bargain for three months at twenty dollars per month & board myself.

On Monday, Apr. 11th, [they] had a school meeting for an election of directors. Over twenty four voters out. Seven candidates for directors, there being 3 to elect; Jas. Porter elected for 3 years, Lewis Potee for two years, & I for one year. I was appointed clerk of the district and now will have all or nearly all the business to do. Board of education met on Monday, Apr. 18th; organized in the afternoon by appointing Mr. Armstrong chairman; levied a tax of a half mill on the dollar to pay teachers in the township. Had a considerable amount of argument on the question of holding meetings in the schoolhouse. The board left the matter in the hands of the local directors, there being no law for anything of the kind. One hundred and forty one dollars in the No. 1 district treasury. . . .

The prospect for corn, wheat, oats, grass, & in fact of every kind of grain is very flattering this spring. . . . I worked one day last week for Wm. Godfrey planting corn. . . .

Maria Andrews still has the ague. . . . She has had it for nearly a year. I am afraid that she will never get over it if she does not look sharp, as drugs have lost their efficacy in her case, as her system has become so saturated with them that there is no room for any more of their qualities to enter into her system. . . .

My lot has indeed been cast in a pleasant place. I am now in good employment, and everything is as well with me as I could wish. I have some friends warm and true. I have star[ted] fair & honest with the world, which does not exactly owe me a living, but I think that there is a living in the world for me if I only make a strong enough effort to obtain it. I think that I have energy & perseverance enough to take me through. If not, I ought to go down unpitied and unnoticed. I now have a home, a circle small to be sure; still, it can contain just as much happiness as a larger one & perhaps more, because there is not so much to see after, not so many chords to keep in harmony, not so many minds to influence for good, & I am now inclined to look at the bright side of the picture & hope that I may always be able to see the bright side. . . .

Tuesday, May 10th, A.D. 1859

. . . I am in very good health at present. I still have the old habit of using tobacco engrafted on my constitution so that I am afraid that I shall never quit it. . . .

Wm. H. Roberts, Allen Anderson, & Valentine Wilson are working at Mr. Jas. Garrards house at this time. It is a $75 job. They are going to have enough work to last them all summer. They ought to lay up some money as they are getting good wages, and of course their money is sure.

There is no sickness around here of any consequence, only some old chronic complaints made so by the use of drugs & medications of various kinds. It seems curious to me that people will continue to drug themselves, when they know that they get no better and that drugs are actually injurious to the organism of the human body. Still, the time will come when the laws of health will be thoroughly understood by all, and by being so it will certainly be practiced by the human family. Then pain and disease will rarely pester the corporal frame. Old age will not then be filled with pains & sleepless nights, but the frame will gradually wear out from age and peacefully fall into the grave.

The time is going off smoothly & pleasantly along at this time. There is no excitement here at this time, nothing to make the blood boil over & the passions inflame, & I am not sure but that it is best that it should be so, as those tremendous storms of religious and political excitement are calculated to leave the minds of the people more sluggish after they are over than they were before they commenced. The mind can be exhausted by these things as well as the body is by unnatural and severe exercise. There is a certain amount of excitement necessary for the mind and body to remain in a healthy state. We need something at times to stir up the inner man to action and to quicken the flow of the blood.

I have had enough business to do lately to keep my blood in circulation, as I have had to run around and get a great many things to keep house with. Still, this is a pleasure to me. . . .

Tonight is lodge night and I must go into London & go into the lodge. If I do not, I will begin to get rusty in the work of the craft, and I am in favor of living up to my profession, . . . & I am sure this is a noble and good profession, i.e., Masonry, when it is carried out as it should be.

. . . Some of my smallest scholars are already getting to be a little too familiar. I must bring them down a peg or two, or I will be outgeneralled by them. It takes a great deal of patience & forebearance to govern a lot of little chaps. I would rather undertake a large regiment of men than a large school of five year old schoolboys. They so soon forget your admonitions. Still, I am very fond of the business and do not complain of it as a nuisance but rather like it, as it puts a man to working his wits sometimes and stirs him up and makes him lively. . . .

Wednesday, May 11th, A.D. 1859

. . . There are some streaks of bad luck attending some of my friends. B.F. Roberts horse has the distemper, not very badly, however, at this time. S.D. Truitts horse has had it very severely. He has been lanced in the head and neck five or six times. The horse is getting some better. He will not do much with him for more than a month to come. This is a heavy blow on Doc, as he intended to make a considerable profit out of him this season. . . . He is keeping him at Father Truitts at this time. John W. Brown is attending to B.F. Roberts horse. . . .

I got some medicine of Dr. Darling for my wife . . . last night. A doctor bill is a bore, not so much on account of the money as upon the account of the suffering produced by the disease and the wrecking of the constitution by the strong medicine. I take it for a truth that more than half of the diseases of the human family are caused by medicine.

I have about twenty five pupils today, not more, however, than I want, as I cannot feel right unless I have plenty to do.

I saw the assessor today, Mr. McCormack. He asked me if I had any taxable property. I told him no and left him. I must have some taxable property by the time the assessor comes around next year. I am not one of those that are unwilling to keep up our government, as I am sure it is bound to support me after I become helpless or unable to do for myself.

This is a glorious government of ours, one of the very best in the world, and I am in favor of paying to keep up its expenses without grumbling. Those foreigners and others that do not like our laws and institutions can just leave as soon as they have a mind to go, and there soon [will] be enough good men found to occupy the spots they will leave unoccupied, & their presence or absence will not make a particle of difference to the great mass [of] freemen in this goodly land.

Semp Saunders has a lot of money in town for himself left there by the railroad co. for wood cut by him & put upon the r[ail]road. He will be on a flush now. The amt., $185.00, [is] a good little pile these hard times. G.W. Saunders talks of coming to school this summer. . . .

Last night was lodge night, and I worked with the craft, took a view of the beauties of the structure founded on wisdom and held together by the strong band of brotherly love, cemented by charity & benevolence, and illuminated by hope. There is no earthly institution that can equal it. Nothing can break its strong chain of beauty and strength. It has the impress of age stamped upon its every feature. I love every feature of it and am always glad to hear of the prosperity of the craft.

They are going to have a celebration on the 25th of next June at Mechanicsburgh. The London lodge is invited to attend. I do not expect to be able to go, as I am engaged in teaching and it will make a balk in my school to attend to it. . . .

They are going on with the new church here again. I do not know whether it will be finished this hitch or not. Mr. Joshua Cory has the job now and seems to be putting it through.

Thursday, May 12th, A.D. 1859

This morning I had enough scholars to commence at half past eight o'clock. I do not get them out hardly ever till nine o'clock and not all of them by that time. I have a tolerably noisy school. . . . The reason of this is because the most of them are as small as the law permits to come to school, and I am not sure but what some of them are under age. . . .

I am not doing much work about home. . . . I am now trying to build a henhouse. . . . I have got it built up three rounds & have enough logs to make it nine or ten rounds high. I would like to have some rails made to fence in my yard. I must pitch into the rail business this week.

. . . The pastures will be very good this season, & I am glad of it, for butter and milk is very scarce at this time. Butter was twenty five cents per pound week before last, but now it is worth something less. . . . There is a fine prospect now for a bountiful harvest of everything in the farming line.

I have not heard from my old friend W.T. Cobaugh for some time. The last time that I heard from him he was engaged in selling fruit trees in Union Co. and was making pretty good wages at it. . . .

I have but twenty pupils today and I feel first rate. It [is] a most excellent day for study. The scholars are getting very good lessons today. I must try the Normal plan as soon as possible, as I think it is the best that I can adopt. I heard from Jos. B. Couples this week. He has a very light school. . . . I have had several teachers graduate under my tuition. J.B. Couples, Jos. Cartzdafner, & Miss Mary Weldon are all my pupils, and they all have certificates for teaching. E. Hull is now holding forth in Somerford. Hull is a fine fellow, sociable and clever, and ought to be patronized by the people.

Jas. H. Roberts is farming this season. I must go over & pay him a visit soon, as I have not been over for some time. . . .

Friday, May 13th, A.D. 1859

This makes the last day of the second week of my school. I am getting pretty near used to staying in the house. I am now taking up school in the morning at half past eight, noon recess from half past eleven till one o'clock, forenoon recess at quarter past 10 o'clock . . . , and half past two o'clock in the afternoon. I am giving tickets this quarter. I am in favor of a reward system if it can be judiciously & rightly applied. I must teach the best I know how this quarter, as I am now in favor of establishing myself permanently in this part of the country. I had a reading match this afternoon. They do not understand the process very well. Still, I shall make it interesting and profitable, I think, before the quarter is out.

I went home at noon after the key to the table which I had forgotten to bring this morning. I must go to mill this evening. Also, I must plant some potatoes, as they say the sign is now right for planting potatoes. I filled a straw tick this morning at Mr. Allens straw pile. . . .

I may have to help Godfrey plant corn tomorrow. If not I must make some rails & finish my hen house.

Monday, May 16th, A.D. 1859

. . . I have 32 pupils today, quite a number for the summer school. There are eight or ten new pupils today from Sam Prughs & Eli Wilsons.

I was over to Father Truitts Saturday night and all day Sunday. The old lady is quite unwell at this time. . . .

P.L. Roberts & Wm. Roberts were at my house on Sunday. I was over at Somerford on Saturday along with John Wm. Brown. I bought some sugar & tea of G. & A.T. Prugh, also a paper of pins & 3/4 of a yard of calico. It goes kind of queer for me to be buying these things. I have been used to buying them when I kept *bach* in days of Auld Lang Syne. I find married life much pleasanter than keeping *bach*, there being many little inconveniences attached to this *baching* business that a person does not have to contend with in married life.

Tuesday, May 17th, A.D. 1859
. . . P.L. Roberts has been dipping into the gift book business. He has made it pay pretty well. . . .

Wednesday, May 18th, A.D. 1859
. . . C.M. Roberts, Ree J. Cornwell, & my wife all went to meeting last night to the Williams Chapel to hear a German preacher by the name of Miller from Iowa. He is the author of the book called Experience of German Ministers in America, a readable book by the way. John Peck bought one. So did S.D. Truitt. They all got home at midnight. It is entirely too far to go to night meeting in the summertime, & I do not know but what it is too far to go in the wintertime. This thing of going 12 miles at night through the mud is not very healthy or good for the organism, and I am going to quit it for my part. S.D. Truitt stayed all night at my house last night. He is the first person that has stayed all night with us since we have commenced keeping house. He also was the first one to eat with us. . . .

The old feud existing between the Clark County chaps & the Oak Run folks received some more fuel on last Sunday. Wm. H. Roberts, Wm. Anderson, & Valentine Wilson went up there to a sing carried on by Mike Wilson & co[mpany] at the brick schoolhouse. The boys went there civilly and peaceably and sat down. . . . Wm. Anderson laughed some during the sing at some girls that were making themselves rather fresh. After the sing was out Mike Wilson took Bill to task about making fun of their women and accused them of coming there to raise a fracas. They denied the assertion and told him if they had thought of raising a rumpus they would have brought more force along with them to weigh against their pork up there. One word brought on another till finally Mike invited them to go down the road so that he could give them a dressing. They did go down, but Mr. Wilson took water and would not fight after arriving on the ground, but he said that he would see them again. This is Henries version of the affair. There is another quite different one, and that is that Wm. Anderson took back what he said & begged off. . . .

Thursday, May 19th, A.D. 1859
. . . I have only about 29 pupils today, one new one from Lewis Potees, one of his twin boys, Hezekiah. Yesterday I had quite a time with Frances Peck and Missouri Tingley. They had a paper doll in time of school & were playing with it. I kept them in after school and talked to them considerable about it but did not whip them. They promised me that they would do better in future if I would only let them off for that time. I did so but told them that they would meet with more severe punishment for the next offence of the same kind.

I am afraid that I talk too much to the scholars. I must be a little more strict with them hereafter. I do not believe in being tyrannical or harsh. I think that school government should be mild but firm. I must fit and qualify myself more fully for the work. It takes a great amount of patience and close application to teach school right. I have conceit enough, however, to think that I can make a good No. 1 teacher out of myself. I intend to try my very best to accomplish that very difficult undertaking, as the teachers profession is one of the noblest callings in the world, and it is also one of the most pleasant if rightly understood. The teacher is at the foundation of our liberty. The teacher and the printer are the two most useful of all the learned professions. Take them from the people and the sun of liberty would soon set forever. Therefore the American people should pay them liberally.

Friday, May 20th, A.D. 1859
. . . Last night I received a letter from Henry Peck from California. He is not doing much for himself. The mines are not a very profitable thing, I should judge. Perhaps it is owing altogether to luck, or chance, rather than industry. He also sent me a couple of papers, the San Andreas Independent and the Golden Era of Sacramento. They are very good papers. All is not gold that glitters, nor is there a fortune for every man in California. Henry talks of coming home or of going to Mexico before long. I rather suspect he will come home. I do wish he would, as his folks are very anxious about him.

. . . I am going to have a reading match today. I had one last Friday but did not do much at it, as it was only a kind of introduction to it. . . .

I finished my hen roost and I must try and get home some chickens to fill it up with. . . .

I received a small poster yesterday from a showman stating that there would be a circus in London June 6th, 1859. It is called Antonio and Wilders Circus. They say that it is a very good institution and pays a person very well to go into it. I will not go, I do not think, as it is on a Monday & I do not want to loose the time.

Monday, May 23d, A.D. 1859

. . . Joseph B. Couples came home on Friday evening. . . . He has . . . got something like the measles. He is not bedfast. I do hope that the measles will not get into my school this term. I had to contend against a great many difficulties last winter, and I want a better time this summer. None of the Couples family are here today, and I am in hopes that they may not come till the danger is past.

Winter before last I had the mumps to contend with. Last winter I had the mud & big meetings to combat, and this summer I must try the measles a round, I suspect. . . .

There is going to be a big meeting up here on next Saturday and Saturday evening. The Methodists are the getters up of the institution, and I suppose we will have an old fashioned preach with a plenty of fire & brimstone in it.

Yesterday I stayed home all the time. Emarine went up to class in the forenoon along with C. Margaret. We had about a dozen visitors in the afternoon, all boys. . . . Jas. Dillow cut my hair and my whiskers. . . . Wm. H. Roberts ate dinner, and B.F. Roberts, John Peck, & Wm. Truitt ate their suppers at our house. The day passed off pleasantly and agreably. It was just about cool enough to be right for comfort.

Godfrey went down to James Andrews in a wagon & took a lot of the women folks with him. Jas. Andrews has had the bad luck to lose his mare. The best one he had died last week. This is a hard blow for him, as his wife has been sick for a long time and he has not had a chance to do much. . . .

I helped Godfrey on Saturday. We laid up a pretty good string of new fence along his new ground. We planted some potatoes for him in the afternoon. It rained like blazes in the afternoon, and I got as wet as a rat, as I was out in it all nearly.

Wheat and flour is very high at this time. Flour is $4 per hundred.

I took a dozen hens over to my house from Mothers on Saturday evening & put them in the hen house; one out this morning. . . .

Religion and religious institutions are at this time making a great stir in the U.S. Revivals are going on in different parts of the country, and men are enrolling themselves under the banners of the different sects and are professing to have a new birth & to be regenerated. Some even pretend to sanctification and being without sin, blameless before God & free from sin of every kind. These poor fanatics are, however, pretty scarce.

I have been applying my mind to the subject for some time past, but I am unable to make anything out of the subject. I am a firm believer in a Supreme Being and in the Bible. I, however, do not pretend to be an expounder of its truths, nor to see more than every other or any other person into its mysteries. This thing of praying to be seen of men I am not in favor of at all. There are many in this little world of ours that pray long and loud in public but never send up the first petition from the closet. Our religious institutions are saddled with so many ceremonies and various hard mystical rites that not one in ten thousand can make out clearly the doctrine that they have subscribed to, and that [they] have solemnly pledged themselves not only to believe but also to support in every situation through life.

Now this thing of a man supporting and vindicating something that he knows nothing more than the name of is radically wrong. Yet it is a lamentable truth even in this enlightened day and hour of the nineteenth century [that] there are many persons who are advocating the doctrine of the Trinity of the Great Ruler & Grand Master of the Universe that do not know what the term means or what it signifies. Still, if a man does [not] say he believes in the Trinity he is called a skeptic and unorthodox, a fit companion only for dogs and harlots. In fact, no good that such a one can do will ever merit a solitary smile or the least favor from the Great Prince of Peace, that is, in the estimation of those Trinity advocates spoken of before. Still, these same Trinitarians cannot produce a solitary argument in favor of their theory. They call it a mystery and pass along. It is the same with those advocates for eternal punishment beyond the grave, for what is this that ought to merit eternal torment? Orthodoxy says that it will fall to the lot of all those that do not get religion or a change of heart. My God, what a fearful multitude there must be in that place if this is so!

Tuesday, May 24th, A.D. 1859

. . . S.D. Truitt was over this morning on his way to help Godfrey plant corn. The prospects for a bountiful harvest are very flattering at this time, and I am in hopes that they may prove true and that abundance may be the cry when harvest comes, as the nations of Europe are about to plunge into a war.

The chains of those tyrants are rusting and nothing short of a war can brighten them up again. I only wish that all those potentates were compelled to fight their own battles, stripped naked and unarmed, and on short allowances at that. They would soon be peaceable enough and be very willing to listen to reason. I presume there will be over a million of men under arms this war in Europe. This will make provisions very high here in this country and will flood this country with emigrants from the desolated kingdoms of Europe who will prefer exile to a foreign land to the miseries of war at home.

Some people are much in favor of the war in Europe, as they think it will be a great benefit to this country. I do not think it is right for us to rejoice over the miseries of those unhappy countries now plunged in a bloody contest for liberty.

I must quit Somerford and go to London for my groceries, as I cannot get what I want at Prughs, and this thing of going to a place for a thing and not getting it is a bore and a big bore too. I must buy my groceries by the wholesale as soon as I can do it, as it is much cheaper and a great deal more convenient. . . .

I am still a little sleepy in the afternoon. I do not live right or this would not be so. I ought to take more pains to live rightly; then I would enjoy myself. I must begin to take a morning bath now pretty soon, & [stop] chewing that vile narcotic tobacco, as I am sure that it is using me up and rendering me nervous & miserable. Still, I continue to use it upon all occasions. I, however, do not carry any of my own in my own pocket but have been a notorious beggar for the last year or two. I am getting heartily ashamed of it and ought to have quit it long ago. . . . Tobacco is more of an enemy to me than ardent spirits. Why it is so is because I have never indulged in the spirits and have in the tobacco. . . .

The nats and musquitoes are getting awful bad here at this time. They are now swarming over this page and into my eyes with a perfect rush. I will have to quite writing on account of them. . . .

Thursday, May 26th, A.D. 1859

As the news is not of a very brisk or exciting [kind] and as there is going to be an exhibition in Somerford on tomorrow evening, I will just copy a piece that I have some notion of putting in as an afterpiece. It is called The Loafers Soliloquy. [JMR quotes a story in dialect of a drunk who falls over a wheelbarrow into a coal cellar and tries to fix the blame for his plight.]

[He adds at a later date:]

Exhibition went off very well. Kept it up till midnight. I spoke the Soliloquy for an afterpiece. I never saw as large a crowd in my life as there was in the Somerford s[chool]house, that is, so many persons packed in a house of that size. I suppose there must have been over 300 persons packed in the house. The house was literally crammed full up.

Their play entitled Irish Assurance was a rich thing and well played for an exhibition. P.L. Roberts took quite a prominent part in the exercises. They had music upon the violin by P.L. Roberts, Ichabod Gardner, Milton Gardner, & Taylor. C. Margaret & wife went over in Mothers spring wagon. I enjoyed myself hugely. . . .

It has been so long since I have written in this book that it goes awkward now to commence.

Wednesday, June 15th, A.D. 1859

. . . Times are getting tight here at this time & no mistake. . . . On the 4th of this month there was one of the severest frosts that has ever been seen by anyone in this part of the country at this time of the year. I have talked with a great many folks about it, and they say they never saw the like before. There was ice frozen more than half an inch thick. Some of the leaves on the trees were killed dead. In fact, some of them were stripped of their leaves entirely. The fruit of all kinds was injured very materially. Apples, peaches, plums, cherries, and berries of all kinds are more or less injured. All those berries that were in the open pastures are killed, but those in the woods are uninjured. We will have some fruit, such as apples & peaches & pears, but it will be of an inferior quality, not half as good as common. Some people are pretty badly alarmed about the wheat crop, as they think it is injured very materially. . . .

The corn before the last frost was in a very flourishing condition. It was, however, cut down level with the earth. Some persons are . . . planting over again. Some of the corn . . . was knee high & was doing finely. The frost, however, leveled it all to the earth. The beans and vines of every description were cut down irremediably, and some fields of wheat are badly frozen. All the wheat in very low black ground is ruined & done for. The most of it, however, is in good condition, and there have been so many good showers since the frost that the corn will soon be as good as it was before the frost.

This frost has extended all over the state of Ohio & Kentuckey in the northern part, also the northern part of Illinois & the whole of Indiana, also into New York and Pennsylvania. . . .

I am nearly half way through with my school. I was up yesterday to see James Porter about taking the job of repairing the s[chool]house. He wants to sell out the job to the lowest responsible bidder, and I do not know who will bid upon the job; no one, I presume, without it is A. Cornwell, & he is not a very good workin[g]man. I have written a note to Mr. Potee about the matter & I expect an answer tomorrow. . . .

The singing school has nearly ran out; that is, the last quarter is nearly out. They talk of having a grand picnic on next Saturday week, on

Charley Littlers place close to his house. This has become very fashionable here of late. They had quite an extensive basket sing down near Midway about two weeks ago. The London brass band was at the Midway picnic. The Midway & Newport choirs were singing to see who could excel. Newport came out first best in the exercise, so I understood from some of the spectators. . . .

We have had some very nice weather since the frost, and I am in hopes that we may have easier times on account of it, as wages are very low at this time. Wm. Anderson is working for Lancisco Peck at $10 per month. He is only going to work at this rate till harvest. He will then put out for harvest wages. I would be glad to hear of a rise in wages of every kind. I am of the opinion that we are going to have good prices after harvest for everything in the farming line, as the Austrian and French war has commenced in Europe & they need all the provisions that they can raise to feed their armies. . . .

The scholars are getting restless. This warm weather makes them very restless and uneasy. I must draw the reins a little more taught and see if I cant straighten them around somewhat, as they begin to need it very much. They are not as bad as some that I have seen. Still, they are not what I want them to be.

Thursday, June 16th, A.D. 1859

. . . My school is getting along first rate. I had 29 pupils yesterday. I have a new pupil today, Rebecca Rodrick. John Peck is not here today. He ought to come more steady, as he never can make much headway by coming as he has come heretofore.

It does seem curious to me that people do not take more interest in school matters and education than what they do. This is the chief thing in life, . . . or at least it should be the main thing to be thought of, because what is a man when he is perfectly ignorant of everything connected with education? He [is] nothing more than a mere animal. He knows no higher pleasures than that of eating and drinking. His soul is stunted, dwarfed, in fact almost so small that it may almost be doubted whether he has any soul or not. Then there are the many pecuniary advantages connected with the possessor of a good education. Why do people overlook this important item? It is worse than madness for a man to think of acquiring a fortune without an education. In this bustling world of ours the thing is impossible. . . .

There are quite a number of nondescripts traveling through the country at this time. They are all begging. I suppose from their appearance they must be Gipsies, as they have the features of that peculiar race of people stamped upon them. They say there is a large encampment of them in this county somewhere. I am of the opinion that they will do some extensive stealing before they leave here.

These people are a very singular set of beings. They never stay long in one place, never build houses, never own any land, speak a strange and mysterious language, and have manners & customs entirely different from any people. They come under no government but submit to every kind of government with a kind of apathy that seems almost philosophical. They never work any whatever, yet they seem to take a delight in withstanding the toils of long journeys and bid defiance to cold & heat. What are they and where did they first spring from? Can it be that they are a part and parcel of the ancient Egyptians that were so famous for their stupendous works of art and for their learning & refinement? If this is indeed so, they must have retrograded sadly since the days of Cleopatra, & if this is the truth, may it not be possible that the European race may run out & become as degraded as they are?

A schoolroom is one of the best places in the world for studying human nature. Here you can see all the springs of our nature laid open. Vanity and high mindedness, cunning, patience & impatience can here be fully canvassed and thoroughly understood. If you make rules, you can see a growing desire in some to break & run over them. If you permit them to gratify some whim or caprice, you will soon see them tire of it & lay it aside of their own accord. For instance, if you allow them to run to the water bucket whenever they please, [you] will hardly ever see them drink much, but just make it a kind of a gift at your option & they will continually be asking you for the privilege. They will never think anything about taking a drink during recess, but the very moment you stop ringing the bell for school to commence there will arise from every quarter of the house a cry for water, not from one or two but from them all en masse, and if you grant them the privilege, they will enjoy it to its fullest extent. This is on account of their combatting principles, I suppose, & I am of the opinion that this is all for the best and is just as it should be. Some people are, however, of a different opinion. They think that this is depravity caused by Adams fall.

Friday, June 17th, 1859

This is the anniversary of the battle of Bunkers Hill. There has been quite a change in this country since that memorable event. The western states were then a vast wilderness unknown to white men & perfectly inaccessible to the approach of civilization. Now every river is covered with boats & barges. Every valley now has its own iron horse snorting & screaming along on its iron track. People think that they have hard times now, but it is not a tithe of the hardships that were endured by those iron men, the pioneers of the great West.

Mother has gone to Darby today to haul up some of her mill timbers. G.W. Saunders took down his ox team. I would be glad to see the mill under good repair and in good working order. Newton is growling like blazes about it, but it does no good for him to make a muss about it, as he cant make the thing go any faster.

I have advertized the letting out of the s[chool]house job per order of directors, sale to be today week. Wm. Truitt wants to go in with me if I get the job. . . . I am handy to it & can be at home every night. It would be a good thing for me to pitch into immediately after my present term is out.

Monday, June 20th, A.D. 1859

. . . We had quite a time here at our Saturday evenings sing. Wm. Orpet was here drunk as a loon. He came up to the window on the outside of the house and commenced swearing roundly at the singing teacher. I went to him and civilly requested him to be still. He immediately commenced cursing me and pulling off his coat. I was sorely tempted to knock him down. He was so drunk, however, that he could not stand still. Old Mr. Couples pulled him down and finally took him off. Bill is getting to be drunken and insolent. Some persons keep selling him whiskey in London, & I am in hopes that they may be jerked up for it and fined severely, as Bill is becoming a nuisance to the whole community. I do wish that liquor laws were ten times more stringent than what they now are.

We also had a singing school on Sunday in the afternoon. . . . There was quite a large crowd of people out. . . . There were quite a number of strangers present, five or six that I did not know.

James H. Roberts, E. Hull, and the Somerford folks have come to the conclusion to have more light & knowledge. They are going to try to get up a select school in Somerford. They met last Saturday evening and passed resolutions to that effect. They have appointed me on one of the committees.

On Saturday I was at Godfreys & helped him measure some ground that he cleared last winter for C. Hornbeck. He has 11-1/4 acres cleared and in corn at this time. He gets $8 an acre for clearing and plowing it up & gives 1/3 of the corn he raises off of it. He has performed a power of manuel labor in those woods over there, and will do an immense amount more if he lives and keeps his health.

I have the most scholars today that I have had during this term. I have 36 here today. . . .

Henry and Allen are making it pay up at Jim Porters. It will take them two months or more to get through up there, I expect. However, they will make good wages all the time while they are at work at that job.

S.D. Truitt, Wm. Truitt, & P.L. Roberts ate dinner with me at my house on Sunday last. Jas. H. Roberts and E. Hull stopped in a few moments to get a drink. They were there for the first time. . . .

The new meetinghouse has again fizzled, and the workmen have again went home. I am of the opinion that it will be some time before they will get anyone else . . . to work on the job. The narrow minded, contracted, and cramped policy of the Methodist Church is a little too much behind the age to drive things just the way they want them.

Wesley Allens strawberries are all gone. He made nearly three hundred dollars out of the patch this season. He is pretty badly nonplussed about several little circumstances that have taken place on or about his premises. He discovered one day last week a very curious kind of an instrument in his geer house. It is supposed to be an instrument used by housebreakers. . . . It is called a jimmy, I believe. He has also missed a couple of hoes taken from the granary at or about the time this tool was left there, and he also got up one night and found his ash house on fire, supposed to be the work of an incendiary, as there had been no fire put into the house for more than a week. . . . I am of the opinion that it is some person who wants to pester Wesley & get him into a sweat just for amusement.

Raspberries are getting ripe. . . . There are not a very great quantity of them, however, . . . as the frost killed all of those that were in the open ground. . . .

I have made a division in my A.B.C.darians today. I must put this small class through and see what I can do for them, as I have the starting of them all myself. I wish I had the phonetic system introduced here. I think that I could certainly advance them much faster than by the old way. I hope that the system will become so popular that it will be introduced into the school system of Ohio by law. Then those tedious, unmeaning spelling classes will be dispensed with, and we will go upon certainties and not be groping in the dark as we have had to do heretofore. I therefore say speed, speed the happy day. Let us have a thorough set of scientific readers, real orators. More than 3/4 of the time spent in school is spent in learning to spell and read. This ought not to be so, and the worst of it is that not one in ten ever acquire a decent knowledge of either of those important branches.

Tuesday, June 21st, 1859

. . . On next Saturday we are to have our picnic or basket sing and everyone is on the qui vive for it. . . .

They are having quite a time down at Newport about their 4th of July dinner. The Methodists and Radicals have made a divide. The Methodists are going down to Midway and throw all their influence down to that place. The Radicals wanted the picnic to go by their name, and so they had a quarrel about the matter. Wonder if they could agree in Heaven if they were there? I am of the opinion that their religion will never take them there at any rate. I wanted to go to Newport to their dinner, but I do not know whether I will or not. Two or three Methodists about Newport have given $50 apiece towards the Midway concern. I go in for home institutions myself and do [not?] approve of the action taken by these gentlemen in this matter.

. . . I presume the new church here has gone by the board, as they have quit working at it and the carpenters have all taken their tools away and are in debt for the lumber already upon the ground. . . . The church over on the pike will soon be under cover, I presume, as they are driving things right along over there, so I understand.

I did not get to work any yesterday, and I am in the same row today, so my work will get ahead of me if I do not look sharp. My garden needs working badly, & I must pitch into it as soon as possible if I want to raise anything. I have got it partly hoed up but not entirely so. My potatoes are doing fine and will make very good ones if they are only attended to in time.

. . . I am somewhat surprised at some things I hear . . . today. One of Rodricks boys wanted to go into the second reader. When I told him if he had a book of that kind he might go into the class, his sister immediately spoke up and said that his mother said that he must still continue to read in the first reader, as Mr. Adams was going to teach here next winter and he was going to have different books introduced. . . . I think that this is counting chickens very fast before they are hatched. I must see the other directors about this matter and see what they will do for me before long, as I am not so sure that Mr. Adams will teach here. . . . It looks a little kind of queer that such word should get out around here and I not get to hear anything of it. Perhaps it has been merely hinted at by Mr. Adams, and some of the others have taken it up on ready wings to annoy me somewhat by it. . . .

The political horizon is very murky at this time. The Republican party has gone more and more toward abolitionism, and I am of the opinion that they will drop the name of Republicans after a while and take up the name of abolitionist, as they are that now in principle at this very moment. I wish for my part that every wooly head was in Africa, not even reserving one to raise tobacco with. . . .

The Oberlin chaps are having a great muss about some runaway negroes. They murdered or attempted to murder the U.S. marshal. It was attempted by two negroes. All this was done just because this man was attempting to do his duty . . . after some fugitives that had escaped from service in Kentucky. I see by the papers that some of their leaders up in Oberlin are for raising an army to resist the officers of the general government. I do wish they would, & that in the first engagement they would all be taken prisoners and the head men all hung upon the very highest trees that could be found. Perhaps they would then learn some sense, or their deluded followers might see them as they really are.

I am getting to be more & more a lover of tobacco every day and still know well enough that it is injurious to my system & that it is a source of vexation and expense to me & my friends. . . .

I have about 30 pupils today. 3 of them, however, have gone home, Louise Cornwell & her two brothers. . . . Adam wants his little chap to set up corn this afternoon. I am not in favor of taking children away from school. It is the worst thing that can be done for them, as education is the life & soul of the community. It is the mainspring that moves the world. Still, people are getting to be very remiss about these things. . . .

Wednesday, June 22d, 1859

. . . They are preparing for the sing which is to come off on Saturday. They say the Midway choir is going to be on hands. . . . John Hornbeck & Peter Timmons are going to have a grocery on the ground. It is all right if they do not sell whiskey or lager. If so they will be compelled to quit, as we do not want to have any drunken men upon the ground. . . .

They raised their new meetinghouse over on the pike near Orcutts mill yesterday. It will be a pretty large house, I understand, and will accommodate quite a large congregation. It was raised without any accident . . . happening to any person. Orcutts are very much opposed to the church there, and I suppose that they have some cause for being so, as the church is uncomfortably near to his premises, & it is quite a bother sometimes to those that live near a church in the country.

Thursday, May [June] 23d, 1859

. . . The weather is remarkably cool for the time of year, which makes it very nice upon the wheat but not very good upon the corn crops. Still, the corn is growing very nicely. The potatoes are doing fine, and so is the most of the garden *truck* in these *diggins*. I hear that the wheat crop down about Dayton is not only good but very good. They say they have never had such good crops since the Mad River valley was first settled. . . . This [is] cheering news to those poor, unfortunate, panic stricken wretches who a few weeks ago were ready to go into hysterics about the frost killed wheat. . . .

I understand that Miss Ann Melvin has quarreled with her sweetheart Hardman. Well, the course of love never did run smooth, and there must be a few clouds for lovers as well as other people. . . . I would be glad to hear of her marriage to some good, clever, industrious fellow, as I think she is a very clever kind of a young woman, and as she is rather in an unprotected situation, and there are hounds enough in the world to blacken peoples character even when they are surrounded by friends that would be fully able to punish them for their mean & despicable conduct; and she being an orphan & poor at that is more liable to be defamed by those hellhounds.

Friday, June 24th, A.D. 1859
. . . Old Leven Jones is dead. He died sometime last week. Dropsy was what put an end to him, so I understand. Well, we must all go someday, and perhaps the sooner we get off the better. If it was not for the uncertainty that man is in as regards the future state, we might be more reconciled to our fate, but I presume that this dread of death [is] natural and therefore it must be all right, as I am of the opinion that everything that is natural is right and just. . . . I am of the opinion that God never intended that anything should be lost that He had formed, & that in His own good time He will bring everything around as it should be.

It is raining at this time & I am afraid that it will be a bad time tomorrow for the basket sing.

Monday, June 27th, A.D. 1859
. . . I have about 18 pupils today & I also have had the toothache for the greater part of the day.

Our picnic sing went off as pleasantly as the most sanguine of us expected. There was not the slightest thing to mar the harmony of the day. The whole ground abounded with mirth and good humor. There never was so large [a] crowd gathered upon Oak Run for any purpose, & none was ever so satisfactorily ended. Wm. H. Roberts, Chas. Littler, & myself had a grocery or lemonade stand on the ground. We had about $34 worth of nuts, figs, & raisins, besides ice, lemons, cigars. We sold about $28 worth & cleared nearly a dollar apiece or perhaps more. . . . We gave away about $6 worth of stuff. Thos. Paice & wagon were over to make a speculation. Littler soon started him from the ground & we had the whole thing all to ourselves.

Nearly everybody was over from Deer Creek, Jas. H. & P.L. Roberts, and I saw my old schoolmaster A.A. Hull from Turkey Ridge. . . .

Tuesday, June 28th, A.D. 1859

An old weather prophet down about Xenia prophesied that on the night of the 27th of June there would be a tremendous hard frost that would kill every green thing, and in fact there would be a hard freeze. Last night was the night, and it was one of the hottest nights that I have ever felt for a year. I fairly stewed. There was no sleeping in bed hardly on account of the heat. So much for the weather prophet. Some people were foolish enough to think that the prophesy would come true. I never once thought of the frost till the warmth of the night made me think about it & wish for some cool breeze to come.

D.B. Wilson was over to the sing on Saturday and he was very drunk. He is a sad drunk, and when he is where he can get whiskey to drink, he would be much better off if he was without money entirely. . . . If he was without money he would be kicked out of company, but he has a few dollars and peo[ple] bow down to them and shut their eyes upon his faults.

I have but 18 pupils today. They come but very irregular. Some days I have 29 or 30, & some days but 18 or 20. I do not know what to do to secure a regular attendance. There ought to be some law in regard to this matter. People ought to be compelled to send their children to school. . . .

Mother has sent down some teams today to Darby to haul up her mill timbers. Godfrey had promised her that he would go down and help her haul some, but he did not go & she got mad about it. It will be very hot on the oxen today to haul, & I am afraid that she will not get her mill repaired for some time yet. . . .

I got a letter from Peter Adams yesterday. He is one of my wifes uncles. He lives in Illinois. He says things are prospering finely out there. The frost did not light in their part of the state but very slightly and did no damage whatever. . . .

John Peck is not here today. He is plowing corn, as Timothy Burt is sick . . . with the milk sickness. They sent for the doctor on Sunday last. I am not in favor of letting the milk sickness have a chance at me. I am very glad that [the] Burts refused to let my wife have any more butter. We have not . . . got any from them for more than a month. Nearly all the Burt family are sick with it. . . . This is the first case of the milk sickness that we have had in this neighborhood for a number of years. It used to be very prevalent in this part of Madison County.

My classes are getting along first rate. My 3d reader class is through the . . . reader three times. The 2d reader class is going through the second time. Some of the members of this class are making a decided progress. Also, one or two in the first reader class are making a very nice improvement, very visible to the most casual observer.

I have not much time to idle away from this time till fall school commences. I have not heard from the Somerford select school for some time. I suppose, however, it is still calculated to go on.

Wm. H. Roberts & A. Anderson are not working at Porters house at this time as he is out of lumber. They expect to get a job of building a barn for him.

. . . Wesley Allen has found an owner for those mysterious tools found in his granery. They were simply some drills brought from Springfield by Mr. Gabriel Potee. His boys having been engaged to haul berries from Springfield, this thing was brought by them & left there, as they were going the next trip to Columbus with berries and they did not expect to use the machine for some time to come. So it turned out to be a very simple thing at last. No robbers nor burglars had ever been around. Still, it was a puzzler for Wesley, & as it was mysterious, he of course put the worst construction on it. . . . People should never be too suspicious. They can make more trouble than a little for themselves. . . .

Wednesday, June 29th, A.D 1859

Harvest has now commenced here . . . in good earnest, and the farmers are now paying their best respects to the laboring man. The worker is now fully appreciated by the independent set who have earned enough by grinding down the faces of the community to buy up & monopolize the earth and the soil. I am not in favor of this thing called land monopoly. It is a dead weight upon the community. It is a curse to the country, a curse to their families, & a curse to themselves. The more land a man has the more trouble he will have. . . .

Harvest wages are now the general topic to be discussed by the community at large. $1.25 is the most that I have heard that has been paid for binders after a reaper. I would like very well to harvest some this season, as I want to get some wheat for bread. Godfrey was to have helped Mother cut down her harvest. . . . I think that wheat will be cheap this fall, as there will be a very good crop of it throughout the whole western country. The croakers are now hushed and we hear no more of their prophecies of evil. Their great frost has not come off. . . .

I am of the opinion that we must have more rain for the corn. . . . Corn is growing very slow at this time. Still, . . . a few more nights as [hot as] last night ought surely to bring it right out of the kinks, especially those kinks made by the frost. The most of the corn is knee high at this time, and it has all a very good color, and if there would only come some good showers now we would be safe enough. . . .

Elizabeth Allen is here today. She has came but very little since the quarter commenced. It is remarkable that the girls around here take no more interest in their studies than what they do. The most of them have very good minds and could excel in many parts if they only would. Some of the boys are very good . . . but the girls are rather upon the dull order. None of them are farther advanced than the fundamental principals of the English branches.

This ought not to be so in this land of freedom & knowledge. . . . This is the model republic and the only one in the world worthy of the name, and as women are the first teachers of the human race, they of course ought by all means to be thoroug[h]ly educated and enlightened.

Women occupy a secondary position in society in some respects, and in others they occupy a higher sphere than man does. I am not in favor of womens rights as advocated by some [of] the modern reformers. Still, they could be fitted for a higher position than they now occupy, & if they were, they would soon be occupying it.

Thursday, June 30th, 1859

The most exciting thing now upon the carpet is the tragical end of Lance Pecks cow, which came off yesterday afternoon. They heard a gun go off in the afternoon and did not expect anything of this kind. Some person belonging to the family having occasion to go into the pasture, they came across the cow with a bullet hole in her head. She lived an hour or so after she was discovered. No reason can be given for this wanton act of destruction, and I do not know anyone base enough to do the deed, especially in this quiet neighborhood. It is an animal that Nehemiah Nedds had last winter and which Mrs. Peck & Nedds had a quarrel about some time since. As Mrs. Peck took the cow away from Nedds just at a time when she would have been of use to him, this little fracas . . . will cause some people to judge Nedds of the deed. Still, I am of the opinion that he is not the guilty party. . . . Peck himself is a man very well liked by all, and why anyone should thus do him a private injury I am unable to say. Time may unravel the mystery.

Friday, July 1st, A.D. 1859

. . . Next Monday is the glorious 4th. I do not know but what I will teach on that day, as they say the black tongue [a fungus] is very bad down about Midway, and the Newport folks may also be getting it, some of them, and I am sure that I dont want the disease nor do I want any of my folks to be exposed to it.

C. Hornbeck has commenced cutting his wheat today. I saw Godfrey this morning with his force going over to help him. He has a machine at work for him. As a general thing people are cutting their wheat pretty green this year. Mothers wheat is not very ripe. Still, she is having it cut down.

Allen & Henry talk of going to Yankeetown tonight. They will have a long ride of it if they do go. Allen has just got back from Darby. . . . He was down at C.C. C[lifton]s and found them all right and kicking. They have an extensive crop this year. Their corn is first rate, & they have quite a lot of good wheat, and are doing the best that they ever did in their lives.

I have only about 15 pupils today, only two boys, John Newton & Albert Trowbridge. Newton has not been sending very regular for some time. His boys have been gathering berries to preserve, so they say. Newton himself has been running around much more than a miller ought to do. He has not been in the mill for four or five days. He is not a very pushing man about his business and will do but very little if he does not keep his eyeteeth cut. Perhaps he will do better after harvest when the new wheat begins to come in. He ought, however, to be pitching in now while flour is up. I hope he may make it pay and do well for himself as well as for Mother. He is a stubborn Englishman & I suspect there is no doing anything with him. The English are proverbial for their stubborn dispositions, & I presume he is of the same stripe with all the rest of the seed, breed, & generation.

I must go to Lewis Potees & get him to sign my school article about the repairs of the s[chool]house. I have articled with Porter, and I suppose that I must try and get Potee on it right off, as I am to have the work completed by the first of September. There are only two months to go upon.

I understand that Wm. T. Jones' mother has actually been on the verge of starvation and that the overseers of the poor were called in to attend to them. They found them in sad destitution. Now, it seems rather singular to me that the rich and powerful Methodist Church should let an old & faithful member starve in this land of plenty. It does not speak very well for their charity. The Good Book says that the man that does not provide for his own household is worse than [an] infidel. Now, if she is not of the Methodist household, then no one in this country has a right to say that they are of that household. So they, with all their boasted goodness, are not even charitable to their own, leaving out all others, and yet they claim to be the only true church. They claim to be the pure church, the world saving church. They pretend to sanctification or perfect purity and godliness, & in the face of all this they let an old, steady churchgoing member suffer for the common necessaries of life, a member grown gray under their banner and superannuated in their service. The Good Book says by their fruits ye shall know them.

Tuesday, July 5th, A.D. 1859

I took my 4th this year down at Newport in this county. They had a very fine time down there. A large dinner was set out upon a table and there was [a] general feast free of charge. Their table was bountifully supplied with every luxury of the season, and everything went off as it should go off. Rev. Mr. Fowler & Rev. Mr. Flood were the orators of the day. They are both clergymen of the Methodist Protestant denomination. Fowler did very well. He had his oration written down and read it to the audience.

My wife & C.M. Roberts went down along with me in Mothers spring wagon. The day was very cool and pleasant, and I enjoyed myself hugely at this celebration. The provisions for the company were not more than half exhausted by them, and there was a great quantity taken home by the getters up of the dinner. It spoke well for the liberality of that part of the community.

John Rea from Kansas was there and responded to a toast. He dragged in the Kansas troubles about slavery and made some remarks not all appropriate to the day and occasion. The London band were on hand and played some tunes pretty poorly. . . .

I got Lewis Potee to sign my article for the s[chool]house repairs, so I am in no danger of getting out of employment for some time to come. I must try and get this school for the fall and winter term. . . . I presume that I can get it, as I have the promise of it already from the other directors.

Negro equality is brewing a ferment in London at this time. Jesse Rea had a skirmish with one on last Saturday. The [Negro] was from Columbus and was acting out Pompey pretty tall down at the depot when some man upset him, and they had a battle in which wooly head got the worst of the bargain. Jesse asked him if he had had a fight. He said he had not & finally he called Jesse a damned liar, whereupon Jesse struck him with his fist. This, however, had no effect upon him. He then ran into the [Negro] and gave him another tanning. After this they took *Cuffee* down to Oak Run and ducked him good. They then took him to the railroad and put him upon the train bound for Columbus and told him his reception in the town of London on his next visit would be warmer than his present one had been.

The [Negro] in London that has been holding forth there as a daguerrean is about to be taken out of the place, and he has actually been warned out and told to leave the place as soon as he can get off. He was a very pompous [Negro], and I am glad to hear of his downfall. He took an active part in the [Negro] *fight* in town the other night. I am not sure about his actual pitching into the muss at the time, but he immediately after tried to protect him and upheld the [Negro] in his assault upon Rea.

I am in hopes that they may clear every wooly head out of the country and not allow another one to come in here for forty years. All this muss comes from the Oberlin philanthropists, or more properly speaking Oberlin [Negro]*loveism*. The Republican party has suffered these fanatics to be a part and parcel of their number, and also to lead their party. Infidelity and [Negroism] are now stalking hand in hand through this country. The great masses, however, are untainted with the malaria, and a few more such cases are calculated to awaken and arouse them from their lethargic slumber and hurl the corrupted officeholders down from their high places. The people are intelligent enough, and they will soon see the folly of these mock benefactors & [Negro] lovers, & they will soon estimate them at their true value. . . .

Henry, Allen Anderson, & John Wm. Brown are cutting Mothers wheat. . . . It is very well filled but it is thin upon the ground. It will yield 15 bu[shels] to the acre. Godfrey has promised to help Mother with her wheat. Still, he has failed to do so. . . . It does not look like the clear grit or the nice thing of him. Still, he may not be to blame as much as I now think he is. I am going to make it a rule hereafter not to judge too hastily, as there are always two sides of the question. . . .

Henry and Allen went down to C. C[lifton]s near Yankeetown and got back on Sunday evening. He says that they are all in first rate spirits and . . . doing first rate. . . . They have in about 30 acres of prime corn and about 15 acres of No. 1 wheat. I am glad to hear of their prosperity. I do not intend ever to go down there anymore.

James Garrard has purchased a machine to reap with, Kirbys patent, I believe. It is at work today on his plantation.

Wednesday, July 6th, A.D. 1859

. . . The great trial of machines went off very well, so Mr. Garrard said, & he was upon the ground. They had some reapers from other states. The eastern states were represented by a host of manufacturers. This will make Madison Co. a grand theater for future exhibitions. There are some reapers now that have the binding and raking all done by persons on the machine as it goes along in the field. Some of the manufacturers say that they have a machine that will rake & bind as they go along and put it up into shock also. This is certainly a progressive age, and we may look for strange things in mechanics, still not as strange as this would be.

American genius transcends everything now in the world. America is the masterpiece of creation. Everything here is carried to its highest extent. We have the fastest steamers, the most railroads, the largest cities to their age, the most extensive system of popular education and free schools. We print more newspapers and make them cheaper than any other nation in the world. We can clothe with our cotton and wool half the world, and we can feed the other half from our corn & wheat fields. We have the freest people and the best government. Still, some people are not satisfied even with all this.

Godfrey was at Mothers this morning, and Mother and him had a pretty high time about their business, he wanting to make all that he could off of her & she trying to do the same. I am afraid that the quarrel will not stop here, as there were other names mentioned by them. I expect myself to be drawn into the quarrel, as I have been a witness to several of their business transactions, & Mother told Godfrey that old man Truitt had told me that Godfrey had cheated Mother in the hay trade & that he said that Godfrey did not give enough for the hay. This brings me right square into the muss. Godfrey accused Mother of dogging his hogs to death. She denies the charge. I am of the opinion that they are both in the wrong and have misunderstood one another. Godfrey is going to charge her eleven dollars for the timber in the addition to Newtons house, when the frame itself would not bring much more than that much money. This charge I think is unreasonable, and I do not blame her for not agreeing to pay it. I am going to keep my tongue inside of my teeth hereafter & try and not get mixed up in the petty quarrels that Mother will sometimes get into.

I helped my wife milk one of Mothers heifers this morning. She is going to let us have her for her milk this fall and winter. I think she will make a very good cow for milk. She is very easy and gentle to milk. . . .

I have not heard from the Somerford select school for some time. I suppose, however, that it is still to go on, as I have not heard anything to the contrary. I ought to go over there next Saturday and see about it, as I am one of the committee chosen to get a teacher for the school. I . . . have not done anything towards it yet. I suppose . . . that they have hired Hutcheson to teach it, as the most of them were in favor of hiring him in the start.

I have only three weeks more to teach after this week. Then I must pitch into the repairing business on the schoolhouse. . . .

Timothy Burts little chaps are here today. They have all recovered from the milk sickness. I do not think that [they] ever had it very bad in the first place. . . .

Some of my scholars have gone off without asking permission of me. I must put a stop to this. . . .

Thursday, July 7th, A.D. 1859

I have the toothache like the blazes this morning, and I do not feel at all like business. . . . Tonight I must certainly go to London and have my tooth plugged.

There is still some trouble for me to encounter. Mother has promised to let me have one of her heifers to milk this fall and winter, but she refuses to let me have the one that she promised me and now wants me to take an old one that is nearly dry. I do not think that this is at all fair, and I told her so last night. They are, however, to let me have cream for my tea & coffee and also to sell me butter at market price. This rather bores me. Still, I must put up with it and do the best that I can. . . . Mother is rather close on me. . . . I think she might do a little more for me than she has done and is now doing.

I understand that Newton intends to sue Mother for damages about the fixing of the mill. If he does he will have a hot time. . . . I am of the opinion that he will not make anything off of her, as she has repeatedly warned him to quit and she would not charge him any rent until it was fixed. . . .

July 8th, Friday, A.D. 1859

I am free from the toothache . . . and will be so till another tooth has a nerve exposed by its being decayed. I have suffered very much with the toothache lately, and I went into town yesterday to have the nerve killed. I got Dr. Brown to examine it, and he was of the opinion that it would ache even after it was plugged. It took to aching while I was in the dentists chair, so I thought that I had better have it drawn and be done with it at once; so I told him he might draw it if he would, and he was not slow in getting his forceps upon the delinquent, and if I had had a leg drawn it would not have been any more severe than the pain was for about 3 seconds. He, however, was not very long in doing it, and there was no stopping when once the tooth got under headway. I would rather have them pulled than to suffer from the toothache.

I made a purchase of a ham of meat and several other little items in the grocery line on last evening. My meat bill will not be very much this year. At least, if I did not use more meat than I have for the last 3 months it will not take more than $10 to get all of my meat for a year to come.

. . . I must try and get some biographical sketches for my journal, as my stock of composition is running out and I must fill up with something.

Monday, July 11th, A.D. 1859

. . . I was over to London on Saturday and made several purchases in the grocery line. We consume a considerable amount of groceries such as sugar and rice. Still, I do not complain, as I am bound to live on good grub at all hazards. Everything is going off with me as smooth as oil. . . . My health is pretty good, and my wife is in pretty good health. . . .

S. Saunders was here this forenoon. He is hunting one of his oxen. The Saunders boys are doing finely this summer, and they will climb out of their difficulties, I think. . . .

I got some ripe blackberries on Saturday last in London. They have been brought from Kentucky and they sell them for 12-1/2 cents per quart when there was a peck purchased. They were sold by Lewis Low at the P.O.

Tuesday, July 12th, A.D. 1859

Harvest in the wheat fields is nearly through. The wheat was not very heavy or thick upon the ground, but it was very well filled and there will be more than an average yield of wheat. The weather is very hot and dry at this time, and the corn crop has been injured some already. . . .

Yesterday I had a visitor. He was a tramping jour[neyman?] shoemaker and was out of money, I suppose, as he wanted me to buy some of his kit of tools. He looked like a man that was somewhat addicted to dissipation.

Godfreys wife has went to bed this morning, and I suppose that there will be one more inhabitant in our little village.

The lodge meets tonight and I would like very well to go, but I am afraid that I cannot get off, as my wife will be at Godfreys at supper time. . . . Dan Orcutt is going to take a degree tonight, so he told me some time since, and I would be glad to be on hands to take part in the ceremonies of the occasion & learn more of the great work. . . .

S. Saunders was here yesterday at afternoon recess. He says there has been no new light thrown upon the Pecks cow case. It was not the cow that Nedds had as was at first reported by some of the neighbors.

. . . School is out on the pike tomorrow. It commenced a month earlier than my school did. Miss Ann Knight is teaching it. There are more male teachers this year than common, and I am glad to see it, as I am of the opinion that the women have spoiled a great many of our schools.

There is a fine breeze springing up at this time which is very refreshing to me. The scholars just sweat all the time in the house. Today the sweat stands in great drops on their foreheads. . . .

I wrote to Wm. T. Cobaugh some time since about the little he owes me but have not received any answer yet.

Thursday, July 14th, A.D. 1859

There have been several little incidents of importance to the chief actors. The first is that Wm. Godfrey has a fine boy. . . . He calls it Dennis Henry, or Henry Dennis, I forget which. The other incident was the death of Jas. Rodricks only child. Thus we see how the different parts of the world are going on. In the one house the funeral is chanted, and in the very next house the blushing bride is saluted by her friends, and in the next house, perhaps, the newborn babe opens its eyes on a new world to it, destined in a few years to be cut down by the all devouring scythe of time. . . .

I was into London and in the lodge on last Tuesday night. One more person was made a Mason. Dan Orcutt was raised to the sublime degree of Master Mason. There was not a very big turnout. The lodge did not close until near 11 o'clock. I rode out from town with Dan on his horse behind him. It was about 1 o'clock ere I got to bed. My wife was over to Godfreys, and I had to go there before I could go home to sleep any. . . .

Truitts are going to thresh tomorrow, so I understand. There will be an immense amount of new wheat threshed right off if it keeps as dry as it is now, as they cannot work at their corn for fear it will be killed by the sun. The pastures would almost burn at this time. They are as dry as powder.

I must go around and see John Wilson about getting a shingle tree for making the shingles for the schoolhouse roof. . . .

Friday, July 15th, 1859

I do not suppose there ever was a dryer time much than there is now. Everything is parched up. The meadows will soon be too dry to cut.

. . . It is too hot for the pupils to enjoy themselves or study hard. Still, they are making some progress. I am glad that two weeks more will wind my school to a close, as this is not the kind of weather to teach in or for scholars to learn in.

There is going to be a picnic down near the Williams Chapel tomorrow, a kind of a Sabbath school celebration. Curtis from Charleston is the orator of the day.

I must pitch into biography or I shall run ashore in my journalizing. . . . John B. Stilwell, one of my smallest boy pupils. He is about 13 years of age and is very small of his age. He has a pretty good disposition. His father met with a tragical end some 8 or ten years ago. He went out to shoot a chicken, and not knowing whether the gun was loaded or not, he put his foot upon the hammer of the gun and placed his mouth over the muzzle . . . to blow into it to see if the tube was open, when his foot slipped off and his brains were blown out. His wife, Elizabeth Stillwell, has been keeping house for her brother, Dan Davis, ever since. She was not more than 14 years of age when she was married, and had two children, a boy & a girl. John is the boys name. He is a pretty good tempered fellow and will be sent pretty regularly to school by his mother, as this will be his only wealth. He is not very far advanced. He is reading in the fourth reader at this time. He knows nothing about writing or arithmetic. He does not improve very fast. He will never make a very hard working man, as he has not enough vitality about him. He will never be large. He has went considerably to school. . . .

S. Saunders is another subject for a biography. Semp is a little, swarthy, Frenchy looking chap . . . and has in his time been deep in my confidence. He is the son of a widow woman long known . . . as a zealous disciple of the Methodist faith. She is a good, pious old soul that has seen better times in her younger days and that still loves to dwell on the good old days of *Lang Syne*.

Semp is about twenty four years of age, with a countenance strongly marked. He has a keen native wit about him that is truly refreshing. His general knowledge is pretty good. He knows a little of almost every kind of business, but he is not thorough enough upon any one thing to make him celebrated for it. His monetary affairs are pretty favorable at this time. He is apt to undertake more than he can perform. He loves popularity and will strive hard for it. He has a good crop on hands . . . and . . . will make something this year. He will never be vastly rich, nor do I think that he will ever be miserably poor. He may marry, and I am of the opinion that he will want his wife to walk very straight and precise. He will not live to be very old, as his constitution will break square down when it does go.

Wednesday, July 27th, A.D. 1859

I am near the close of another term & I am glad of it. I think that I have honestly earned my wages this term, as I have had a pretty large school and the most of them have made a decided improvement in knowledge, book knowledge at least. Some of them have advanced very rapidly. C. Hornbecks little girl has made a remarkable start in reading. She could scarcely read any in the start, and now she reads quite fluently. James Porters little [girl] has also mad[e] quite an improvement in her reading, and in fact they have all done first rate.

I have been giving tickets this term, a thing that I do not know as I shall do again, as it is a great pother and trouble to me, more than it is a benefit to the school. I have nearly 3000 tickets out at this time. I will not average over 18 per diem this term. Yesterday I had about 30; today I have only 13 pupils. I do not know why folks do not send more regularly, as I do most candidly think that education forms the common mind, and this is free to all & everyone. I would be in favor of putting upon the pauper list all those that do not make any provisions for the education of their offspring. Let the state take them under their own especial care & compel the parents if they are able to educate their children.

The weather is remarkably dry. . . . The ground has never been any more parched. . . . It has been weeks since we have had any showers here to do any good, and the sun has been tropical in his heating propensities. The roads are almost suffocating on account of the dust that has accumulated in them. All the ponds are dried up in toto. The corn is badly curled and twisted up in the blade. The pastures are dry enough to burn and the meadows are all dried up. There will not be one third of a crop of grass this season. In fact, most of the meadows are mowed at this time. Potatoes are nothing. The early ones were killed by the frost, and now the drought is taking the latter ones, so we must not expect to get any potatoes this season. The fruit must be very indifferent if we do not soon get rain. Still, I am of the opinion that by the next change of the moon we will certainly have rain.

. . . I will not get to write in this book for some time to come. . . . I will have to go to work as soon as I am through here. I am going to put the s[chool]house job right through and get it done as soon as possible. Wm. Truitt says that he will be ready as soon as I am.

Mother has not heard from that old Geo. Lee, the millwright, yet. . . . Newton is getting to be very uneasy, and I am afraid that there will be trouble about it yet, as Newton has considerable bull about him.

I was over to Uncle Jas. H. Roberts on last Saturday night and Sunday all day. His wife presented him with a 10 pound baby on the fourth of July. It is a girl.

Grandfather is . . . unable to do much anymore. He says that he will come over pretty soon to see the mill to see how it can be fixed. There will have to be 3 sills put under the mill.

Henry & Allen are still working on Porters house. They are fixing to put on the roof. They are sheeting the rafters today. . . .

I saw V.C. Wilson there [at a baptizing in the creek]. He looks very much bloated, and he will not certainly last many summers more ere he is carried to the boneyard.

The Christian Church in Somerford is in a prosperous condition. . . . They have a very flourishing Sabbath school there; Gabriel Prugh superintendent, James Palmer vice superintendent, and Jas. H. Roberts secretary. Eld[er] Griffon is their preacher in charge at this time.

I heard Morse preach a sermon on the sure foundation on Sunday last. He handled the subject very well, I thought. He has made quite an improvement in his preaching, I think. His text was taken in the first Epistle to Peter, 6th chapter, & 19th verse.

Some of the young converts around here are falling back to their old standing points. They have backslidden woefully. There are a few bright exceptions, however, to the rule. . . .

The Methodists are not doing much in this neighborhood at this time. Their new meetinghouse has gone to pot or somewhere else. They have spent their subscription money and have not got the house raised nor the lumber paid for that they have used. . . . It is the biggest balk that ever happened, in this neighborhood at any rate.

Thursday, July 28th, A.D. 1859

. . . The drought is now the only topic that seems to engross the public mind. . . . Everyone is grunting about the great scarcity of rain. Now, I think that we ought to take these things patiently, as what we lose this year we must make up the next. I am of the opinion that the dry weather will make the soil more productive, and that this dry spell is actually a benefit to us instead of an injury. Although times are somewhat gloomy just now, I do think there is a better time coming, and I for one am willing to wait a little longer. . . . I am inclined to think that [it] is all for the best.

I was up to Jas. G. Porters today to see him about signing my order on the township clerk for my pay for this quarter. He was not at home, however, and I did not get to see him till I came back to the s[chool]house, where I met him with a load of lumber. He signed my order, which will save me a trip up there. I must go to Mr. Potees tomorrow night and get him to sign it, and then on Saturday I must make a draw upon the treasury for sixty dollars, which is not quite enough for the service rendered. . . .

I understand that the European war has ceased for awhile. They want to see if they can make peace. I am of the opinion that they will manage to make it up so that the tyrants will still hold the reins of government in their own grasp. The people in this glorious country do not know what they are talking about when they talk about the government being bad and the times being hard. Let them go to downtrodden Italy or Hungary if they want to see hard times. There they will find not only hard but miserable times, not only find high but exhorbitant taxes, the people not only ignorant, but debased and vicious in the extreme. Their mobs have to be put down with the bayonet.

This will be the last day that I will get to write in this book for some time to come, as my school will be out tomorrow. . . . I have had a very pleasant time during this quarter, and everything will go off smoothly I hope on the morrow. I am going to redeem my tickets [issued for attendance] then and go to town in the evening to draw my money and pay up some of my debts. My money will not pay all of them, . . . but as far as it will go it must go, as money that I have when I owe it is not mine.

I am in pretty good health . . . and have been all summer. My weight is 140 pounds avoirdupois. I did weigh 146 pounds in the spring, or forepart of the summer rather. My wife weighs 97 pounds. She weighed 100 pounds when we were married. . . .

Giles James is going to have a sing here tomorrow night. He wants to get up a class to sing here during the summer. I do not know whether he will get one up or not, as the nights are so short and the days are so warm that there is no comfort to be had anywhere. I wont sign till fall anyhow.

The Summerford select school has gone by the board. E. Hull has been teaching there this summer at $20 per month and board himself. He is not getting rich, nor can ever become so at such very low wages. I cannot say anything on that score as I am in the same row of stumps myself. I must try and get my wages raised somewhat, as I must live and I also want to lay up a little for a rainy day or a cut foot. Still, there always has been a way provided for the virtuous poor of the country. Still, charity is cold and unpalatable to anyone possessed of the least bit of independence of spirit. . . . I do not anticipate any such calamitous future for my part.

E. Hull is too diffident. He thinks everyone is looking right at & also criticizing his every action. I . . . fear not the carping of critics. Their jeers fall unheeded by me & my works. Still, I want to have the praise of good men.

I once in awhile see the Clark Co. boys Wash and Mike Wilson. . . . Wash was not in the singing school scrape, but Mike and Jasper [were]. They do not speak to me nor I to them. I just pass by them as I would by a wolf, give them a good half of the road and pass by on the other side. I am bound to have no lot nor part with them hereafter in no shape nor form. Some people may say that it is wrong to hold a grudge against anyone, but I am of the opinion that when people act the dog we ought to treat [them] as dogs and not as men or human beings. . . .

I will soon have this book a year. On the 11th of next month I shall have completed a year of my diary, and on the 21st of next month a year of my journalizing in this book. I am not tired of it, however, and I am now in for keeping it the ballance of my life.

9

Neighborhood Affairs
August 21–September 29, 1859; August 5, 1860

After the last entry in this chapter, Roberts writes in his big journal only on his birthdays. During the period recorded here, he works at repairing a schoolhouse and begins teaching another term. He resolves once more to quit using tobacco and again fails in the attempt. (He succeeds in 1866.)

His own marriage runs smoothly, but not those of some couples in the community. There is a scandalous episode of adultery in a cucumber patch. Another incident—the surprise under the hoopskirts, or "the efficacy of black pepper"—sounds like the synopsis of a Sut Lovingood yarn.

Henry Roberts and Allen Anderson still go to camp meeting binges, and young fry rob watermelon patches, but John's youthful frolics are ended. He shows an increasing interest in the neighborhood's early settlers and enjoys hearing one of them sing "Barbara Allen" and tell its history.

The big event in Roberts's political life is his trip to Columbus to hear Illinois Senator Stephen A. Douglas speak on squatter sovereignty. Roberts hopes to get a chance to vote for the Little Giant for president.

Sunday, August 21st, A.D. 1859

Today I am about to pass another milestone on the great highroad of life. This makes the 26th one that I have seen come & go past on eagle wings. I have made many promises upon this day to begin anew the tenor of my life, to make some decided stand in favor of some better course of things for myself, but each succeeding anniversary has found my schemes as far from realization as the preceeding ones found them. I find that I resolve & reresolve & perhaps I may die the same. . . . Still, I must make some reforms this time or my feeble powers will not recuperate by the next anniversary.

My habits are getting to be more regular than they were, as I am now settled for life and have something to live and hope for. This year has passed pleasantly & profitably by, and I am more advanced than I was this time last year. I have performed more manual labor and accomplished more this year than I ever did in my life. My health as a general thing has been good. . . .

I have kept my diary faithfully during the last year, & I have also taught nine months school and have received $235.00 for the same. I have also built me a house on Mothers place and have been very busy generally. I am better off in one respect this year. I am married. This is the most important thing that I have accomplished this year. I do think that I have had more real satisfaction since my marriage than I have had during the last 10 years of my life. In fact, I know that I have. I can now fully appreciate the charm said to exist around the home fireside, and it is those only that have experienced these things that can fully appreciate them or know their true value. I now see more real satisfaction in a month than I did in a year of single life. The expense of keeping a light establishment is not much over that of a single mans outlay.

I have just about finished the s[chool]house repairing. Wm. Truitt & I took the job. We had to have the most of the work done, so we made but very little on the job. Still . . . we made about 75 cts. per diem. . . . We have got a new roof upon it and shutters to all the windows. The catches are not yet put upon the shutters, nor is the weatherboarding put on yet.

I made several resolves that I have failed to live up to. I must try and make the same ones over again . . . and see if I cannot do better this time. . . . I have someone now to help me if my resolution should fail, someone to give me aid and strength to withstand the temptation, one to remind me of my faithlessness to my own interest and my own happiness, and I do think that I shall certainly with her aid and help make my reforms more permanent and deeper seated. My will is good enough, but my appetite gets the advantage of me and conquers my reason.

My only vice I have is that of using *tobacco* to excess. . . . My wife says that she will quit drinking coffee if I will quit chewing tobacco. I must & I will quit. . . . Theo. Smith has quit since last year, & he has not taken a chew since, & why cant I quit? And I am sure that I have as much nerve about me as he has, and I can quit if I only *will*. But enough of this. I must do and not say so much about it.

Today those persons that were joined to the Methodists last year at the Williams Chapel during the great excitement there, the greater part of them have gone back to the beggarly elements of the world. Even those that do belong do not know what their faith is, and their confirmation in the faith will be a mockery. They subscribe to articles they do not understand, and those that do understand do not believe—the Trinity, infant baptism, eternal punishment, total depravity, and various other articles that would make any person stark mad if he was to believe them fully. . . .

Jno. Rush ran away last week. He is bound for Indiana, so I understand, and he will never rue it but once in his life and that will be all the time. He had some difficulty with his stepmother, and his father scolded him for it, & he not relishing it saddled up his nag and put out.

I am going to commence school again about the first of next month. I want them to give me $27 per month and me to board myself. I want to commence for a 6 months term. . . .

Mother & G. Newton have not come to an understanding yet, and I am afraid that they will not till they get into a lawsuit about the mill. I must go next week to see about a millwright to fix up the mill.

Henry & A. Anderson have just returned from camp meeting on Little Darby. They are having a good time generally down there, plenty of whiskey, cards, & fancy women, besides an overflow of religious excitement. Some of the boys got on a big drunk and played hob in general. My camp meeting days are over with, and I am glad of it, as I never made very rapid progress in a moral point of view, & I am sure that my body was not much refreshed by the spree.

Harveys mill below London was burned down the other night. This is a heavy loss to the owners and a very great inconvenience to the neighborhood, as a mill is a very important thing in a neighborhood. Links mill is rented to a man by the name of Miller from Springfield. He is an old acquaintance of Newtons.

Mother was taken quite sick last week, but she is now much better and will soon be about again. C. Margaret was also taken sick at the same time. She is . . . slowly mending and will soon be . . . as well as ever, I hope. . . .

There has been quite a time here about the new Methodist meetinghouse. Cory, the mechanic, sued the trustees for his pay and recovered a judgement off of all of them except Wesley Allen. He was cleared by the court on the ground that he had resigned his commission & refused to act as a trustee. Some people blame Allen & some Potee. The latter person, however, had the funds in his possession at one time and did not pay them to Cory as he agreed to do. He was unable to do so as he had spent the money.

Monday, September 5th, A.D. 1859
Today I again find myself at my old business teaching in Dist. No. 1, for the sum of twenty seven dollars per month and board myself at that. The best that I hear is thirty dollars per month & board themselves.

Times are pretty dull at this time, not much money going, and but very little work is going on. Still, there is enough slander to make up for the slackness of business life.

They have had a very bilious time of it over in Somerford. It seems as though the whole town has been thrown into a commotion by the sudden discovery of a criminal connection between G.W. Prughs wife & Wm. Teeter. It is a parallel case to the Sycles [Daniel E. Sickles] & [Philip Barton] Key case. Mrs. Kate Prugh has been noticed for some time to be very intimate with Wm. Teeter, & on last Wednesday some persons concluded to watch them and see if they were engaged in anything of this kind. They followed them down to the cucumber patch and caught Teeter & Mrs. Prugh in a peculiar situation, and upon this being made known to G.W. Prugh, he commenced making an investigation, and his wife immediately swore a rape against Teeter. This oath, however, was overruled by the defence bringing up a positive proof of connection with Teeter prior to this time, and Teeter of course went free.

The old adage that says when a dog begins to go downhill everyone gives him a kick is truly exemplified in the case of Mrs. Prugh. I have heard all sorts of hard tales about the woman since her mishap with Teeter. She is now accused of being rather loose before marriage. She was at one time about to take up with old man Hendrickson of this neighborhood, so it seems from the evidence of the trial. It also seems as though her connexion with Teeter has been of a years standing and that she has been in the habit of waving her handkerchief & her basket to him for a long time. This was proven in open court, so I understand.

George W. still intends to live with his wife, so I understand. He talks of killing Teeter if he can lay hands on him. I am not so sure, however, that he will ever be able to do so, as Teeter could maul him to death. Prugh has quite a considerable little family, some five or more children, & was making quite a good living. His wife heretofore had borne a very fair character and was a very tidy, industrious woman, very well respected and esteemed by all that knew her before this transaction. She is a daughter of Ludwig Rodricks.

. . . We have had several remarkable frosts here of late; not frosts, but northern lights that some folks think are prognostics of cold weather. It is said that the telegraph refused to operate during the time these lights were seen. I suppose that this was caused by there being so much more electricity in the atmosphere than is usual.

The political horizon is getting pretty warm at this time. There is to be a governor elected this fall. The Republican candidate for governor was in London on Saturday last and gave them a speech, also the Hon.

Mr. [Edwin M.] Stanton, a congressman from this state. . . . It was a prosy affair, so I left. He is not a very flowery orator nor a very profound reasoner. . . .

They had quite a time over on Deer Creek week before last about a young woman over there. She is some connexion to Geers and has been living with Joshua Geer for some time, who appears to have been perfectly innocent of the girls situation. This girl wore tremendous hoops and was considered a very nice kind of a girl. She was taken very badly with a spell of the colic some time during the week before last and sent Joshua out to get some medicine from some of the neighbors to cure her. He came to Grandfathers, and Grandfather told him to give her some pepper tea or a spoonful of black pepper & that would ease her. He went home and administered the pepper, when lo, it soon fell into her arms. This is a remarkable instance of the efficacy of black pepper. Her brother in law, Geer, swore roundly about the matter and said that his wife never more should wear hoops. This is a very queer kind of a world. So much for hoops.

Tuesday, September 6th, 1859

. . . This is sale day in London, and I suppose that the most of the farming part of the community will be in to see the stock and talk politics over their *Lager*. I do not know how the election is going to go, but I presume that it will be mixed as usual in this county. . . .

Tomorrow the justly celebrated Steven A. Douglas will speak in Columbus. I want to try to go and hear him if I can possibly do so.

Mothers millwright is coming on tomorrow or today, so he wrote her some time ago. Henry and Allen are going to work for her as soon as he comes. There is quite a job for them to do there. They have run out of lumber at Porters and are now idle, have nothing at all to do. . . .

I saw quite a number of Brush boys in London the other day. . . . Benjamin Briley was there. He looked a little on the seedy order. He has been going to Antioch College some this summer. He says there has been several changes down there in the Brush. . . . I would be very glad to see all of them down there once more, but I suppose that I shall be unable to do so at this time. . . .

I hear that one of Jewels girls has gone crazy & that there is not much prospect of her getting well. Her name is Charlotte; she is the youngest one in the Jewel family. . . .

I must try and write some biographies in my book, as the news of the neighborhood is not sufficient to . . . fill it up rightly. . . .

The life of James Garrard, Sen., is the first one that I shall notice. He was the oldest son of Jacob Garrard and was born in Virginia, I believe. His father then moved down on the Miami in this state, in Green Co., where the younger days of Mr. Garrard were spent. The country at that time was poorly supplied with schools, and so he was unable to acquire a thorough education. He, however, was taught reading and writing and the rudiments of arithmetic. His father moved into Madison County 30 years ago and bought a large tract of land 3 miles west of London, where he built a mill & distillery.

Here the subject of our narrative lived for some time, working on the farm & driving teams to Cincinnati with produce. In the year 1819 or 20 he married Polly Buckles, a daughter of one of the pioneers of this state, and made an improvement for himself from this time forth. He commenced gaining slowly but surely, making no rash ventures nor living higher than his income. He had a family of six children. Five of them reached the age of adults. Two married and two are dead.

He has been a staunch member of the Old School Baptists for 30 years and is now the sole survivor of that sect in this neighborhood, that is, himself & daughter are. He is also a staunch Democrat, never has been known to indulge in alcoholic drinks, and is considered a good citizen and a patriot by one and all.

He is at this time the most wealthy man in this neighborhood. He is somewhere in [near?] 55 or 56, never has held any office higher than supervisor or s[chool] director. He is, in fact, one of the old school, one of the ancient regime, that are fast disappearing before the sway of young America. . . . He is one of those strong links in society that are never appreciated until they are lost. . . .

Thursday, September 8th, A.D. 1859

Yesterday I did not teach, as I wished to hear the justly celebrated Judge Douglas of Illinois make a speech. I stayed all night Tuesday evening at Father Truitts and walked from there to London in time for the nine o'clock train for Columbus. S.D. Truitt went with me from London. D.J. Cartzdafner went with me from Pecks crossing down to London. We soon found that the half fare business was all a humbug & that the Republican road would charge full fare to Columbus. Joe Cartzdafner would not go on this account.

We got over to the capital city in good time and had ample time to make investigations for ourselves. We went nearly all over the city. Saw the *great bore* in the state yard, namely the artesian well, which is twenty three hundred & sixty feet deep, & still no water can be had to run out at the surface. We also paid the penitentiary a flying visit, walked around it and saw the convicts at work upon the walls. They are making very extensive additions to the prison yard and house. The convicts that we saw were not working hard at all. Some of them were bargaining for a melon with a countryman. They were having a very easy time of it to my notion.

It was very dusty in the city and also upon the cars. The roar of wagons and vehicles of various kinds in the city must be very annoying to its inmates. It would be to me, I am sure.

The great man of the day, the lion of the occasion, was Judge Douglas, a little short man, apparently about 50 years of age, rather inclined to be corpulent, about 5 feet 4 inches in hight, with a massive forehead and a very firm look about him. There is no coward in his looks. He has a heavy brow & sharp gray eyes, not a gimlet eye but an eagle eye. His hair is thick upon his head and mixed with gray.

He has a powerful voice and can make himself heard by a very large crowd. He is a very emphatic speaker and makes some very good points. In fact, his speech makes everything so plain that everyone that heard him thinks that they always thought as he speaks. They imagine that they have always had such principles. His argument seems to be impregnable. He leaves no unguarded place for an enemy to attack. He never lacks for words to express his ideas. His language is not flowery but tinctured with strong common sense. Everyone understands him, and you know by intuition what the next word will be. . . .

The whole of Douglas'es speech was upon the squatter sovereign and fugitive slave business. . . . He showed that slavery was a domestic institution and ought to be governed by local laws. His arguments were very sound & logical throughout.

I am . . . a Douglas man and will vote for the gentleman for president if he offers for that office. I will also do all I can for his election, as I am of the opinion that he is of sound principles and that he will do all that is in his power to preserve the Union and promote good feelings amongst the states.

Garrards plasterer has come on and is now at work on his house. He has just finished his chimnies & is going to work at nailing on the lath. He is an Englishman by the name of Self and possesses considerable shrewdness for a foreigner. I must get him to do my plastering for me if he will only do it.

Our mill business dont seem to progress much. Wm. Orpet was talking to me this morning about helping to do the [schoolhouse] work. I do not know whether Porter and Potee will hire him or not, as they want the job to be performed too cheap.

I have thirteen pupils today, 3 Porter children from Mr. Rushes. I feel a little agueish today. Perhaps . . . it is on account of my trip over to Columbus yesterday. . . .

Friday, September 9th, 1859

I have but twelve pupils today and times are a little dull.

Jacob Wilson was here today and wants me to go before the board of education and try to get him cut off from this district and put into Clark Co., as it is too far to send his small chaps down here. . . . I am not sure that the thing can be done, but . . . I am willing that it should be done, as he seems very anxious to have the change made. He says that the board of education meets next Monday. If so, I must attend to the matter and be on hands to see to the interests of Sub Dist. No. One. . . .

Zeph Webb has advertized a sale to be held sometime during this month. . . . He is bound to move west as soon as he can get off.

I understand that James H. Roberts is going to move down upon A. Rankins place and is going to teach that school down there this winter. It is not a very strong district, and there is not much of a fund down there. Still, they seem to be willing to foot the bill while the money lasts.

Monday, September 12th, 1859

I am full of business today. I have Orpet digging a well for the s[chool]house and 21 pupils. . . .

Mr. Randall & his wife were up here on Saturday and Sunday last. He and I went down to Jas. Andrews on Sunday last to see Maria Andrews, who is . . . still sick and not able to do much. . . . She has had the ague for nearly two years and has been drugged nearly to death by the doctors of this and Clark Co. They have given her every kind of poison known to druggists. She has taken calomel, arsenic, strychnine, aqua fortis, and ether, and still has the ague. Randall, however, thinks that he can cure her. He is going to try hydropathy on her case and has left some pills to give her a natural appetite. He is not a pure hydropath.

We got our dinner down there and came home at about 3 o'clock. Randall broke down his bugg[y] just as we were leaving the pike beyond the chapel as we were going to Jim Andrews. We mended it up with a nail and went on our way rejoicing. We broke the side of the bed off just forward of the seat. . . .

The Republicans of Madison Co. are getting pretty sick of some of their nominations. Philis is a hard pill for some of them to swallow, and it seems as though Stutson is growled at by some, as they think that Simpson ought to have had it this time. However, they must grin and bear it, as there is no help for them now that the thing is done for & gone before the people.

The Republicans are too much of a mixture to do much good. No one knows what their real platform is. Everyone of them stand upon a separate platform. Some of them are in favor of the Fugitive Slave Law, and some of them are bitterly opposed to that law of our general government, made with a view to carry out the provisions of the Constitution of the U. States. I am in hopes that they may be defeated and that the Fugitive Bill may be enforced to its fullest extent and the slave returned as he should be to his lawful master and put to work as he should be so that he would [not] be here to overrun the white population of this country. I do hope the Republicans may be signally defeated in the coming election.

Tuesday, September 13th, A.D. 1859

. . . The town of Somerford still keeps boiling over about the G.W. Prugh affair. I understand that Prugh is going to take his wife home. She is most undoubtedly a hard case from all accounts, as she has not only abused Prughs confidence but has actually perjured herself in the bargain. Still, we must allow something for her excitement and fear under the . . . public exposure of her crimes. She must, of course, have been rendered desperate by her situation or she never would have acted as she did at the trial. It is indeed a sad affair and may terminate fatally for some of the parties.

I must try and study some this winter, as I will have a most excellent chance to study. I will be at home and have no one to bother me. Still, I am not very sure that I can do much at studying, as I am naturally inclined to idle away my time after school hours. I must try and study some while I am engaged in teaching this quarter. I might put in an hour or two each day very handily. I must not, however, take up all my time in books. I must have enough exercize to keep my blood in a good circulation.

Last Saturday night was the first night upon our new quarter of singing by James. He has twenty two dollars made up at this time. I must try and come during this present quarter and see if I cant learn something. I have been coming for some time and have not as yet learned much; in fact, nothing. It is my own fault, however, as James always did his best and has very sensibly advanced the singing class in this neighborhood.

G.W. Saunders, G.H. Webb, & Smith Couples went along by here awhile ago on a hunting expedition. They can make it pay shooting pigeons as they are very plentiful.

Wednesday, September 14th, A.D. 1859

I was at Father Truitts last evening. So was my wife. We went from there to Mrs. Saunders and stayed there till nine o'clock. [We] heard old Henry Asbury sing Barbara Allen and recite the history of the same. He is a quizzical oddity. I laughed heartily at some of his queer expressions.

Semp Saunders and John Peck had a knockdown last night. The quarrel originated about the oxen. John Peck accused the boys of driving the oxen in a trot with a load on. John collared Semp & Semp knocked him down and pounded him some. Semp is a little too much for John.

We got as many watermelons as we could eat at Saunders. . . .

Wm. Truitt is now engaged in hauling wood to town. He has engaged about 30 cords to be delivered this fall.

The Madison Co. Agricultural Society meets today to show the domestic manufactures of our country, and more particularly the farming interests of Madison. Kissing, however, goes by favor with them generally at these fairs, as the richest men get all the premiums and the poorer class must stand back, not having the ghost of a chance to win the prize. So the beaten ones always say, & of course they are unprejudiced.

Thursday, September 15th, 1859

. . . The road is lined with carriages and vehicles going to the fair at London. I do not know whether I shall go or not, as my monetary affairs are not the most flourishing at this time. . . .

I have only twelve pupils this morning, three new ones from Eli Wilsons.

The news of this part of the world is very stale. . . . No new scandal is going. Down at Charleston they have another Somerford affair, Mr. Malot & Mrs. Thomas, also Mr. Malots wife. I have not heard the full particulars. They are all . . . strong church members and made loud professions last winter at the Williams Chapel. If these are fair specimens of their converts, God help them, as they are not much changed, only for the worse. These things are creating quite an excitement in the little town. These little scrapes are getting to be alarmingly frequent. We will have to coop our wives up the same as the Turks and guard them with eunuchs as they do their wives. I am not afraid, however, of my domestic arrangements or my honor, as I think there is no danger.

Tuesday, September 20th, 1859

For the last 3 or four days I have been trying public matters, such as going to the fair and attending to the board of education to transact business for the different subdistricts in the township.

I was at the Madison Co. fair on Friday last. There was quite a crowd out, and the fair was as much as an average for this county. They are getting to be very particular about their entrance or admittance fees.

I, however, was bound to try and escape paying it, as they are making more money at this time than is necessary for the vitality of the institution, and I presume that the extra charge goes into the officers pockets. I managed to walk in at one of the gates past their gatekeeper, unnoticed by him. He was busily engaged talking to a man, and I stepped up & walked in and stood and talked to the gatekeeper awhile, then deliberately walked off into the ground and soon was as deeply interested in the trotting against time as any of the rest of the crowd. My wife went in with Mrs. Hornbeck and Mahala Godfrey. We ate dinner with Godfreys. There was a numerous quantity of mountbanks on the ground, fellows with swings, snake shows, and bird shows. I went into one of the shows and saw a man swallow, or run down his throat rather, a sword 22 inches long, no sleight of hand about it but a reality.

The board of education for this township met on Monday and returned the enumeration of pupils from each of the subdistricts. No. One is the strongest of any in the township. The board met at 1 o'clock and appointed Smith Warner president or chairman. They would not let Jac. Wilson off from this district to go to Clark Co. to school, nor would they let Peck off from the pike.

After considerable debating on the question of 65 days for a quarter, the board finally passed a resolution in favor of the 65 day plan, resolving that each and every district should make this the standing rule of action. I have always been in the habit of teaching 65 days for a quarter. The only difference this will make will be that teachers will [put] the tariff on a little stronger, as their terms will be that much longer. There are but two districts in the [township] that have no teachers, Smith Warners district & Armstrongs district.

J.B. Couples was up to the fair on Friday. He has no school engaged yet, & got me to sound around the board for a situation. Warner offers $30 per month & Armstrong offers $25 per month. Both want the teacher to board himself. I wrote to J.B. today & sent the letter in by Jac. Gaither, who stayed all night at our house last night along with S.D. Truitt.

. . . We got some books for a library in this district. . . .

Wednesday, Sept. 21st, A.D. 1859
. . . I hear of various depredations being made upon melon patches in this neighborhood. W. Allen has had his patch robbed and his sweet potatoes *grabbled* by some vagabonding boys. This was performed in broad daylight on Sunday last. Who they were no one knows. S.F. Saunders had his melon patch entered on last evening by some mischief lovers. They put a candle in a pumpkin and sat it up in the patch. There

were four of them, as they saw the larks in there but were not close enough to recognize them. I am a little surprized at their entering Saunders patch, as they have not sold a melon this season and have given to all that came. These chaps, however, did no particular damage. . . . Some people are naturally mean and despicable. I dont know as they can be blamed, as nature has refused to do her part by them and they were born Ishmaelites.

Thursday, Sept. 22d, A.D. 1859

. . . I suppose that I will have more pupils today than yesterday, as I have some 8 or 9 present. Our s[chool]house well is progressing slowly at this time. The rainy weather . . . is getting to be quite a detriment to the work.

Henry & Allen are at work at my house floor today. They are laying it down without planing any, and I see that they can make a pretty good job of it. There will, however, be a few cracks to be seen through. . . .

I must try and manage my business so as to go to Darby one of these days for lime to build my chimney, as cold weather will soon [be] here & I will need some fire.

Friday, Sept. 23th [*sic*], A.D. 1859

. . . Godfreys family are not very well. . . . His two children are sick. . . . My wife went over this morning to help set things to rights. . . . Isma Timmons is still working there at his clearing. He got a letter from the north the other day. They are having the ague good & strong up there this fall. They have had no frost, however, to do any damage there yet. Neither have we had any biting frosts as yet, & in fact we have had none at all this fall yet. If the frost would only stay away until sometime in October, we would have much more corn. . . . The greater part of the corn will be out of the way in a few days.

They are drilling in the well at this time. They have got down about 30 feet altogether, and still no permanent stream has been found. . . .

Mother has some five hands at work upon the mill at this time, G. Lee, Wm. H. Roberts, A. Anderson, Jno. Brown, & Val Wilson talks some of helping next week.

Saturday, Sept. 24th, A.D. 1859

. . . Last night we had a sing here by G.A. James. He has a class of fifty here at this time. The house was crowded to its utmost capacity.

I am teaching today, as I have lost three days this term already, and I want my time to go on as expeditiously as possible, as I am in need of the funds to pay current expenses. This term will, however, let me out pretty well. In fact, I think it will let me clear out. I did want to be clear by Christmas, and I think that I shall be by that time.

I must try and finish up my s[chool]house job next week if possible, as the job has been hanging on hands long enough as it is.

I am not sure but that I shall have but four pupils today.

P.L. Roberts was at our house on last evening and stayed all night. They are still working at D.B. Wilsons house and are making extensive repairs upon it. Danl. B. Wilson is on an extensive spree, and has done nothing but drink whiskey ever since the 4th of last June. He will soon be as far gone as his brother V.C. Wilson. They say that he is very much bloated at this time.

Thursday, Sept. 29th, 1859

The times are very tight just at this present. No money to be had hardly at any price. . . .

Geo. W. Prugh has taken his wife back to her fathers to stay. This is rather a sad affair for her and will be a warning for future delinquents.

I got Mr. Garrards plasterer, Self, to put on some plastering for me at the s[chool]house this morning. He put a crock in the chimney of the stove.

I have several new pupils this week. . . . We also got the s[chool]house well finished yesterday. Orpet put in eleven days and L.D. Couples five days, Wm. Porter about four days, and C.C. Roberts about 6 days on it.

Charles was down on Darby this week. He says that Lydia Ford is married to Sam Waters. I know that they cannot be lawfully married, as L.D. Ford is still living and is . . . in Illinois. Such trash as they are, however, are not worthy of notice by the community, and I suppose no one will say anything about them even if they are not married, so they keep to themselves.

Sunday, August 5th, A.D. 1860

Many long busy months have rolled over my head since last I wrote in this old book. There have been almost a thousand changes in our little neighborhood. We have had a great many weddings, and alas, the scythe of time has mowed down some of the loved ones in our midst. . . .

Grandfather Roberts is dead. He died April 26th, 1860, after an illness of only a few days. He was upwards of 78 years of age and had been a resident of this country for over 40 years. . . . Daniel B. Wilson died on the same day, . . . aged about 22 years. Dan's death was brought on by intemperance. He walked around till within an hour of his death. Dr. Randall was there at the time . . . and gave him a dose of morphine, which some think hastened his dissolution. I am of the opinion, however, that it was whiskey that killed him. Elder Griffon preached Grandfathers funeral & Dan's also. . . .

Valentine C. Wilson is very sick. . . . He has something like an inflammation of the stomach caused by excessive drinking, and I am of the opinion that his days are very few, and that ere we see the sun ten times he will be under the sod. I am truly sorry that this is the case, but he would not listen to reason. . . .

10

Civil War on the Homefront
August 21, 1860–December 31, 1865

In the birthday annals recorded in his journal, Roberts reflects on the coming of the Rebellion and his distress during its long ordeal at being called a Copperhead traitor. He rationalizes his failure to enlist in the federal army, and when finally called by the wartime draft, he is exempted because of a hernia. His "military experience," recorded in greater detail in diary entries, consists of six days at Camp Chase when Confederate General John Hunt Morgan invades the lower Midwest.

Although Roberts's diaries for the three years 1860–1862 are missing, his wife, Emarine, kept a diary for 1862 and 1863. Her brief entries, some of which are included in this chapter, display the domestic chores of a young wife and mother and her escape from loneliness by frequent visits with family and neighbors.

John's diaries for 1863–1865 provide glimpses of everyday activities that go unnoticed in his journal's birthday reflections. In the cramped daily entries he notes such troubles of keeping school as shortages of stove wood, falling stovepipes, and noisy scholars, and their exciting triumphs in spelling matches. On neighbors' farms, he plows, plants, harvests, and shears sheep. At home, he gardens, chops wood, makes shingles for his porch roof. His family responsibilities grow when Emarine bears two daughters, Flora and Alma, during the war years. His purchase of lozenges and a syringe to get rid of pinworms reveals an irritating problem that will last for years.

Roberts deplores the disruption of the Union by zealous abolitionists and secessionists and avows his loyalty and patriotism in angrily answering accusing neighbors. Eastern and western battlefronts loom constantly in his thoughts, and he frets when he hears no war news.

His moods shift quickly from "the blues" to euphoria, or the reverse, as he hears of success or defeat on the battlefield or at the polls. His fear and loathing of blacks intensify his hostility toward Radical Republicans, in Congress and at home. He cries "Bully for Grant" and other northern generals when he hears of their victories, but he longs for President Lincoln's defeat by the Democratic party's nominee, General

George B. McClellan, in the election of 1864. Lincoln's calls for more and more troops and the local attempts to raise bounty money for substitutes cause Roberts to see a rising antagonism of poor men against rich and a growing war weariness which he hopes will bring Republican division and defeat. But the war provides a supplement to his own small income when he helps enforce "an odious law" by collecting military fines.

Although Roberts escapes the draft, friends and family members serve in the Union army, and several are wounded or killed in battle or die of disease. He travels to a military hospital in New Albany, Indiana, and to Governor John Brough's office in Columbus to try to get his wounded brother Charles discharged from the army.

Lee's surrender to Grant in April 1865 brings Roberts joy, though it does not last. He hopes for an early reconstruction of the old Union, but by August he foresees troubled times for his country. "Heaven frowns, Hell yawns, & vice triumphs," he cries on his birthday. By year's end, however, his unfounded partisan optimism has returned. "The Radical element is nearly floored & everything looks as though it would prosper," he believes. "Long life to our noble president, Andrew Johnson."

Tuesday, August 21st, A.D. 1860

Today I am 27 years of age, another milestone on the road to eternity.

Two years ago I made my first entry in this book. Many and great have been the changes since then, but none for the worse in my case, I believe. I am in tolerable fair health . . . and my prospects are very good. . . . I have no great evil habits to contend with. My passions do not very often get the better of my judgment. . . . My wife is as good as I could wish her to be, and perhaps much better than I really deserve. The Grand Master of the Universe has indeed dealt kindly with me, and I feel very thankful that it is so. . . . I have no children, thank heaven, and by this means I have not been the author of any more misery. Time speeds away and leaves some marks upon my face, but none upon my happiness or my peace. . . .

The great topic now is . . . who shall be next president of the U.S. The two great champions of the present canvass are Abe Lincoln and Stephen A. Douglas of Ill. I am a Douglas Democrat out and out, and I am of the opinion that he will be the next president . . . and that he will be elected by the popular vote. The country is now on the brink of a revolution, and if Douglas is not elected I am afraid that the Union will be endangered. I hope he or John Bell of Tenn. may get into the office. If it should be otherwise, woe be unto this government as a nation and as a people.

I have not been doing anything at all for the last month, but as soon as corn cutting comes in I will then be able to get some[thing] to do, I think. There will be more grain raised this season than there has been for years. Oats, corn, and wheat are profusedly abundant this season. Besides all this, there is a vast quantity of mast in the barrens. We must have good times this winter. Money will be plenty and everything must flourish. . . .

I think some of making a few speeches this fall on politics. I do not know as I can make it pay. Still, I want to talk some so as to improve my speaking. G.W. Saunders and I will be together in this matter. He is in strong for Old Abe & I for the Little Giant. We have to elect county officers this fall, and there will be some sharpshooting done on all sides. Ez Tullis, Geo. Bowen, A.J. Coover, and myself had quite a debate over in Somerford on last Saturday night. Bowen is running for the recorders office again and will electioneer some this fall.

Wednesday, August 21st, A.D. 1861
     Today I pass the 28th milestone on the road to eternity.
     What a change a year can bring forth! Last year I lived in a happy, free, glorious republic. This year I live in a distracted, dishonored, dismembered country. The abolitionists and Breckinridge disunionists have succeeded in arraying the North and South against each other in deadly combat. We on the side of the federal government have over two hundred thousand men in arms to support the Union. The South has nearly as many.
     . . . I was for peace on the Crittenden Compromise. I was hooted at by my Republican friends. Now we are in a bloody civil war, brother against brother, father against son. Rivers of blood must now flow & hundreds of millions of money must be spent before this unnatural rebellion can be put down. . . . .

1862
     Emarine Roberts began keeping a diary January 1, 1862, and faithfully continued to fill the tiny pages (2" x 3-1/2", 3 days per page) until December 31, 1863, when she wrote: "So the last of my Dira is gon. I dont think I shall kepp one next yeare all though it is a good thing. So far well for this yeare." Her brief, often illegible entries for 1862 begin during her pregnancy with her first child. Her spelling and capitalization have been retained, but initial capital letters have been inserted at the beginning of apparent sentences and periods at the end.

Saturday, January 4, 1862: Went to pap['s] and staid till in the afternoon. The[n] went to London. Got a new pair of shoes. Give one dollar and sixty cts. Staid all night at paps. Cold.

Wednesday, January 8: Did nothing of eney a count. Soad on my shime [chemise] and made a sack. Mary C came down and brung me a turkey. Cold, rainy.

Thursday, January 9: Baked some pise in the forenoon. . . . Lade in bed all the afternoon with the hedach. Warm.

Monday, January 20: Made some homney to day in the forenoon. Worked at my quilt in the afternoon.

Tuesday, January 21: Churned this morning. Mad one and a half pound of buter. Cut John out a shirt. Went to Minervas this afternoon. . . .

Wednesday, January 22: . . . I washed to day and took up my carpet and scrub the flore. . . .

Friday, January 24: I irond in the fore noon and went to Jim Clelens in the afternoon. Came home and got super. John went to the debate. . . .

Saturday, January 25: . . . I and John went to london in the afternoon. G W Sanders has got home on a furloug. Valentine Wilson has a son.

Sunday, January 26: . . . Staid all night at Mothers on saterday night. Godfrey and famly at paps to day. John is not well to day.

Monday, January 27: . . . Soad some on John shirt. . . .

Sunday, February 9: . . . John got me a pair of shoos yesterday at longs. He give one dollar and 15 cents. . . .

Friday, February 14: Went to London. . . . Jeff Postel[?] . . . was buried in solgers close. Buried in the semetary at London. . . .

Wednesday, February 19: Soad on my Dress. They had a Voluntair meeting hear last night. Did not get one to Enlist. . . .

Saturday, February 22: . . . John went to his Mothers to ring the pigs. . . .

Wednesday, February 26: Meeting still going on at the Chapel. Some got religon. Some joined. I dont no how many. . . .

Friday, March 7: . . . Did not do much to day. I was not well. [John's] Scholl out to morrow. I am so glad I dont no what to do.

Monday, March 10: . . . Going to move to day. John is a going to take one load to day. I will stay at paps.

Wednesday, March 12: I am heare in our littel house and got all clend up.

Thursday, March 20: Did not do much to day. Raney all day. I finished Emadoras shime sleavs. John lent unkel Jim 10 dollars to day to pay the miller with.

Wednesday, March 26: . . . B F Roberts hear for Diner. Thank the good lord I have lived to see another birth day. I am 23 to day. Finished my pillers and bake two cakes.

Thursday, March 27: The last day of uncle Jims school. John went to the school house. I did not go. I went to Godfreys. Spelling school last night. I went to Mrs Roberts. . . .

Wednesday, April 9: . . . John went to Sanders. Got some tobaco seds. I soad some. Had the hed ach all day to day.

Saturday, April 12: Irond to day in the forenoon. Mary E and Estel hear for diner. John soad his tobaco sed to day. . . .

Sunday, April 27: Staid at home all day. Awfel lonsom. John went to Sanders. . . . No body hear to day.

Thursday, May 1: Mary Webb sent me a seten of guinea egg by Caroline. I set them to day. Laid in bed all fore noon.

Monday, May 5: Big victery. Yorktown taken. . . .

Saturday, May 10: The baby borned 15 minets past twelve. Oh I was glad. Several hear to day. Child cross. It is not well. I fele ofel. . . .

Sunday, May 11: Dont fele much better. Lide [who has been with Emerine much of the time] went to meeting. John went to John [illegible name] for Ann Newman. Did not get hir.

TUESDAY, JANUARY 7, 1862.

went to paps then
mother and Jimes
went to wellbs
staid all day Mahly
was oper thair I
mued my saph got
to pupa our dark came ha
me after night cold

WEDNESDAY 8

did nothing of eney
a count saad on my
shime and mode
a Jack Mary
came down and brus
me a turkey cold rainy

THURSDAY 9

baked some pise
in the forenoon
and cruped of the
fire and got
dinner lade in
bed of the afternoon
with the hedack warm

Emarine Roberts visits her family, sews, and bakes pies.

SATURDAY, APRIL 1, 1865.

All fools day. I worked hard all day putting up the kitchen. Wm Brandlin also worked all day, we raised it and put the roof on. William Brandlin went to Jefferson after supper. H.C. Roberts rode to Jeff & got our mail there. Big every appearance now that the rebels will soon be conquered.

SUNDAY 2

I remained at home nearly all day & wrote a letter to Peter Adams & enclosed my photograph in it. It is rather lonesome down here at this time. The Creek is falling rapidly it fell over three feet to day. Charlie crossed over the creek to day for the first time since the rise.

MONDAY 3

Fine day. I worked till noon & then went to Louton & Jefferson to mill & to the election. Great news to day. Richmond was evacuated by Lee & his army to day. Every one is firing or ringing bells. I must go to mill again tomorrow as I did not get my grinding

John Roberts puts a roof on his kitchen, sends his photograph to a friend, and hears guns firing and bells ringing in celebration of Lee's evacuation of Richmond.

Monday, May 12: Lide washed. John went and got Rachel Shockney. Then went and took Mary E home. I did not fele well.

Friday, May 23: Mother staid all night hear last night. Mrs Willson hear for super. . . . I felt bad all day with my brest.

Saturday, May 24: Mother went to Godfreys to day. I went out and walked around some. Doc and May and pap hear to night.

Sunday, May 25: Pap and Mother hear for diner[,] Mrs Willson[,] Jim Roberts and famely[,] Godfrey and his. . . . Twenty seven in all.

Tuesday, May 27: Set up right smart. Rachel ironed. John is plowing to day. Went out and walked around the yard.

Wednesday, May 28: Set up all day but one half hour. . . . Felt awfel tired.

Thursday, May 29: John worked the road for uncel Jim. I set up all day. . . . Felt perty well. No one hear to day.

Friday, May 30: Set up all day and till nine oclock. Caroline hear in the after noon. Rachel went to Godfreys and staid night.

Monday, June 2: Got up [and] got breakfast for the first [time] since the child was borned. Felt perty [tired?] at night. John worked for the miller. Rainy.

Friday, June 6: Paid Rach Shockney fore and a half dollars. Churned for the first [time]. Felt perty well.

Monday, June 9: Took a chill at fore oclock and took the weed in my brest. Got no brekfest till noon.

Tuesday, June 10: Not beter. John had to do all the work. Did not get to milk. No one hear all day. Felt lonly.

Wednesday, June 11: Brest awfel sore. Milked a littel. Hale [Mahala?] milked at night. Clare [clear]. John worked at the field.

Friday, June 13: Did nothing to day but tended to the baby. . . . I felt prity well all but my brest. It is not well.

Thursday, June 19: My brest is vary sore. Mary Jane Trobridg washed for me to day. She charged 20 cents. Hail hear this eving. I feal awfel weak.

Monday, June 23: Feal some beter. . . . I have not set up eny yet. Brest awfel sore.

Wednesday, June 25: I did not do eny thing. I am geting beter I think. . . .

Thursday, June 26: Tride to iron some but the babe was so cross I did not get to do it. I had to hold hir all day.

Wednesday, July 2: Washed to day for the first time since the babe was borned. Got don by noon. Felt tired.

Saturday, July 5: Went to london to day. Got me a Dress. . . .

Monday, July 7: Maid John shirt bosem and that was all I got don. No new war nuse yet nor no raine. . . .

Wednesday, July 9: . . . Soad some on John shirt. . . .

Saturday, July 12: Scrubed the kichen . . . and baked bred. Went to Godfreys for molases. Left the babe with John.

Sunday, July 13: Went to Godfreys. Staid all day. . . . Went to the school house to meeting in eving.

Tuesday, July 15: Cut out my Dress. Went to Godfreys in the eving. John worked for Dave Turner. . . .

Monday, July 21: Soad some on my Dress to day and laid down and took a good nap. I am a fraid of a draf.

Thursday, July 24: . . . Bad war nuse. Want more men.

Saturday, July 26: . . . Meeting in london for to get volentiers for the war.

Friday, August 8: . . . John help Dock to stack wheat.

Saturday, August 9: Laid in bed all forenoon with the hed ach. Churned in the eving. Did not [do] eny thing more.

Wednesday, August 13: John went to help paps folks thrash thare wheat.

The chronicle for 1862 continues with John's journal entry:

Thursday, August 21st, 1862

 . . . I am twenty nine years of age and I am getting old. . . .

On Saturday, May 10th, my wife had a child. . . . It was rather puny at first, but in a few weeks it improved very much and is now a fine hearty child. We think of calling her Flora. Wife had an awful hard time. She was sick two nights and one day. She had quite a trouble with her breasts. . . .

I taught school 6 months in Newport this season and had some difficulty about whipping some of the aristocracy. It blew over, however. . . . I moved from Newport March 11th to my house on Mothers place, and I have lived here ever since. J.H. Roberts and I rented about five acres of ground on the run bottom below the mill and put it in sweet potatoes, Irish potatoes, corn, and tobacco. It was not put [in] till tolerably late on account of the wet spring. We got our tobacco plants from Germantown below Dayton, and they did not do very well. . . . There has been a drought for the last two or three weeks, and I am afraid that our potato crop will be very short. . . .

War! War! War! is all the cry now. Money is being spent by the million dollars. Thousands and tens of thousands of the best citizens are being killed off by . . . cannon & by fell disease almost daily, and yet there is still a cry going up . . . for more men & more money. Business is at a standstill on account of the call recently made by the president for 600,000 more men to be marshaled into the field against the fiend secession. . . . May God speed the cause of the Union!

There is great excitement here on account of the drafting of soldiers for nine months. Madison County has not quite filled her quota yet. . . . The draft is to commence on the 6th of next month. If I am drafted I will go cheerfully to my post and do my duty to the best of my ability. This government has made me what I am, and I owe all that I possess to her fostering and protecting hand; and for me to refuse to do my duty now when called upon by the necessities of my benefactress would be Judas ingratitude. Not one of all our family are in the field yet, and I am ashamed to own to the fact. My reasons for not volunteering are:

1st, I have a wife that I have sworn to support and defend through life, also a helpless dependent babe. Now, if my wife would be willing to try her fortunes alone and would let me go, I would do so immediately; but as she is unwilling to do this I do not feel like going off and leaving her to the cold charities of an unfriendly world, for if misfortune should overtake her I would never forgive myself by being instrumental in bringing on her misery.

2d, I have of late been accused by some enemy of being Secesh, opposed to the war and also of dissuading persons from volunteering in the U.S. army. This being a wilful, malicious lie, I must of course have a deadly enemy somewhere who wishes my destruction. All liars are cowards, and I know that this person will not volunteer. Therefore, if a draft comes, he as well as myself will both have to go perhaps. I will therefore be better satisfied that the villain can do me no private injury or sacrifice my family.

3d, nearly all the able bodied men are gone already, and every grain saved is as good as two raised; and my strength not being equal to the average, I can do more by working here than by fighting. This being the case, I have not volunteered.

I believe in the ultimate success of the Union and that eventually this Union will be permanently reestablished and every traitor banished from the land. Party spirit still tell[s] its malicious tales to poison the minds and hearts of the people. The everlasting [Negro] is still harped upon by the quasi philanthropists and demagogues. I do sincerely wish that every negro and abolitionist and secessionist was in Heaven or Africa. They . . . wont help themselves, and I am in favor of their remaining as they are. They are emphatically an inferior being and ought to occupy an inferior position. My doctrine is, down with secession first, but dont let negro equality get too big a start while you are at that job. Next, down with fanatical abolitionists such as Wendall Phillips, Lloyd Garrison, &c. Next, down with sectional distinctions in congressional action and party politics. Let us have a broader, deeper, and more extensive fraternal Union feeling cultivated after the tiger strife is over and the Rebels have received sufficient punishment for their crimes. Set the press and the schoolmaster to work in their midst to renew the old regard for the old flag.

This war has brought out several things that were in doubt before. One of the most prominent is the feeling expressed by aliens, or rather the foreign born citizens. Nobly have they responded to the call of their adopted country. They have never failed us in a single instance. Irish and German regiments are to be found in every camp and amongst the foremost on every battlefield. Also, the remarkable repugnance that the real, straight out abolitionists have to going into the field of battle to fight those that they hate so intensely. Also, the remarkable fatality that seems to follow the track of the generals in the field that are antislavery in principle. The faithful historian will have no bright pages for them in the history of this Rebellion. Also, the envy and treachery of the crowned heads of the old world. . . . We as a nation today have hardly a single royal friend in the civilized world; but on the other hand they are gloating over our calamities with ill concealed satisfaction.

But I must close for this time. Union forever! The old flag, long may it wave!

Emarine's 1862 diary continues:

Saturday, August 23: Went to London with Mrs Willson. Got John too pair of pants. Got a pair of glovs for me.

Thursday, August 28: Soad some on Johns pants this fore noon. . . .

Tuesday, September 2: Did nothing to day. Took the ague to day. John had it to. Both shook with it at one time.

Wednesday, September 3: Feal vary bad this morning. Had the head ache. John . . . mist the Ague. I had it bad.

Saturday, September 13: Irond some and went to Godfreys a littel while in the forenoon. John went to london and got one dozen cans.

Monday, September 15: Went to Mrs Roberts to can peches. Got five cans up. She got 8 cans. Good war nuse. Mclen [McClellan] gained a victery. Good for him.

Wednesday, September 17: Did not do eny thing to day the baby cryde so much. John has not found our colt yet. I expect it is ded.

Monday, September 22: . . . The baby is no vary well. I have a bad pain in my sid. I dont no what to do.

Tuesday, September 23: Dont feal much beter. John is a going to london to get somthing for me to take. . . .

Wednesday, September 24: John went to town. Got a box of pills for me. I took one at night. It may help me some.

Thursday, September 25: Mahala came hear to do hir wash. Their well has give out. . . .

Friday, September 26: Sisey sick all night with a bad cold. I did no sleap eny of a count.

Wednesday, October 1: Staid at home and soad on the [illegible] skirt. Cut some tomatos for kechup. Awfel pain in my side.

Friday, October 3: Irond to day and finished Flora petcoat and did no more I felt so bad.

Tuesday, October 14: Election day. John is a Cox man. I dont no hoo will get it yet.

Thursday, October 16: James Andrews and famley hear to day. Went to Godfreys for diner. Went to Mrs Roberts.

Friday, October 17: . . . Flora is not well. She has broken out. I dont no what it is.

Sunday, October 19: Went to Roberts and boild don sider for to make apel buter. . . .

Monday, October 27: Went to Godfreys to day. Staid for diner. John worked for his mother. Set out frute trees.

Tuesday, November 4: Show in London. Will came down for me and I went home with him. Caroline came home with Hail.

Monday, November 10: Washed to day and went to Godfreys. The baby is six month old to day. I am so tird I dont no what to do.

Tuesday, November 11: Comenced Johns pants. . . .

Thursday, November 13: Finshed John pants. . . .

Monday, November 17: Cut out John shirts and made one. John school comenced to day. . . .

Wednesday, November 19: Finshed John shirt and cut out my Dress. . . . No war nuse of eny a count.

Thursday, November 27: Finshed my dress. Snoad to day. Dont feal well to night. Thanksgiving day. John teaching school to day.

Sunday, November 30: . . . Went to Godfreys. John and me thair for diner. S D Truitt thair to all day. . . .

Monday, December 1: Washed to day and scrubed the flore. Irond some and got rada to go to Webbs soing.

Tuesday, December 2: Went to Webbs soing to day. Severl was thair. 10 women I think. . . .

Wednesday, December 3: Went to Godfreys. Will and Caroline came up and help kill hogs. . . .

Thursday, December 4: Renderd out my lard and that was all I got don.

Saturday, December 6: John went to London to day. Will brought up a load of corn. 8 bushel.

Monday, December 8: Will came up to fix to build the chimney. Mason did not come. . . .

Thursday, December 11: . . . Grate trubel about the work. Will had to go to Somerford for a iron to build the chimney.

Saturday, December 13: Finshed the chimney yesterday. . . .

Tuesday, December 16: Knit on John sock some to day and some on my Dress.

Wednesday, December 17: . . . Some nuse of some batels being fought.

Monday, December 22: Cut out Flora sack to day and made hir apron. Pap bucherd to day. Warm.

Thursday, December 25: Went down to paps with Mahaley. Jas Andrews and Godfreys and Dock and May ware thair.

Saturday, December 27: Went to meting at Newport Friday night. Not meny out. . . .

Wednesday, December 31: This year is coming to a close. I hope be fore a nother year may pass that the war may be don with and pece be a gain in Amarica. I have had a good time this year and if I dont see no more trubel in this next to come I shal be glad. . . . Good by old year.

Excerpts from John Roberts's brief daily diary entries, supplemented by birthday reflections from his journal, continue the chronicle until the close of 1865:

Thursday, January 1, 1863

30 pupils today. Happy New Years to one and all. I treated my scholars to 2 lbs. of candy and 1 lb. of almonds. Someone got into the s[chool]house last night and burned up all my wood so that I had a very poor fire in the forenoon. Jacob Wilsons wife had a fine girl this morning, a New Years gift for Jacob. Very dull day in Somerford.

Saturday, January 3, 1863

. . . Lincolns proclamation freeing the slaves in the rebellious states & parts of states . . . is an idle threat and will only serve to divide the North. Lincoln is now a Radical. Lincoln puts arms into the hands of the freed negroes and calls them American citizens of African descent. This is suicidal and dangerous.

Thursday, January 15, 1863

No wood at the s[chool]house today & therefore no school. Snowed all last night and all day today. . . . The snow is about a foot deep and still there is more coming. No one is stirring around any more than is necessary. No paper today. Mr. Crawford hauled a load of wood to the s[chool]house in the afternoon.

Friday, January 30, 1863

46 pupils today. Mr. Ferree came in the evening with a magic lantern apparatus. I staid at Somerford to see the show. He gave me two tickets to distribute. I acted as doorkeeper. David Tullis came home last night. All the boys are well in the 40th Regt. I got supper at Mr. Palmers. I had a spelling match in the afternoon. Raw, snowy day.

Saturday, January 31, 1863

. . . B.F. Roberts helped me haul a load of wood at night. I got 52 lbs. of flour of Lamon today. I also sold Bill Ritter one pound of tobacco on the leaf. This is my first sale. I did not work much today. [Negro] is taking up all the time in Congress.

Thursday, February 5, 1863

41 pupils today & an awful snowy day too. I took my scholars to the Lafayette school. We spelled in the Campbellite church. We all went in sleds and sleighs. Squire John Jones was moderator. Wallace Martin

pronounced. I had 12 and Shepherd had 12 pupils. Six of mine remained standing after all his were down. Very exciting time. I got home at one o'clock. The Secesh have broken the Charleston blockade.

Friday, February 6, 1863

40 pupils today. It was very cold nearly all day. I did not get to my school till ten o'clock. I got up pretty late & had to chop down a tree for wood. My scholars are very much tickled over their victory over Lafayette. Not much war news. The abolitionists are coming right out in favor of disunion. So we go.

Wednesday, February 11, 1863

41 pupils today. I got up very late this morning. It rained all the afternoon. I had some fun in trying to keep my scholars still. I had one boy read a love letter. There is no war news [of] any importance. The negroes are making trouble in the army. . . .

Wednesday, February 18, 1863

44 pupils today. I had no wood in the afternoon so I did not teach any after dinner. The Congress has passed a conscription bill taking everyone into the army except those able to pay $300 into the U.S. Treasury. It is a rich mans law. The army is doing nothing. . . .

Saturday, February 28, 1863

Fine warm sunshiny day. Wm. Truitt came up and helped me to haul 3 loads of wood. Wife went down there with him. I went and staid at Mothers all night. I sat up till after 4 o'clock this morning. I read three dime novels through. . . .

Wednesday, March 4, 1863

40 pupils today. It was an awful cold day; mostly clear, however. Dave Tullis started for the 40th Regt. The most of the boys went with him. . . . The U.S. Congress expired today. They have done almost as much mischief as they could. Their adjournment is a relief to the country. . . .

Saturday, March 7, 1863

It snowed like blazes all forenoon. I did nothing till about two o'clock when I cut some wood. I also got 15-1/2 lbs. of tobacco from the mill. There is trouble brewing all over the North. There was a riot in Columbus last Thursday night. Some citizens broke open the Crisis office at Columbus and tore up the books of that concern. The editor had a flaming reception last night. I am afraid of a revolution here in the North.

Tuesday, March 10, 1863
      33 pupils today. . . . Joseph Yardley was brought home dead today. He had the typhoid fever. The boys are dying off rapidly. I want this war to stop as all our young men will be gone if it keeps on. Two provost guards were in Somerford today after deserters.

Thursday, March 12, 1863
      30 pupils today. I had no school till noon on account of having no wood till 10 o'clock. The stovepipe fell down and the crock in the flue was broken. I got a sharp lecture from Mr. Geer about noisy recesses. I deserved the lecture perhaps. . . .

Friday, March 13, 1863
      34 pupils today. . . . I had a spelling match this afternoon. . . . I am still threatened with an arrest by a provost guard for being true to the Constitution. The darkest hour is just before day.

Monday, March 23, 1863
      I went over to Somerford in the morning and staid all day. I collected my school money and paid all my debts over there. My school money amounted to $112. . . . The Somerford women have had quite a time about politics. The South are getting tired of the war. There is a reconstruction newspaper started in Georgia. Things are more favorable for peace. . . .

Thursday, March 26, 1863
      . . . Godfrey is going to make Sally Rankin smoke for talking about him. Slander suits hardly ever amount to much. I read Washingtons Farewell Address, which every man ought to read over at least once a week. Wife is 24 years old today.

Saturday, March 28, 1863
      . . . They have reported in Somerford that I am in jail for treason. They are threatening me very hard just now because I am for the Union & Constitution. There is no war news. Election time is drawing nigh. That is why I am being abused by the blacksnakes.

Thursday, April 2, 1863
      . . . Geo. Bowen showed me what he said [Ezra] Tullis wrote about me, saying that I said this was a damned abolition war and nobody would join the army. I wrote to Tullis tonight.

Saturday, April 4, 1863

. . . I went to London & paid off the Dr. Jones note which amounted to $5.15. I also sent E. Tullis a letter about what he has been writing about me. Wife was in town also and spent $3.00 for dry goods. I am on the Democratic ticket for justice. I do not want it. I got another Agricultural Report. . . .

Monday, April 6, 1863

Cloudy, cold, and stormy day. I went to London in the morning and took in 3 doz. eggs. Wolf (my dog) got killed by the cars running over him opposite Boyds. . . . Great excitement over the election. I run the strength of the Democratic ticket and no more. I expect Coover is elected by 40 votes. I rode out with Coover. . . .

Tuesday, April 7, 1863

. . . The Democrats have met with a Waterloo defeat in this township, but they have made it up in other townships. Somerford went Democratic. So did Paint and all the southern townships in the co[unty].

Thursday, April 9, 1863

. . . I went to London in the forenoon. I bought a spade for $1.35 and a quart of onions for 12-1/2 cts. Everything was quiet about town. The vampires about town talk about arresting me for treason. I am prepared for them unless they go into downright perjury, which they will hardly do. So I feel safe on that score.

Monday, April 13, 1863

. . . I slept till 11 o'clock today and then I ate dinner and then went up to the school election. We voted in A.J. Coover for one year as director and Eli Wilson for 3 years. We had some sparring about dividing the school district. There was nothing done in the matter, and more angry words were all that was accomplished. 25 votes were cast. . . .

Thursday, April 16, 1863

. . . I sowed some tobacco and cabbage seed in the forenoon. I took over a pair of boots in the afternoon. I also paid V.H. Prugh 37-1/2 cts. for tea. I paid Wesley Geer 70 cents for mending my boots. Aquilla T. Prugh [and I] had a quarrel. He abused me and called me a traitor and secessionist & said he could prove it. I will sue him tomorrow if I live. I paid John Wilson for cow pasture $1.05.

Friday, April 17, 1863
. . . I went to London in the forenoon and saw my friends about my A.T. Prugh case. I have consulted a lawyer about it. He thinks I have a very good case but wants some more things on hands before he commences suit. . . . I am on the track of some liars and I think I will catch them yet.

Saturday, April 18, 1863
. . . I got J.H. R[oberts] to get a sight of the Tullis letter and got a quotation from it. Wife got Flora's likeness taken today. There was a negro infanticide in London yesterday. Jury sat on the case today. The wench lived at Jno. Dungans when the murder took place. . . .

Monday, April 20, 1863
. . . I made garden all forenoon. I then went to London to see the board of education about dividing the s[chool] district. We had a hot discussion over it. . . . We argued a 1/2 day about the matter. They have arrested nearly all the storekeepers in West Jefferson for selling clothes to soldiers so that they can desert from the army. All Repub[lican]s but one.

Tuesday, April 21, 1863
. . . I sold my cow to Isaac King for $25 in cash. I got my heifer from Truitts today. . . . The Jefferson merchants all got off except the Republicans, who were bound up or over in $100.00 each. Good, better, best. The shoe pinches in the right place this time.

Wednesday, April 22, 1863
. . . I am accused of persuading A. Anderson to desert. It is an infamous lie.

Saturday, April 25, 1863
. . . Things are getting pretty scaley here. I heard a man abused like a pickpocket because he said he was a Butternut [i.e., an opponent of the war] and that he would wear a pin of that sort if he saw fit.

Monday, April 27, 1863
. . . Gen. [Nathaniel P.] Banks has thrashed the Secesh like blazes. He got 3000 prisoners and a large amount of stores. There are some provost guards in London. They are poking up all the chaps that have military suits on. . . .

Wednesday, April 29, 1863

. . . I got a letter from E. Tullis today. He says I did write what was reported. They are bound to crush me if they possibly can. I wrote a letter to G.W. Saunders today [to get him, and perhaps other soldiers, to vouch for Roberts's loyalty?]. . . . The political excitement is unabated. I hope we wont come to blows about it.

Saturday, May 2, 1863

. . . The French have been whipped at Puebla, Mex[ico]. Bully for old Mexico. Aztec is coming out. I hope old [General Joseph] Hooker may do something, as he has been a long time about it. I made an onion bed and put some brick in the milk house.

Wednesday, May 6, 1863

. . . There was a little riot in Dayton this week. [Clement L.] Vallandigham was arrested. No one killed, I believe.

Monday, May 18, 1863

. . . I went in the afternoon to help Hornbeck lay the foundation for his barn. There was about 20 hands there. . . . They say that Port Hudson is taken by Banks. Bully for Banks. Hit them again.

Tuesday, May 19, 1863

. . . Hornbeck raised his barn today, or partly raised it, with a block & tackle. He sent for me to come & help him finish in the morning. I must help Godfrey finish planting tomorrow. I am very hoarse hallooing at the old mare. Port Hudson is not taken yet.

Friday, May 22, 1863

. . . I got two letters, one from P.L. Roberts & one from C.C. Roberts, Charles's letter containing a certificate of the loyalty of my letter, signed by four or five of the soldiers in the 40th. This clears myself of the infernal machinations of my enemies. There is a good report from [Ulysses S.] Grants army. Bully for Grant.

Tuesday, June 2, 1863

. . . I went to London in the forenoon to the cattle sales. There was quite a large crowd in town. I was in to the Democratic convention. There was no resolutions offered or speeches made. . . . It is reported that 1100 negroes have been killed by the Secesh in Missouri.

Tuesday, June 9, 1863
   . . . I am afraid that C.L. Valingham [*sic*] will get the nomination for gov. of Ohio. Defeat is certain if he is nominated.

Thursday, June 11, 1863
   . . . The Democratic convention has nominated Vallandigham for governor. This knocks the party cold this fall. It was so reported in London tonight at any rate. I expect they have adopted a peace platform. If so the whole ticket has gone to Davy Jones'es.

Friday, June 12, 1863
   C.L. Vallandigham is nominated sure enough and on a war platform at that. . . . He will be defeated without doubt. I was enrolled today by the marshal, Robt. Withrow. . . .

Saturday, July 4, 1863
   Militia election in London. I acted as one of the clerks. A.J. Coover was elected captain. . . .

Monday, July 6, 1863
   . . . Glorious news from the Potomac army. They have defeated [Robert E.] Lees army at Gettysburg, Penn. Rebel loss reported at 40,000 in killed, wounded, & prisoners. Most too good to be true.

Wednesday, July 8, 1863
   Hot and clear. I bound wheat from morning till night. Sally, Nancy, Betsy, & Mary Clifton helped from noon. The first two raked & the last two shocked. Jas. Baker & B.F. Roberts cradled. Augustus Anderson & myself bound wheat. Vicksburg is taken sure enough. . . . Bully for Grant.

Friday, July 10
   . . . Everyone is rejoicing over the fall of Vicksburg and the defeat of Lees army. We hope the Secesh may all be driven into the sea and the Abolish [abolitionists] on the other side of the Jordan.

Saturday, July 11
   . . . Matt Tanner[?] . . . told me about Tullis wanting to injure me by writing a letter to V.H. Prugh to be read by him in public. I will attend to the gentleman.

Monday, July 13

. . . John [Hunt] Morgan has made a raid into Ohio & all the militiamen in southern Ohio are ordered to report forthwith. . . .

Tuesday, July 14

. . . I start today for Camp Chase. . . . Everything is in commotion & confusion. We stayed in London till near night. . . . Jacob Goings is about crazy. He is afraid of being shot for deserting the Rebel army. There are many pale faces to be seen on the streets.

Wednesday, July 15

. . . I was in London early and bought a tin cup & some straps to carry my blanket. Half the men in Madison Co. were in London today. There are a thousand rumors going about Morgan. We got on the 10 o'clock train & arrived at Camp Chase before noon. The whole face of the earth is covered with militia. The[y] are pouring in by hundreds.

Thursday, July 16

Last night I slept under a tree on the ground. I slept but very little. Every man in the camp was cheering & singing. John Morgan is said to be coming this way. I do not feel very well on account of not getting any sleep. We drew field rations this morning. We got beef, rice, soft bread, sugar, pork, & browned coffee. We have miserable water to drink. Smoky weather.

Friday, July 17

Cold, disagreeable nights & agueish days. I wrote home today. Some of the men are getting the diarrhea. There are a thousand rumors about Morgan. Todd [Governor David Tod] made a speech today & dismissed half the militia. It was decided by lot & I drew to stay in camp. Our company is to be consolidated tomorrow. The lucky men are skedaddling for home.

Saturday, July 18

Very cold last night. We have had no tents and are about to give out sleeping on the ground. Dave Turner had a hard fit right in our quarters. There was another man fell at the same time. John Shorley[?] also had a hard fit in the afternoon. Wm. Teeter also fell at the same time Shorley did. They had two really hard fits. I wrote home this morning. We got tents today.

Sunday, July 19, 1863

Fine, pleasant day. We are consolidated with the Amity company, they to have the capt. & orderly & we to have the lieutenants. We are to have the 2d, 3d, & 5th sergeants. Finley preached in our regt. this morning. Nearly all the men came out to hear the sermon. It was short and to the point. Jac. Goings is in great distress. I fear he will go crazy.

Monday, July 20, 1863

Last night was warmer than any night yet. We drew guns and ammunition yesterday. They are old Prussian muskets and have been in the service. I went swimming in the river yesterday. Our regt. does guard duty today. I & Goings are cooks. Quite a number of our boys have deserted. We were discharged this afternoon and gave up our guns. Morgans men are routed & nearly all captured. . . .

Tuesday, July 21, 1863

I started from Camp Chase yesterday & got home at 11 o'clock last night. . . . There was three engines to our train last night. One man had a fit at the railroad. Everyone is satisfied. Deserters are to be returned to the adjutant general. I have a very bad cold & have done nothing today. Morgan is captured. The militia campaign is over.

Friday, July 24, 1863

. . . John Morgan still has a thousand men at his command and he fought a battle at Zanesville yesterday.

Monday, July 27, 1863

. . . I pitched hay all forenoon. We put up two stacks. Wm. Truitt stacked; Caroline Truitt & Harford Rankin hauled; Jas. Truitt hitched. John Morgan was taken through London today as a prisoner of war. His whole band are captured. One man was arrested for abusing Morgan. . . . I am tired. I made hay all the afternoon till starlight.

Thursday, July 30, 1863

. . . I went to London today and saw the great gurilla John Morgan, Maj. Gen. in C.S.A. He is a very pleasant looking man, about 35 years of age. He shook hands with quite a lot of folks. He laughed & chatted very friendly to all. . . . There was a big crowd to see Morgan.

Friday, August 7, 1863

. . . Add. Cornwell is being bored extensively in London about shaking hands with John Morgan. It is a good thing to bore the great mogul of the Republicans in this neighborhood. . . . Allen Anderson was at Darby the other day. He has been on the gunboats. He is going back to his regt.

Wednesday, August 12, 1863
. . . Some of the boys in the 95th Regt. are home detailed to take drafted recruits to the army. Vallandighams prospects are getting worse every day.

Friday, August 21st, A.D. 1863 ("Evening before") [from Roberts's journal]
I am now . . . thirty years of age.
The past year has passed away pleasantly enough. . . . The worst thing I have had to deal with is my political opponents. I have been abused by them like a pickpocket, especially by the abolition portion. I have been called a Butternut, Copperhead, traitor, and every epithet that the malignant ingenuity of the administration fanatics could invent, all because I do not say that abolition is god & Abraham Lincoln is a true prophet. There is a better time coming, I hope, as I do not believe that the mass of the people are against the Constitution & the Union, which guarantees freedom of speech and the press.
The Rebellion is still abroad in the land, although there is light behind the clouds. . . .

Saturday, August 22, 1863
. . . I went to London in the afternoon to a militia election. I voted the Sawyer ticket, which was defeated by 60 votes. Vallandigham [partisans] were plenty in London today. Cap Timmons wore a Butternut pin on his coat right in front. Coover resigned his captaincy. I did not like the idea of serving as sergeant, so I declined. I was sworn in [as school(?)] director.

Monday, August 24, 1863
. . . They say there will be no draft here in Ohio. Only 12,000 men are called for from this state. . . .

Tuesday, August 25, 1863
. . . I went to London in the afternoon to our militia election. John H. Hornbeck & Jacob Petrey were candidates for captain. Petrey was elected by two majority for the high office . . . . I am of the opinion that the draft will not go off in this state at all.

Friday, August 28, 1863

I went to see Eli Wilson & Coover about the school in this district but failed to close the bargain as there is no money in the treasury for them. I sent a note to Dave Lewis about the school in Oak Run Township. I rode in with a darkey and rode out with Dave Garrard. . . .

Tuesday, September 1, 1863

. . . I went to London in the morning and stayed all day. We had a Democratic convention today and made up a splendid ticket: Capt. Jas. Watson, representative; Maj. Squires, treasurer; Marsh P. Beach, clerk of court; B.F. Clark, probate judge; & Erwin Philer, recorder, and Geo. M. Athey, sheriff. It is a bully ticket and will triumph. Hurrah for old Madison.

Wednesday, September 2, 1863

. . . I went to London early in the morning to help arrange the seats & speakers stand for the Democratic mass meeting to [be] held there tomorrow. . . . We got everything in good shape. A fine day is much to be desired. . . .

Thursday, September 3, 1863

Cloudy in the morning and fine in the afternoon. Wife & I went to London in Kellys wagon to the great Democratic mass meeting, the greatest that was ever held in London. There was said to be over 10,000 people there. The Democracy had a procession as much as five miles long. I never saw so many wagons in one string. There was several wagons with 24 girls in them. There was not a drunkard in town.

Friday, September 4, 1863

. . . The Republicans are very sore over the mass meeting. They say it was the biggest meeting ever in London.

Friday, September 11, 1863

Fine day. Wife & I & Mothers folks went in Jonah Trowbridges wagon to the county fair, which was a very poor concern. The jugglers & mountbanks were the saving feature of the fair. There was a small crowd out. . . . There is to be a Republican meeting in our s[chool]house tonight.

Saturday, September 26, 1863

. . . This is my [first] day of living in Oak Run Township. I drilled all day at Harveys mill under Capt. Rea. I drilled the company some myself. There was about 25 men out to drill. Harveys mill is only about a 1/2 mile from where I live. Everything passed off peacefully. Wife scrubbed and set things to right.

Monday, September 28, 1863
. . . I went up to London after my cow & calf. The cow could not be brought as it is nearly dead with the milk sickness. The news from the 26th is sad enough. More of my old friends have been stricken in this last battle than ever I heard of. G.W. Saunders lost a leg; Joe Morris wounded in the hand; B.F. Tyler in the back; Pat Graham both legs broken & an arm. Co. K only had 11 men at roll call at night after the battle.

Tuesday, September 29, 1863
. . . I was up to London to general or regimental muster. I acted as orderly. I rode to town in Biggs Thomas wagon. Major W.H. Squires drilled us some. We had no fights. The news from Rosecranz [General William S. Rosecrans] army is not very cheering. The Madison Co. regts. are terribly cut up. A great many of our wounded are in the enemys camp. I borrowed ten cents of Biggs Thomas.

Saturday, October 3, 1863
. . . I went up to the grand abolition Republican Union anti-Constitutional mass meeting. They had out their whole force. About 390 wagons were in the procession. It exceeded the Democratic meeting in numbers. Wife went up with Father Truitt, who came down in a buggy after her. No war news.

Monday, October 5, 1863
. . . I cut up 11 shocks of corn & got some scaffold poles for my chimney. My house is in a very poor fix for cold weather. . . . Winter seems to be rapidly approaching. C.C. Roberts was wounded in the wrist at the battle of Chicamauga. . . .

Tuesday, October 6, 1863
. . . I went to London today after my colt. I got a horse & saddle of Biggs Thomas. I bought a bridle of Lotspeich for $1.90. . . . There was a row in Jefferson yesterday. Some soldiers were made drunk & set upon the Democratic meeting held there. Two men were badly hurt. They threw stones at the women & children.

Monday, October 12, 1863
. . . Wife & I rode up to London in Dave Lewises wagon. . . . A man called me meaner than Jeff[erson] Davis because I did not intend to vote for [John] Brough or Vallandigham. The excitement is very high.

Tuesday, October 13, 1863
. . . I went early to the polls & voted the Democratic ticket except Vallandigham. There was 62 votes cast in the township. Vallandigham got 36 of the votes, Capt. Watson 39, also Major Squires & B.F. Clark, the rest of the ticket, 37 apiece. I was appointed clerk. . . . All peaceable at the election. I am afraid our county ticket is defeated.

Wednesday, October 14, 1863
. . . Vallandigham was beaten 60,000 votes in the state. Madison County goes 500 majority for Brough, but 3 townships gave Vallandigham a majority, viz. Range, Stokes, & Oak Run. The Republicans are jubilant, Democrats despondent. . . .

Friday, October 16, 1863
. . . I went down to the s[chool]house to help clean it up. D. Lewis, three of Mr. Fellows children, and Miriam Leach all were there with soap and pails & broom to wash all the stains away. . . .

Saturday, October 17, 1863
. . . The Republicans had a grand blowout in London last night. The big wagon that came from Newport overset opposite Boyds and injured two or three of the girls that were riding in it seriously. . . .

Sunday, October 18, 1863
. . . I remained at home all day & read L.A. Hine's tale of the Law & the Profits. Some good things in it. Tomorrow I must commence my labors in the schoolroom. I do not hear any news of any kind. I am afraid I shall be afflicted with hernia. The war is at a standstill. There is no telling when there will be peace.

Monday, October 19, 1863
Very fine day. I commenced teaching today in the new s[chool]house on Turkey Run, Oak Run Township. I had 10 pupils, 7 girls & 3 boys. It was rather a dull time . . . ; too light a school for me.

Friday, October 23, 1863

    13 pupils today. . . . I got a letter from J.F. Peterman and one from N[ancy] Clifton. Peterman is wounded in the left leg & is now in the hospital. . . . The draft comes off on next Tuesday in this county; 51 men are required under the last call.

Saturday, October 24, 1863

    . . . Biggs Thomas helped me to haul two loads of wood. I then got a horse of Thomas & went to London. I went to see Dr. Coblentz about my incipient hernia. Dr. Jones has obtained a short furlough & is now at home. I saw him. He says G.W. Saunders is getting along tolerably well. . . . I got some flour of S.H. Cartzdafner. I also got $1.50 as clerk of election.

Sunday, October 25, 1863

    . . . I hear good news. . . . The leaders of the Republican party are quarreling over their ill gotten gains. God speed the happy day, as rogues quarrels are honest mens gains. . . .

Thursday, November 5, 1863

    22 pupils today. . . . All my scholars are bright. I have no dull ones in the school. . . . My grammar class is getting into deep water; they are in the relative pronouns. I must post up on geography and give some lessons on the outline maps.

Saturday, November 14, 1863

    . . . I got my Camp Chase money, $4.78. . . .

Sunday, November 15, 1863

    . . . G.W. Saunders is dead. He died in the hospital from gunshot wound in the leg. Gam was a clever fellow. Peace to his ashes. He was almost like a brother to me.

Monday, November 16, 1863

    25 pupils today. . . . I read a dime novel through today, called The Golden Arrow. I had to make my two spelling classes stand on the floor to study their lessons. We have no broom at the s[chool]house, and the floor is getting to be very dirty. I only had on[e] scholar in my advanced grammar & arithmetic class today.

Sunday, November 22, 1863

    Fine day. I went all over the woods to find a wild cherry tree to get the bark to make syrup of. I finally went to Dave Lewises and got some bark off of a tree close to his house. . . . I used too much tobacco today. It makes me weak & nervous and gives me a pain in the breast.

Wednesday, November 25, 1863
    32 pupils. . . . I kept about a dozen of my scholars in at noon for whispering. . . . I got some wild cherry bark today at noon. Geo. Lewis came to my house after dark. He was coon hunting.

Thursday, November 26, 1863
    32 pupils. It was a very nice day. This is Thanksgiving Day. The scholars had a dinner sat on the table. It was a nice affair. They [had] chicken, pies and cakes, & quite a number of good things. Biggs Thomas & his wife came down to visit the school, also Mrs. Fritts. I had two hours noon recess & compositions and declamations in the afternoon. I had a spelling school at night. . . .

Tuesday, December 1, 1863
    23 pupils today. . . . Jno. Morgan got off to Toronto, Canada, so report says. He certainly dug out with his pocketbook. . . . I put the zinc under the s[chool]house stove today at noon. . . .

Thursday, December 3, 1863
    28 pupils. . . . The drafting day is rolling around & I must prepare for it. I played ball some today. Corn is up to 80 cents per bushel now ready cash in London. Everything else is up in proportion.

Friday, December 11, 1863
    25 pupils today. . . . I brought in a stick today into my school for the first time. I may have to use it yet. Quite a number of my scholars came up minus compositions today. I read the Life of Charles XII of Sweden by Voltaire. It is a very fine composition. The book is in the township library.

Tuesday, December 15, 1863
    27 pupils today. I posted up a bill on the s[chool]house door for a meeting to raise volunteers in this township so as to avoid the draft. The meeting is to be Friday evening at the Turkey Run s[chool]house. . . .

Friday, December 18, 1863
    28 pupils. . . . The people of the township met to see about the draft of the 5th of next month. I staid at the s[chool]house till after the meeting. Mr. Rea & Lewis signed my order for my school money. . . .

They did not get any volunteers. They raised $20 for soldier sick [for sick soldiers?].

Saturday, December 19, 1863
 Bitter cold and windy. D. Lewis helped me to kill my hog. I shot it with my pistol three times before I killed it. . . . The men at the s[chool]house last night raised the bounty for volunteers to $400, agreeing to pay in proportion to their taxes for the present year. . . .

Sunday, December 20, 1863
 . . . All the talk now is about the draft of the 5th of January. They are raising some volunteers in London. I understand that J. Fletcher Chapman has volunteered as well as John Rea and a lot of negroes. . . .

Friday, December 25, 1863
 Merry Christmas. I was at James Andrews. There was upwards of 30 people there, several from S. Charleston that I had never seen before. Nearly all of the Truitt family were there. We had a superb dinner, two roast turkies & other things in proportion. . . .

Saturday, December 26, 1863
 . . . Wesley Allen is in great trouble about his traitor son John.

Sunday, December 27, 1863
 . . . J.M. Allen voted for C.L. Vallandigham. Good, better, best. Old Wesley's chickens are coming home to roost. Bully for [Samuel S. "Sunset"] Cox and every other good Union man. . . .

Monday, December 28, 1863
 . . . They have about half of the volunteers made up to meet the draft.

Tuesday, December 29, 1863
 . . . I could not get a diary for next year, so I bought a pocket ledger for twenty five cents. Geo. B. McClellan is nominated for the presidency by the Constitutional & Union Party.

Thursday, December 31, 1863
 . . . I got 105 lbs. of beef of B.D. Thomas at 4 cts. per pound. I also ground my ax at D. Lewises. I also went out quail hunting with Dave Lewis. I also helped cut down a tree for squirrels in Lewises pasture. We got one fox squirrel. . . .

<u>1864</u>
Sunday, January 10, 1864
 . . . John H. Jones & his wife, Miss Margaret Kidney, & Caroline Truitt came down to see us. . . . My chimney caught fire & I was busy all the time they were here putting it out. I had an awful time to keep my house from burning down. I boiled two pots full of mud & daubed it up so that it is safe to have a fire in once more.

Saturday, January 23, 1864
 . . . I subscribed $5.00 to the volunteer fund.

Sunday, January 24, 1864
 . . . Miss Saline Schofield is said to be enciente. Such things are common these days. . . . Several of my scholars are sick at this time. . . . They have lung fever or pneumonia.

Tuesday, January 26, 1864
 19 pupils today. . . . War meeting at the schoolhouse. There was upwards of 50 persons at it. . . . I was secretary. . . . 15 persons subscribed $27 apiece & the others made up the remainder of $6.25 to pay extra bounty for 5 men to fill up the township quota. The meeting was last night. Nancy Lewis staid with my wife. I got home at midnight.

Saturday, January 30, 1864
 . . . I cut wood nearly all day. In the evening I went over to David Lewis's and wrote down the names and ages of his children in his new Bible. I . . . paid Nancy Lewis 20 cents for knitting my wife a net for her hair. Union Township lacks 7 men yet to fill her quota. . . .

Wednesday, February 3, 1864
 21 pupils today. . . . The president has called for 200,000 more men to be drafted by the 10th of March. He is bound to have the last dollar if not the last man. This makes 500,000 men that he has called for in the last six months. Hiring volunteers is all the talk now. Money is the cry. . . .

Thursday, February 4, 1864
 22 pupils today. . . . There is to be a war meeting at the s[chool]house here tonight to raise money to hire substitutes or volunteers to clear the township of the draft of the 11th of March. . . .

Friday, February 5, 1864
 21 pupils today. . . . The meeting last night was a failure. They did not raise any money for the purpose of paying additional bounty. They

talk of having another meeting. . . . I had compositions and declamations [today]. Several of my pupils failed to get their declamations ready.

Saturday, February 6, 1864
. . . B.D. Thomas brought my paper and a speech of S.S. Cox on confiscation. It is a splendid speech and one of Coxes best efforts. I cut down a large tree for wood and tried to get a team but did not get one. . . .

Friday, February 12, 1864
21 pupils today. . . . The smallpox is in London very bad. There are two cases, Sam Cramer and a negro. The negro in the frenzy of the fever killed his wife with an ax by cutting her head open. The smallpox was brought to London by a negro. This makes twice that the negroes have brought the smallpox there this winter.

Sunday, February 14, 1864
. . . There is no news except it is about the smallpox that is raging in London. I have heard of no new cases there lately. Sam Cramer is getting some better, I understand. Dr. Strain came to D. Lewis and never changed his clothes after visiting Sam Cramer. The negroes are dying at the rate of 100 per diem in Washington.

Monday, February 15, 1864
21 pupils today. . . . I intercepted a love letter today and had the author read it before the school. I put it to a vote whether I would have a spelling school tonight. The vote was nearly a tie so I deferred it.

Tuesday, February 16, 1864
14 pupils today. . . . There is no further news about the smallpox. It is still confined to London, I believe. Some of the people here are alarmed about the smallpox breaking out in the school and have hinted about having the school stopped. I am not afraid of it myself. The London school was going on at last account.

Wednesday, March 2, 1864
20 pupils today. . . . An Irishman named Roach called to treat me to a dram of whiskey. They have raised $200 for another man in this township to fill up their quota of the last draft. . . .

Saturday, March 5, 1864
. . . I started for London early in the morning & walked up there by 10 o'clock. The roads were very slippery. I went up and got a [teacher's]

certificate for two years. Emma Thomas & Miss Martha Kidney were being examined when I went up. I was asked but very few questions. . . . I had to get a 5 ct. stamp on my certificate.

Wednesday, March 9, 1864
20 pupils today. . . . Wm. & Jas. Truitt came down in the evening with a spring wagon and a two horse wagon to move my things up to my own house on Oak Run on Mothers place. The roads are rough but fine and dry.

Thursday, March 10, 1864
19 pupils today. I worked like a Turk till nearly 10 o'clock loading & packing my household stuff on the two wagons. B.D. Thomas started off with his load early in the morning. It commenced raining last night and rained slightly nearly all day. I was awful tired at night. B.D. Thomas reported all safe up at my house. The roads are very slippery. I had everything moved this time except a headboard to one of my beds & several other little items such as two chairs & a pair of old gears. . . .

Friday, March 11, 1864
18 pupils today. . . . I killed a snake yesterday which was the first one that I have seen this season. . . . There is a report that the president is about to call out 200,000 more men. There is quite a quaking amongst the dry bones. I had a little spelling match after recess, but no other exercises.

Saturday, March 12, 1864
. . . There was a Democratic convention held at the courthouse. . . . I was appointed secretary and Geo. Nolan chairman.

Sunday, March 13, 1864
Wife & I staid all night at Godfreys. Mrs. Webb, Mrs. Levi Watson, and Mother were all over there in the evening. They had a very warm discussion of politics. Everyone got mad. . . . W.H. Roberts has sold out his drugstore and has gone into the picture business. . . .

Wednesday, March 16, 1864
19 pupils today. . . . This day five years ago I was married & have seen no reason to regret the transaction. I hear no news and am in a poor condition to write a diary. I am and have been staying at B.D. Thomas house. We go to bed at nine o'clock & get up at five. Breakfast at six. I feed a few sheep some shelled corn and some in the ear. I have been in

the habit of cutting stove wood for the house. Altogether it is a pleasant place to board but not quite like home.

Friday, March 18, 1864

. . . I had a spelling school last night. Only about 15 pupils out. We had a very good time. . . . My school was victorious over all competitors last night. . . .

Saturday, March 19, 1864

. . . I came to London in the afternoon and brought home a copy of the Agricultural Report for 1862. . . . The soldiers are committing a great many lawless acts on the citizens of the country. I would not be surprised if we did not have civil war right here in Ohio before six months. . . .

Saturday, March 26, 1864

. . . The Republicans are fretting hugely over their Fremont factionists. Bully for the Fremonters. They have started the first fissure in the ranks.

Wednesday, March 30, 1864

15 pupils today. . . . Oak Run Township is clear of the draft, as they hired two men day before yesterday to fill out the quota for the last call. There is a report that Geo. B. McClellan is ordered to the field, where to or in what department I do not know. Gen. Fremont has also been assigned a command. This is done to kill off both of them. . . .

Friday, April 1, 1864

. . . A peddler of sewing machines, Mr. Harris, is a devout admirer of Abraham Lincoln and his acts. He calls the president an instrument in the hands of God to convert the world to righteousness. I call this idolatry.

Saturday, April 2, 1864

. . . Harriet Maria had a fit of apoplexy this week. Mother was away from home at the time. . . . Levi Watson had the cool impudence to ask me to vote for him for assessor, after doing all he could to bring the hatred of my neighbors on my head & denouncing me as a traitor. . . .

Sunday, April 3, 1864

. . . There are 31 men to be drafted out of Union Township. This will make some of the black Republicans howl. Go on, Honest Abe!

Monday, April 4, 1864

13 pupils today. . . . My scholars have to pick up all the wood we burn. I am in hopes we may get so that we will not need any more wood. . . . The township and county elections go off today. I suppose the black Republicans will be overwhelmingly in the majority. I will not get to vote. . . .

Tuesday, April 5, 1864

12 pupils today. . . . B.D. Thomas father in law was at his house last night. . . . He is going to send his son to Delaware College. . . . The Democrats elected every officer in the township yesterday. . . .

Wednesday, April 6, 1864

12 pupils today. This is too small a school for me. . . . B.D. Thomas was at London today. The 40th Regt. veterans were in town, very drunk most of them. There was some fears entertained about the Democrat office. I have not heard of its being destroyed, however, by anyone, soldiers or citizens. . . . The draft is inevitable in Union Township. Well, let her rip. I can stand it if the rest can. Gen. Geo. B. McClellan is gaining popularity every day. He must be the coming man in the Democratic party. I hope so, as I feel that this is the one hope of the country. . . .

Saturday, April 9, 1864

. . . John Hornbeck was buried today. He died of measles in a military hospital somewhere South. He had only been in the service one month. Wm. T. Cobaugh was buried yesterday in the Turner graveyard. He was an old acquaintance and friend of mine. The victims are multiplying very fast. I do hope that the war will come to a close this summer as I every day hear of some old friend going to a bourne from whence no traveler ever returned, a victim of disease or killed by the enemy. . . .

Sunday, April 17, 1864

. . . Jas. Rankin was there [at S.D. Truitt's]. . . . He stirred up a political discussion with me & intimated that he would send the soldiery on me when they returned &c. Alex[ander] Long of Cincinnati is making strong peace or secession speeches in Congress. [Salmon P.] Chase, Secretary of the Treasury, is panic stricken and has made quite a doleful face to Congress about the finances of the country. The London Independents are called out to muster on the 2d of May.

Monday, April 18, 1864

 14 pupils today. . . . Stationery is getting to be very dear. They charged me 5 cts. for two sheets of letter paper.

Friday, April 22, 1864

 14 pupils today. School is out. Bully for Cox and McClellan. . . . I must get my money tonight and be off bright and early tomorrow. Farewell to Turkey Run.

Sunday, April 24, 1864

 . . . D. Lewis hauled up my goods from B.D. Thomas's yesterday. . . . The president talks of calling out 200,000 men for six months in the western states. The abolitionists are in a big stew about the last call from the West.

Tuesday, April 26, 1864

 . . . There is great excitement in town about the draft of the volunteer militia. I paid off my commutation fee of four dollars. This lets me right out of the volunteer militia business.

Thursday, April 28, 1864

 . . . I walked down to Jim Andrews to see about colt pasture but did not succeed. Jim Andrews has hired a substitute for $150 to go in his place. Every man that can raise the money is buying a substitute. Everything is in a perfect fever of excitement about the war. There is a report out now that there is to be a big draft on top of this one. . . . I have turned my colt into the road.

Sunday, April 29, 1864

 . . . The war fever is still unabated in London. . . . Substitutes are in great demand just now. $150 is the going price. I saw John Hughes in London. He is reenlisted. . . . I received a speech from S.S. Cox on the Long expulsion case. It is sound to the core.

Sunday, May 1, 1864

 . . . They say that the big draft for the U.S. army is to come off on Tuesday next without fail. The vigorous prosecution men will get their fill of war before long from present appearances. . . .

Tuesday, May 3, 1864

 . . . I went to London in the afternoon. A great crowd of people in town. A large lot of cattle were offered for sale. I was introduced to Mr. Joshua Nickerson, agent for Wilsons series of schoolbooks, who wants me to take an agency for Madison Co. to introduce these books into the common schools of the county. He gave me my supper at the Phifer House. The National Guards are still in London.

Wednesday, May 4, 1864
. . . I went to London to see Joshua Nickerson. He agreed to knock 40 cts. off of the wholesale price of the books, I to pay 30 percent of the money & he to pay or lay out the remainder. The independent military companies went for Camp Dennison today on the 11 o'clock a.m. train. There was quite a crowd of folks there to see them. . . . 34 men were drafted out of Pleasant Township, Franklin Co. . . .

Friday, May 6, 1864
. . . 22 men drafted in Midway, 20 Democrats in that number. Butternuts are all being drafted. . . .

Thursday, May 12, 1864
. . . I went to London in the afternoon. I saw Major Gen. Rosecrans in the cars. He is a very quiet, common looking man and does not look much like a great general. The 154th Regt. went through London today on their way to western Virginia. The London independent companies are in this regt. . . . There was a circus in town today, Robinsons. S.D. Truitt is in the 154th Regt.

Thursday, June 2, 1864
. . . I went to London in the morning and got a dollars worth of sugar [and] a pair of sheep shears which cost me $2.25. John C. Fremont is nominated for president by the Radicals . . . . They have a very good platform with the exception of the [Negro]. . . .

Wednesday, June 8, 1864
. . . I started for Rankins at half past five o'clock. I sheared 15 sheep only today. I am not doing any great things at sheep shearing. The Great Baltimore Miscegination Abolition Abe Lincoln Shoddy Convention is now in session & will nominate Abram, I suppose, and I rather wish they may. . . .

Saturday, June 11, 1864
. . . I went again to shear sheep. I sheared 10 head. . . . I sheared 82 altogether. I got $6.55 for 5-1/2 days work. . . . They are having a heavy time with the negroes in Butler County. . . . They ran a lot of them off from their work. I do not expect to shear any more sheep this season. . . .

Monday, June 13, 1864

. . . The Democrats had a convention at London to nominate delegates to Chicago. They had a stormy session. The Peace Democrats made a heap of noise but were defeated by the Cox men. S.S. Cox was nominated on the first ballot for delegate. His opponent was Sam Medary. On the next ballot Medary was nominated, as several men ran at this time. The peace men tried to get a set of resolutions endorsing Long passed but failed. . . .

Tuesday, June 14, 1864

. . . I started tolerably early to go to Columbus to be examined by the enrolling board. . . . I immediately went to Millers Building on Town Street and waited about 3/4 of an hour for my turn to come. The surgeon examined me in about 5 minutes and gave me an order to the other members of the board to have my name struck from the roll, which was done. I then made tracks for the cars, which started out at 12 o'clock M. I just had time to make the connection, as the cars were in motion when I got on board. . . . I am now free from the draft, so I was told at Columbus. Therefore they need not trouble me anymore.

Thursday, June 16, 1864

. . . It is reported that Vallandigham has got back to Dayton again. I am afraid that this will breed a disturbance in the state, as it will be a more difficult job to arrest him this time than it was before. It was a bad move for Vallandigham to make in my judgment. . . .

Sunday, June 19, 1864

. . . I wrote a letter to Joshua Nickerson today defining my political status or opinions. He is a stiff Lincoln man and I am opposed to Honest Old Abe, as they call him. . . .

Sunday, June 26, 1864

Hot & sultry the most of the day. It rained some in the afternoon. Wife took sick at about 10 o'clock & gave birth to a girl baby at ten minutes past 2 o'clock. Godfrey went after Dr. Dan Wilson. He did not get him, however, as the Dr. had went to Darby sometime last week. So Godfrey went after Dr. Dennis Warner, who got here about a half an hour before the child was born. Mrs. Peck, Mrs. Goings, Mrs. Trowbridge, & Mrs. Ships were here, also Mrs. Levi Watson, when the child was born. Mahala Godfrey came afterwards. . . . Izma Timmons was here this morning when my wife took sick. It has been a very hot day. I took Flora to Mothers. I am glad the spree is over.

Wednesday, June 29, 1864

. . . Jacob Goings came over to my house in the morning & showed me how to make shingles. . . . I went over to the railroad in the afternoon & got Levi Watsons paper, the details of the fight this side of Atlanta, Georgia. There was a great list of wounded. Chas. C. Roberts was wounded in the hip on the 19th or 20th of this month. I saw an account of Charlies being wounded in the Commercial. I shaved 30 shingles today. . . .

Saturday, July 2, 1864

. . . I cut some stove wood & made about a dozen shingles. . . . Gold went up to $300 premium yesterday but fell again to 260 & 265 today. There must be a financial breakdown shortly. . . . Nothing but groans & curses are heard concerning the greenback defeat. This hue & cry will operate very much against Lincoln at the presidential election. . . .

Monday, July 4, 1864

. . . There was some very good war news. Sherman has succeeded in driving the Rebels from Kinesaw Mountain. Oliver Watson is wounded and so is Jesse Dungan. All the stores in London were shut up today. A great many of the folks went over to Springfield to a celebration over there. The Kilgrove picnic did not amount to anything at all. H.W. Smith made a very short & a very poor speech. There was a platform to dance on just large enough for 8 persons. This was the center of attraction to the crowd. . . .

Wednesday, July 6, 1864

. . . I bolted up two shingle bolts & made about 116 shingles. . . . Wife is getting along fine. She was up around the house the most of the day. The baby is very good. It rarely takes a crying spree. . . .

Thursday, July 7, 1864

. . . I made shingles all day. I made 116. . . . P.L. Roberts wrote to J.H. Roberts. He says C.C. Roberts is pretty severely wounded in the hip. S.S. Cox sent me a Congressional Globe. . . .

Friday, July 8, 1864

. . . Mother received two letters from C.C. Roberts. He has a bad flesh wound in the thigh. He was some time on the road from Kinesaw Mountain & suffered very much from his wound as the flies got at it. The cars were very filthy & the mud and filth nearly killed him. . . . He is in the General Field Hospital, Ward L, Chattanooga, Tenn. . . . Jesse

Dungan is dead and J. Fletcher Chapman is badly wounded in the head, besides several others of the Madison Co. boys. The Rebs are said to have 30,000 men in Maryland.

Tuesday, July 12, 1864
    . . . The news today is not very good. The Rebels have cut every wire of the telegraph going north. . . . Railroads are torn up that lead into Washington. It is rather a gloomy time for true patriots, although they may not have much sympathy for Honest Old Abe as an individual. I am fearful of the result.

Monday, July 18, 1864
    . . . Charlie is getting better & is expecting a removal from Chattanooga shortly. He writes that he is very tired of lying in bed in one position. . . .

Tuesday, July 19, 1864
    . . . There is another call for 500,000 men. This along with the percent will make a million men to be drafted by the 5th of Sept. It is an awful heavy pull & will make a breeze amongst the people. I am of the opinion that this draft will knock Uncle Abes election into a cocked hat this fall. I hope so anyhow.

Friday, July 22, 1864
    . . . Mother got a letter from Allen Anderson today. He had received one of the letters we sent to Chas. C. Roberts. Allen is tolerably well. He says the most of the boys have the scurvy. He is hard down on old Abe & the rest of the negroes.

Sunday, July 24, 1864
    . . . I went over to Mothers. . . . The people here are try[ing] to raise money to pay bounties to volunteers to clear the township of a draft. We have not heard from C.C. Roberts for some time & we do not know whether he has been moved or not.

Tuesday, August 2, 1864
    . . . Gen. Grant has met with a reverse near Petersburg. There was a division of [Negroes] that caused the defeat, so the papers say. J. Fletcher Chapman goes to Tenn. tonight.

Thursday, August 4, 1864
    . . . I helped Paulus drive his hogs down from Dave T. Garrard's pasture. This took 2 hours to do the job. Mary E. Truitt came & washed

for my wife. In the afternoon I rode to London & bought 75 cts. worth of tobacco & sent it to Allen Anderson's by mail. . . . I bought a box of worm lozenges for 35 cts. I also bought Davidsons patent gum syringe for $2.25. . . . Grants army was badly defeated at the Petersburg fight on account of the [Negroes].

Friday, August 5, 1864
. . . I used my syringe today for the first time. It is a good one & no mistake. I must make shingles tomorrow.

Saturday, August 6, 1864
. . . I went to London in the forenoon & bought a gallon of sorghum molasses & a gallon of coal oil. I had to pay a $1 a gal. for each. I also bought some paper, 20 cts. worth. . . .   The O[hio] N[ational] G[uard] 154th Regt. has been in a fight at New Creek Station. Our boys lost 29 killed & 50 wounded. John Jones, Esq., rather intimated that I was a traitor because I felt badly about our want of success.

Monday, August 7, 1864
. . . Everyone here is anxious about the 154th Regt. O.N.G. John Jones, Esqr. give me a round about sympathizing with our army & intimated that I was a Rebel traitor.

Monday, August 8, 1864
. . . I read Ben[jamin F.] Wades & Hen[ry] W. Davis pronuncimento against Lincoln. It is rich & strong.

Tuesday, August 16, 1864
Warm day. I started to London bright & early in the morning & helped Peetry with the militia rolls nearly half of the day. I made three men pay up their commutation fee. This brings me $3. . . .

Wednesday, August 17, 1864
Very hot. I was collecting again today. Did not make much speed in the forenoon. I got 4 men to pay in the afternoon. . . . I find some difficulty in getting commutation out of the hotel keepers of this place. I have some trouble in finding some in of these men. . . .

Saturday, August 20, 1864
. . . I was collecting again today. I made $3 at it. This is rather slow work. . . . Everyone is conjecturing about the draft. The Peace Democrats are making big efforts to defeat McClellan. I do not think they will succeed, as the probability is very strong the other way.

Sunday, August 21st, A.D. 1864 [from Roberts's Journal]

. . . The hiring of substitutes is the great business of people here at this time. Any quantity of negroes are being bought up by the recruiting agents in the rebellious states. The refuse & trash of the western world are now floating into the northern army. Every patriot in the land ought to feel sorry for this state of affairs, as defeat is inevitable if this system of recruiting is persisted in by the people. Negroes wont make good soldiers nor good, substantial citizens. Abe Lincoln is losing friends every day. His defeat is acknowledged by his warmest friends, & his enemies are rejoicing daily over their promised delivery from his imbecile administration. I think that day is breaking in the political horizon, & I sincerely hope that Gen. Geo. B. McClellan will be the nominee at Chicago on the 29th of this month. Thousands of Republicans are hoping & praying that McClellan may be the man so that they can vote for him. . . .

Nancy Cliftons child is dead. It died of flux sometime during last month. Poor Jeanette. She is much better off as it is. I feel sorry for her & would have taken her home if her mother had been willing. . . .

I have been engaged for the past week in collecting military fines in this township. This is a very odious law and one whose enforcement will make sad havoc on the Republican ranks. . . . This law ought to be repealed immediately by the legislature. . . .

The governor of Ohio, John Brough, called out 30 regts. of National Guards for 100 days. Their time is now about out and the most of them are coming home. J.H. Roberts was a member of the company, but owing to his being sick at the mustering in of the regt., he never went out. This 100 days business is a heavy drag on the Republican party. . . .

Clement L. Vallandigham is at home in Dayton. The Republicans swore he could not live an hour in Ohio after his banishment, but lo and behold, he has lived here for two or three months and remains unmolested. I am of the opinion that Lincoln & Vallandigham are in partnership to break up the Democratic party this fall. . . . Politics makes strange connections sometimes, it seems. . . .

Monday, August 22, 1864

. . . I collected about $20 today. . . . I rode at least 20 miles. . . .

Tuesday, August 23, 1864

. . . I collected $15 today. . . . I bought a bottle of Mrs. Winslows Soothing Sirup [for 35 cents].

Wednesday, August 24, 1864
. . . I went to see Grandmother in the afternoon. She is very low & lays & sleeps continually. I do not think she can live very long. . . .

Friday, August 26, 1864
. . . I paid over to Jacob Peetrey the sum of $60.00 of the commutation money. The O[hio] N[ational] G[uard]s come back today from New Creek Station. They look very hearty.

Saturday, August 27, 1864
. . . Grandmother Roberts died last night at 10 o'clock. She was buried today at 3 o'clock in the graveyard near the mill by the side of Grandfather. There was a great many people there. She had slept 3 days & nights before she died. She died sleeping. That is, she never woke up. . . .

Sunday, August 28, 1864
. . . The great Chicago convention goes off tomorrow. I am anxious to hear from it & hope that Little Mac will be the nominee. . . .

Monday, August 29, 1864
. . . There is great excitement about the Chicago convention. The Republicans are praying for a split. . . .

Tuesday, August 30, 1864
. . . I went up into Deer Creek & Munroe Townships. . . . All the men in Munroe Township that I had bills against were either enlisted or aliens, so I made a water haul in this township. Chicago is all the talk among the people. McClellan stands the best chance to be nominated.

Wednesday, August 31, 1864
. . . I made an early start & made 2 collections, one from Mr. Van Ness up in Pike & one from David Llewelyn of the same township. I was in Liverpool today. I ate dinner at Mr. Newmans for which I paid 35 cts. Little Mac is nominated on the first ballot. Hurrah for the good old Union! . . .

Thursday, September 1, 1864
. . . I made 3 collections today in Pike, which finished up the township. Every one is hurrahing for Little Mac. I hear of many changes in politics, many turning from Uncle Abe. . . .

Friday, September 2, 1864

. . . I . . . bought a McClellan portrait for 75 cts. . . . There is an order prohibiting the sale of firearms & ammunition for 60 days.

Saturday, September 3, 1864

. . . I worked for the miller a half day fixing up his smut machine. Semp Saunders has got back from his Kentucky recruiting expedition. He got off on account of his loyalty. . . . The draft in this township is almost clear. They lack about 6 men. Jefferson Township is 40 men behind. They intend to let the draft rip. . . .

Sunday, September 4, 1864

. . . I went over to Somerford to hear Rev. Forshee preach Grandmothers funeral. Text was the 3d chap. & xvi verse of Malachi. There was quite a number of folks at the funeral. Rev. Randall, Methodist preacher, said a few words by way of exhortation. I ate dinner at Mrs. Saunders. Semp denies being in limbo & says he has not been in Kentucky at all.

Monday, September 5, 1864

. . . The 100 day boys got home yesterday. Harriet Maria has had two hard spasms, one last night & one the night before. I am afraid she will be subject to them hereafter. There is no news of any kind as the cars could not come up from Cincinnati on account of the washing away of a bridge.

Tuesday, September 6, 1864

. . . Joshua Nickerson came to see me. . . . Our babe has had an awful spell of the colic & cried till after 8 o'clock. No news.

Wednesday, September 7, 1864

. . . Nickerson stayed at my house till after breakfast. I gave up my book agency . . . [but not] entirely, however. I was over to Mothers in the evening & saw some persons coming from the fair, which is a poor affair, so they say.

Thursday, September 8, 1864

. . . McClellan stock is at a premium, so Jake [Wilson] says, as he has been in Logan Co. & all through that section of country. . . .

Friday, September 9, 1864

. . . I had the pleasure of reading Geo. B. McClellans letter of acceptance, which is a masterpiece of composition. . . . There is a McClellan ratification meeting in London on Monday. . . .

Monday, September 12, 1864

. . . I went to London to the Democratic convention which was held to nominate a congressman & to ratify the nomination of Gen. McClellan & Geo. H. Pendleton. Sam Cox was nominated for Congress by acclamation. He made two speeches, one on accepting the nomination & one afterwards. Cox sent in a letter refusing to run, but the convention would not take no for an answer. I never saw more enthusiasm in my life. We had a good band in attendance but no procession. Everybody seemed pleased.

Tuesday, September 13, 1864

. . . Vallandigham has refused to stump for Little Mac. Well, let him rip. His loss will be the Democracys eternal gain. [Samuel] Shellabarger spoke in London today. Slim attendance, so I understand. Bully for Cox. I think we can increase his last majority several hundred this fall. . . . The 40th Ohio Regt. is reported as all prisoners.

Wednesday, September 14, 1864

Fine day. I made a few shingles in the forenoon & then went to Father Truitts along with my family in Truitts spring wagon so as to go to the state fair. C.M. Roberts & Mary Elizabeth Roberts went along as it was reported that the extra train was to leave London at 4 o'clock in the morning. Will Truitt went to London & purchased our tickets in the evening. Paid out $2.70.

Thursday, September 15, 1864

Very pleasant day. The train got started from London at 10 o'clock in the morning. We got to Columbus at 12 o'clock. An awful crowd of people were at the fair. The exhibition was very ordinary. We went all over the State House, even to the top of the dome. The crowd was composed of Will, Mary E. & Caroline Truitt, C.M. & Mary E. Roberts, & Mrs. Sallie Dingin[?]. There was a perfect jam on the railroad & streetcars. I never saw so many people in my life. We came back to Truitts at 9 o'clock. Very peaceable times on the fairgrounds & in Columbus. I did not see a half dozen drunken men in Columbus. Spent $2.00.

Wednesday, September 21, 1864

. . . I cut corn all day. I went down to see Jacob Goings in the evening. He is very wild at this time. The trustees were to see him today. He ought to be taken to the asylum or placed in confinement, as it is dangerous to let him run at large. I staid with him till after dark and left Jonah Trowbridge to take care of him. I cut 27 shocks of corn today & was very tired when I got home.

Thursday, September 22, 1864

. . . I went to London to see Peetrey about when this collecting was to be finished. He gave me all the time I wanted. . . . Lincoln is dead in the shell & so is Shellabarger also.

Saturday, September 24, 1864

. . . Mrs. Goings came over after dinner for me to go to town to get Jake Goings off to Columbus to the asylum, as he is very crazy now. I went to town with Tom Davis's boy. Jake was examined; will be sent to Columbus on Monday. . . .

Monday, September 26, 1864

Fine day. I went up to Jno. Wilsons & bought 3 bu. of apples to thicken apple butter with. I pared apples some in the afternoon & then went over to Somerford to hear glorious old Sun Set Cox & Geo. Lincoln make a speech apiece. We had a good meeting. Very enthusiastic & more people than could get into the schoolhouse. . . .

Wednesday, September 28, 1864

I went to Somerford in the afternoon to see about the Somerford school. I saw all the directors but did not hire. I agreed with one of them, but one was drunk & the others wifes cousin had said something about the school. I am to get $36 per month if I teach . . . a 4 months school. . . .

Saturday, October 1, 1864

. . . I went over to Somerford to see about their school. I finally struck up a bargain with the directors. I am to get $36 per month for 4 months to commence on the last day of this month. I saw 2 of the directors, Clingan & Carter. . . .

Saturday, October 8, 1864

. . . I was at the Republican mass meeting held at the fairgrounds [in London]. It was a very slim affair. Horace Maynard of Tenn. spoke. He is a very dark complexioned, spare built, Indian looking man & a fair speaker. . . . There was an extra amount of whiskey drank today. I saw several heavy quarrels. Everything is favorable for the Democracy yet.

Tuesday, October 11, 1864
. . . The state election went off today. I went to London tolerably early in the morning. There was a full vote polled; 447 votes were put in. . . . The Democrats lost the county by over 200 majority. . . . We gained on Vallandigham but lost on the two year ago vote. I suppose Ohio has gone Republican by 20,000 majority. B.F. Roberts has volunteered for one year; bounty $650.

Wednesday, October 12, 1864
. . . Cox is said to be defeated & Ind[iana] is said to be lost by 20,000 majority as well as Pennsylvania. I hope this news is premature. I feel very gloomy over the news & hope it may be better when all the returns come in. . . . Disunion is inevitable if the Republicans continue in power.

Saturday, October 15, 1864
. . . Election news . . . is anything but cheering to real Union men. Abolition is on the rampage. I got a letter from Chas. C. Roberts today. He is still at New Albany, Ind., & is not very well at this time. . . .

Sunday, October 16, 1864
. . . I stayed at home & wrote two letters, one to E.M. Stanton, Secretary of War, & one to C.C. Roberts. . . . It is now reported that Pennsylvania has gone Democratic by 10,000 majority on the home vote. Bully for the old Keystone.

Monday, October 17, 1864
. . . I started to go to [New Albany,] Indiana. I got $30 of Mother, who borrowed it of Wm. Tingley. . . .

Tuesday, October 18, 1864
. . . I started for Cincinnati on the six o'clock train. . . . I got there at 11 o'clock a.m. . . . I then went to Gen. Hookers headquarters but did not get to see him as he was out of the city. I then made a search for Dr. Triplett, the medical director of the department, but could not find his office. I went down to the steamboat Rebecca in the afternoon & engaged my passage for Louisville, which cost me $3.50. . . .

Wednesday, October 19, 1864

Foggy morning & smoky all day. I travelled all last night on the steamer Rebecca & till 11 o'clock today. There was quite a number of army officers & Jews on board. The passengers played cards till after midnight in the forward cabin. This is a fine steamer but not as good as I have seen. It is a mail boat. We had to lay by for two or three hours in the morning on account of the fog. I crossed over from Louisville to New Albany and saw Chas. Roberts. He is looking very well & is able to walk around. He went back to Louisville with me to see Cap. Horr.

Thursday, October 20, 1864

Cool day but fine weather. I put up at the De Paw House in New Albany. I got my bed & breakfast for $1.25. I went with Charlie yesterday to Capt. Horr, Ohio military state agent, & got a paper for a special transfer to Camp Chase. We then went to Major Hay, or something like that name. He is the medical inspector for the district. I then went over to Louisville & took cabin passage on the mail packet Gen. Buell, which is a very fine steamer, much better than the one I went down on. Grand Lodge of F.& A.M. Masons in Louisville, I saw several of the members on board. They were a fine set of men, all of them Kentuc[k]ians. I gave C.C. Roberts $10 of Mothers money.

Friday, October 21, 1864

Smoky & rainy in the morning. I arrived at Cincinnati at 2 o'clock in the morning. We had a majority of Democrats on the steamer. Kentucky is good for McClellan by a big majority. New Albany is a great place for boat building. Louisville is as dirty a place as I ever was in in my life. I started from Cincinnati on the 6 o'clock train for home. I got to London at 1/2 past 9 o'clock & went to Truitts, where my wife was staying. . . . Mother has moved to Darby. She went this week. I did not sleep a bit last night as I could not get a berth to sleep in.

Sunday, October 23, 1864

. . . The political horizon is improving somewhat & there is some prospect for McClellan's election. I hope & trust that it may be so, for this is the last chance for our country at this time, in my opinion.

Thursday, October 27, 1864

. . . I worked at my porch in the forenoon. I finished it up & had about 36 shingles left. I also patched up the leaks in my house roof. . . . Stealing is becoming prevalent in this neighborhood again. Hen roosts are being robbed.

Tuesday, November 8, 1864

Rainy day. Today decides the fate of our country, as it is the presidential election. I am afraid that McClellan is defeated. . . . The election passed off very quietly. . . . The abolitionists are jubilant & Democrats despondent here. . . .

Wednesday, November 9, 1864

30 pupils in my school, this being the first day of the term. . . . The news is unfavorable to the Union & McClellan. Kentucky is Democratic as well as Missouri. Somerford gave 31 majority for Lincoln. Everything has gone abolition in Ohio. God help the country if Lincoln is reelected.

Thursday, November 10, 1864

. . . I went over to Columbus to try to get Charley a discharge. Lib Kelly went along with me to see about drawing some of Wm. Kellys back pay, as he is a prisoner of war and has been for 17 months. . . . I went to see old Brough. He gave me no satisfaction whatever. There was no chance for an extension of furlough at Columbus. Old Abe is reelected, I suppose. . . .

Friday, November 11, 1864

. . . 27 pupils. I got me some cloth or jeans for pants. I got it of V.H. Prugh on time. I also got a lot of candles of him. Cloth is very dear. I must have something to wear, however, let it cost what it will. . . . I have the blues the worst kind about the election.

Wednesday, November 23, 1864

40 pupils today. . . . I am going to have a hard time to break the noise up in my school. I got a letter from C.C. Roberts today. He did not get a discharge, not being healed up. . . .

Thursday, November 24, 1864

34 pupils. . . . This is Thanksgiving Day. No one observed it that I know of in Somerford. The stores were all open as usual. . . .

Friday, November 25, 1864

42 pupils today. . . . McCaula, a tailor in London, killed himself yesterday by drinking something he used to clean clothes with. He had the tremens. . . .

Sunday, November 27, 1864

. . . Dunkard meeting today at the Garrard s[chool]house. The abolitionists are begging the Democrats to help them to make peace.

Wednesday, December 21, 1864

45 pupils. . . . There is another call for 300,000 more men by Father Abraham. This is as I expected it would be. Bully for the draft. Let her rip. Some persons are offering one thousand dollars for a substitute. . . .

Friday, December 23, 1864

46 pupils. . . . I had an immense sight of noise in the schoolroom. I had spelling match in the afternoon. I had a dance at my house at night. S.S. Dunseth[?] was the originator of the frolic. There was about 25 persons at my house. They staid till 11 o'clock. . . .

Saturday, December 24, 1864

. . . I must try and post up my diary for next year, as this year will soon be done gone as the American citizen of African descent would say. . . .

Monday, December 26, 1864

50 pupils today. . . . There is glorious news from [General William T.] Sherman. It is reported that Savannah, Georgia, is captured with 800 prisoners & over 100 cannon, with immense stores of ammunition &c. A great victory. I hope it may bring us nigher peace than we have been. I hope the war may soon be over.

Saturday, December 31, 1864

. . . I am afraid that this war will continue for one year more & perhaps longer. The prospect is gloomy at this time. This currency business will crush down this summer certain. Then comes the tug of war in earnest. . . . C.C. Roberts is going to try for an extension of his furlough.

1865

Sunday, January 1, 1865

Happy Newyears to one & all. . . . S.F. Saunders has hired a [Negro] substitute for $200. I went to see Jac. Goings this afternoon. He is still somewhat deranged. . . .

Monday, January 2, 1865

49 pupils today. . . . I whipped Austin Guysinger & Wm. Archeson for fighting in the s[chool]house during recess. My scholars will be noisy. Jno. M. Palmer has gone to Antioch College.

Tuesday, January 10, 1865

34 pupils today. . . . The s[chool]house stovepipe fell down and smashed both the elbows so that we had to quit school an hour or two in the forenoon. . . .

Wednesday, January 11, 1865

40 pupils. . . . There was a magic lantern exhibition at the s[chool]house at night. Admission 25 cents. . . .

Wednesday, January 25, 1865

No school today. There was no wood and I dismissed till noon, & none coming then I dismissed till night. I never saw much colder weather in my life. The roads are in excellent condition, & people are doing nothing except feeding, getting wood, going to meeting & to balls. There is a big meeting here at the Newlight church.

Monday, January 30, 1865

35 pupils today. This is a fine day for winter. Nancy J. Wilson, Harriet Williams, & Wesley Geer were baptised in Deer Creek today & a great many of my scholars went to see them. . . . The sleighing continues good.

Tuesday, January 31, 1865

42 pupils today. The big meeting broke up last night. There was about 13 members added to the church. . . . I saw Wm. H. Roberts & was up in his gallery on Saturday last. He is getting up a splendid photographic & daguerrean gallery. It will cost $200. He has the room rented for five years at $75 per year.

Wednesday, February 8, 1865

38 pupils today. . . . Everybody is awaiting the draft with all the stoicism they can command. Substitutes are scarce and dear & there is talk of raising the liables up to 50 years of age. Everybody seems to be apathetic on the subject.

Thursday, February 9, 1865

35 pupils. . . . There is a great deal of excitement in the community about the draft. Vast numbers are trying to evade it by different means. Quite a number are running away and more are talking of doing so. No one is volunteering & substitutes are scarce & high priced. So the poor men must go. No one wants to go to war. Substitutes command from $400 to $1,000.

Saturday, February 11, 1865

I had a reading match in Somerford last night. There was a great crowd. My school came off victorious. . . .

Sunday, February 12, 1865

. . . This township will stand the draft, as they are making no effort to raise the troops by bounty.

Monday, February 13, 1865

40 pupils. . . . The draft is the chief topic now. About 70 men have left London within the last two weeks. . . . Geo. S. Cornwell & Wm. Trowbridge went to Cincinnati to enlist today.

Wednesday, February 15, 1865

41 pupils today. . . . It is rumored that the draft is put off on account of the volunteers going into the service. They are trying to raise money to clear Union Township. Geo. Cornwell came home yesterday from Cincinnati. He could not get into a cavalry regt. . . .

Thursday, February 16, 1865

34 pupils. . . . Quite a number of the Somerford boys liable to the draft went off today to volunteer. . . . The draft will fall very heavily on the remainder. . . . Union Township has $12,000 made up for the bounty.

Tuesday, February 21, 1865

33 pupils today. . . . Most of the persons liable [for the draft] are making preparations to leave for the army or for parts unknown. It is sure to go off next week in this district. The Good Templars have organized a lodge of about 30 members in this place. This is a heavy commencement. Francis McGarry has gone to Antioch to school. He was the most advanced of any of my scholars.

Wednesday, February 22, 1865

35 pupils today. Peter Bigelow volunteered yesterday . . . for one year. So did [Frank] Niswaner. . . . This makes 6 or 8 that have gone from this township. They think that the township will clear itself before the draft, as they are raising money very fast so that they can pay $450 per man for volunteers.

Friday, February 24, 1865

33 pupils today. . . . Union Township has $2,000 to raise before it can have the ghost of a chance to get clear of the draft. Somerford is a thousand dollars behind yet. I had a reading match in the afternoon. I will have two weeks more school after this & then I shall be free.

Saturday, March 4, 1865

. . . I went to London to get some photography taken of my children, but they would not remain still long enough to have it done.

Saturday, March 18, 1865

Chas. C. Roberts came home. . . . He has a discharge. . . .

Monday, April 3, 1865

. . . Great news today. Richmond was evacuated by Lee & his army today. Everyone is firing guns or ringing bells. . . .

Saturday, April 8, 1865

. . . I hear cannon firing at night at Camp Chase. Some great news, I suppose.

Monday, April 10, 1865

Great news again today. The report is that Gen. Lees army is captured & Gen. Lee also. Peace will be here presently if this should be the case, & I hope it is true. There has been some firing of cannon all day. I hear cannon yet tonight. . . .

Saturday, April 15, 1865

President Lincoln died today. He was shot last night whilst he was at a theater. The man who shot him was named [John Wilkes] Booth, an actor. Secretary [William H.] Seward was also assassinated [a mistaken report]. It is an awful occurrence. . . .

Wednesday, April 19, 1865

I plowed all day. . . In the afternoon all the [other] folks went to Jefferson to hear Lincolns funeral preached. Randalls young folks & all of Mothers folks & my wife went up in a big wagon. . . .

Thursday, April 20, 1865

. . . Charlie shot Mothers old dog Trim this morning and I buried him in the bottom. Mother feared that he would kill sheep, as he was running about & had brought home some dead lambs. . . .

Tuesday, April 25, 1865

. . . It is reported that Sherman offered [Joseph E.] Johns[t]on, the Rebel general, an armistice & offered to let them have their negroes & their guns.

Friday, April 28, 1865

. . . The abolitionists are getting down on Gen. Sherman. They wish to kill him off as he is not radical enough to suit them on the [Negro] question.

Tuesday, May 2, 1865

. . . I paid [M.L.] Bryan for a years [newspaper] subscription on Saturday last & also signed for Sam Cox's book, which is to contain all his speeches since the war [began] and a history of the congressional proceedings.

Sunday, May 7, 1865

. . . The country is full of Rebel soldiers who have taken the oath [of allegiance]. Hostilities will soon cease, I hope.

Tuesday, May 16, 1865

. . . It is reported that Jeff Davis went through Jefferson last night a prisoner. I hope he may be caught and made an example of for the benefit of traitors.

Saturday, May 20, 1865

. . . The southern cause is played out at last. They have only the remnant of an army left in Texas & Jeff Davis is on his way to Washington a prisoner.

Tuesday, May 23, 1865

I finished planting on this side of the creek today. I have ten acres or more in at this time. . . . Barb Clifton dropped the corn and I and

Mary and Betsy Clifton covered it with hoes. . . . We planted a lot of sorghum. Mother dropped that. . . .

Friday, June 30, 1865
    . . . Marsh Cory came down today to let us know that Henry Roberts was very sick with the typhoid fever & inflammation of the bowels. Mother went to see him. The soldiers [are] getting home every day.

Tuesday, July 4, 1865
    Independence Day. Wife & I went to a picnic got up by the Jefferson folks. . . . It was nothing but a dancing party. No speeches or reading of the Declaration of Independence. Charlie went along with Mothers folks to see Henry, who is not much better.

Sunday, July 9, 1865
    . . . Mahala Johnson had a miscarriage yesterday. She is a widow & has been for a year or more.

Monday, July 24, 1865
    . . . Dr. George Becker of N.Y. City came to see Harriet Maria. He says she has a tapeworm. He took a fee of $22 and left her some medicine. . . .

Friday, August 18, 1865
    . . . Miss D. Evans school is out today. She taught 3 months for $40, which was very low wages. . . .

Monday, August 21st. A.D. 1865 [from Roberts's Journal]
    I am 32 years of age today. . . . All of Mothers family were in the house today for the first time for 5 years or more. Brother W.H. Roberts has just recovered from [a] severe spell of sickness. . . .
    On the 15th of April Abraham Lincoln . . . was shot & killed in Fords Theater [in] Washington City. . . . This event . . . cast a gloom over the whole country. Every paper in the country went into mourning, & the body of the president was taken to all the principal cities of the United States.
    Andrew Johnson . . . immediately took the presidential office. He was an old line Democrat and acted with them up till the breaking out of the Rebellion. He was very much intoxicated on his inauguration as vice president, & many of his Republican friends asked him to resign. He is generally liked as president by all parties except . . . some of the rabid Republicans known as Radicals. They are down on him heavily.

A great topic here in politics is that of negro suffrage. A large portion of the Republicans are in favor of negro suffrage, and quite a number of them are against the measure. The matter will create a division in that party which will result in its final overthrow. This event may not take place this fall, but it will most assuredly take place before the next general election. . . .

The most of the Madison Co. soldiers are now at home. . . . Allen Anderson is dead, I suppose, as we have heard nothing from him for a long time. A good many of the boys who have went from here are sleeping the last long sleep in southern soil without a stone or a line to mark their graves. Some have returned who were long since given up for dead. Several women have married under these circumstances and have had their first husband to make his appearance.

I find that I am not able to follow the plow and do any great amount of farming, so I must get into some other kind of business. I have what is called inguinal hernia & expect to have to wear a double truss. . . . If I was not so old I would try and study law.

I look for a grand crash in money affairs, as the country has more paper money afloat than there ever was before. . . . But come what may, the soil is still left and strong arms & resolute hearts will always be able to dig a subsistence out of it. . . .

Public morals are at a low ebb just now. The papers are filled with details of horrible murders committed in all parts of the country, as well as heavy defalcations by officials in the government employ. Crime is more prevalent than I ever knew it to be before in this country. Heaven frowns, Hell yawns, & vice triumphs.

Tuesday, October 10, 1865

. . . I went to Jefferson early in the morning to the election. I voted the Democratic [ticket] throughout & did not scratch any. . . . The soldiers voted the Democratic ticket almost unanimously. Quite a gain for the Democracy in this township. Everything seems favorable for the white mans ticket. . . .

Thursday, October 12, 1865

. . . The election news is rather unfavorable. Cox is supposed to be elected by a reduced majority. Nothing certain, however.

Friday, October 13, 1865

. . . Flora & Alma still have the ague. I got some pills from Randall. . . . This county is 230 majority for Cox.

Tuesday, October 24, 1865
    . . . There is a great spiritual doctor in Columbus who is performing miracles equal to the apostles of olden time. . . .

Friday, October 27, 1865
    . . . The great charm Dr. is a humbug, the people say. Mrs. Tom Cullumber went to him but was not cured. . . .

Thursday, November 9, 1865
    . . . I got S.S. Cox's Eight Years in Congress. . . . 40 [Negroes] in the courthouse hunting places.

Saturday, November 11, 1865
    . . . I got a letter from Somerford today from Clingan saying that I could have their school at my terms, $40 per month.

Wednesday, November 22, 1865
    I cut some wood in the woods in the morning & in the afternoon. I also went to Mrs. Hornbecks to see about getting some wood. She said I might have some. Godfrey ordered me to quit cutting wood in the woods. He swore at me at a terrible rate. I must go to London tomorrow [to see a lawyer]. He called me a liar & I returned the same.

Thursday, November 23, 1865
    . . . I went to London to see B.F. Clark about the Godfrey scrape. Clark advised a conciliatory policy. . . .

Monday, November 27, 1865
    42 pupils today. This is my first day in the schoolroom for this season. I had an awful dirty house to go into. However, I got the dirt out at last & commenced operations. I had to whip one boy for stealing a penknife from my desk. His name is Chas. Sanford. There was no broom nor bucket at the schoolhouse, but at noon we got a bucket. I had no bell & sent mine to the shop to get it fixed.

Friday, December 8, 1865
    47 pupils today. . . . I have not read the presidents message. I see that the radical abolitionists are shoveing the most ultra doctrines of the party right in Congress. They are taking time by the forelock. I think the people will repudiate them.

Monday, December 11, 1865

50 pupils. . . . Sarah Cartzdafner was married on last Thursday to a stranger, a man that she got acquainted with by an advertisement for correspondence in a newspaper. He was a soldier during the war.

Wednesday, December 20, 1865

50 pupils today. . . . The irrepressible [Negro] is all the topic in Congress at this time. President Johnson is a mere cypher, it seems. Lincoln was all powerful; Johnson is the reverse. . . .

Friday, December 22, 1865

50 pupils. . . . President Johnson has issued an extra message to Congress concerning its action on the Reconstruction question. The president intends to stick to his policy of Reconstruction. I am glad of it. The Radicals must go down. I had a spelling match in the afternoon. We had considerable noise in the operation. . . .

Monday, December 25, 1865

Merry Christmas. I fixed up my cow stable & fed my cow hay for the first time today. I went with Troud & Coover to mill. . . .

Sunday, December 31, 1865

. . . About midnight the Dutch in London commenced firing off guns & making a big noise generally. This year has been very full of remarkable events. A great rebellion has been crushed & the Constitution itself changed in regard to slavery. One president has been assassinated and his successor has been duly installed without a jar or murmur from anyone. The reconstruction of the glorious old Union has been carried out to a point which the most sanguine friend of the Union could hardly have expected under the circumstances. The Radical element is nearly floored & everything looks as though it would prosper. Long life to our noble president, Andrew Johnson.

Epilogue
1866–1914

For the years after the documents printed here, John Roberts's annual birthday reflections, and especially his diaries, often make discouraging reading. Three of his and Emarine's children survived the hazards of infancy, but their son Frank, who grew to manhood, died after a long, distressing illness. Their two daughters who lived, Flora and Alma, married and had children, but Alma's husband deserted his family and never returned. Flora died while her children were young and long before her parents.

The immediate postwar diaries show Roberts's continuing disputes with neighbors who had earlier accused him of disloyalty. Some former friends became enemies; one thought killed (Allen Anderson) came back. Other disrupted friendships were repaired. Radical rule in Washington and the South ruined Roberts's dream of restoration of the old Constitution and Union; and at home, close election victories by Republicans were made more bitter when he saw scores of blacks in the courthouse seeking job appointments.

Roberts's racist views became less virulent as the years rolled by. Blacks were among the most frequent customers at his gristmill. On his trips to London, he often walked with them or rode in their wagons or buggies. At the lyceum, he and Horace Tyre, a mulatto farmer, debated, sometimes as colleagues, sometimes as opponents. Once, Tyre brought his cousin, "another light mulatto," who played the guitar and sang three songs. When Tyre moved away from the neighborhood for a while, Roberts wrote: "Tyree is a very good kind of a negro, and got along very well with the people here."

Light skin color made Roberts's acceptance of African Americans as neighbors easier. In Missouri, he boarded with the families of Alva Rush and his son John, the latter a former pupil of Roberts's in Ohio. The chivaree party which had cheered Roberts and his bride also visited the Rush house, since the widower Alva had just married the widow Porter. There "they sung several negro songs that ruffled Rush somewhat." That cryptic comment of March 27, 1859, is clarified by Roberts's diary entry of August 11, 1892, when news came of Alva Rush's death: "He . . . was said to be of mixed blood, about 1/16 negro.

But he always associated with white people." Very dark skin aroused Roberts's anxiety and interracial marriages disgusted him, but he evidently had no racial qualms about persons whose light skin enabled them to pass for whites.

John Roberts struggled against debt all his life. He quit teaching soon after his return from Missouri in 1881, but his efforts to make a living in other pursuits—as miller, farmer, traveling book agent, fish hatcher, fish and game warden, reporter of livestock sales, harvest hand, and odd-jobs laborer—barely enabled him to scrape by, and he had to sell off much of his share of the family property. None of his money-making schemes succeeded.

Emarine's life was perhaps even harder. As her diaries show, she was barely literate and surely did not share many of her husband's kinds of intellectual curiosity. Hers was the main burden of caring for Frank in his tormented illness and of raising Alma's children. Largely imprisoned by household routines, Emarine must have resented her aging husband's outside interests. She grew peevish when she thought he was feigning illness to avoid work, and he contemplated seeking a divorce; yet nearly always on their wedding anniversary, he forgot his marital problems and wrote in his diary that he did not regret a day of his married life.

The closing years of John Roberts's life brought him some moments of pride and of homage from his friends and neighbors. On his seventy-third birthday they gathered in a park near the old family gristmill and organized the West-End Home Coming Association. They elected him president, and returned each year to honor him and hear his reminiscences and readings; many of them had been his "scholars" in his schoolteaching days.

He never lost his interest in learning and in enlightening the public. He devoured newspapers—Democratic, Republican, independent, and socialist—and when rural free delivery came early in the twentieth century, the time of the mailman's arrival was important enough for noting in the daily diary. Newspapers and magazines, congressional and presidential documents, borrowed books, and a memory bolstered by carefully preserved diaries provided grist for Roberts's newspaper essays. So, too, did his purchase, in 1906, of the *Encyclopaedia Britannica*. (He worried whether he would be able to make the $3 monthly payments and instead of telling Emarine of his purchase, he had Alma write her.) His will suggests how he treasured the set: "Item Fifth: I give and bequeath to my beloved grandson, Norman Overturf, my Encyclopaedia Britannica, consisting of thirty-one volumes."

Roberts's will, made in 1907, left the rest of his small amount of property to Emarine. At her death, half was to go to Alma, and half to

Flora's children when the youngest reached the age of twenty-one. A codicil later provided that after Emarine's death Alma should receive the 7.6 acres of his land and his house next to the state fish hatchery, the site of the family gristmill; the other ten acres of his land should go to Flora's heirs. Wanting "no unnecessary expense and vain display" at his funeral, he asked that "a memorial of native stone" costing no more than $40 mark his grave and that another no more expensive be placed at Frank's grave.

Their simple gravestones, John's bearing a Masonic emblem, along with one over the grave of his father-in-law, Handy Truitt, stand at an edge of the Kirkwood Cemetery west of London. On the other side of the graveyard, separated from Roberts in death as they were in life, stand the tombstones of the Tyres and other black families. Ironically, in view of the importance John Roberts attached to his birthday, it appears on his stone as August 26, 1833, rather than August 21. His death on July 17, 1914, was duly entered in his diary on that date by his wife: "J M Roberts died this day at 3 oclock."

Index

(John M. Roberts is designated by JMR)

10/21